AF807467

THE ŒDIPUS COMPLEX

This book examines the contentious relationship between psychoanalysis and anthropology as it has played out in disputes surrounding the Œdipus complex. Here, Éric Smadja explores the complicated historical and epistemological conditions leading up to the emergence of the conflict between the two disciplines. He considers the origins of each science, the "creation" of the Œdipus complex, and the place, role and influence of Freud's key and controversial work *Totem and Taboo*, both in the history of psychoanalysis and as it connects with anthropology internationally.

Focusing on such key figures as Bronislaw Malinowski, Ernest Jones, Franz Boas, Georges Devereux, Émile Durkheim, Claude Lévi-Strauss and Jacques Lacan, Smadja charts the course of the debate as it unfolded during the twentieth century and tracks its contemporary status, with a focus on figures in both France and the United States. Discussing the divergences and convergences between the two fields, he compares and contrasts their historical, epistemological and methodological features and reflects on the new "acculturative" disciplines emerging from their interaction. The book concludes with a look at what the conflictual history of these two human sciences can tell us about the history of ideas and their processes and modes of communication.

Exploring a dispute which reaches back to the very beginnings of psychoanalysis and anthropology, *The Œdipus Complex* will appeal to psychoanalysts in practice and in training, psychotherapists and academics and students of psychoanalytic studies, anthropology and the history of ideas.

Éric Smadja is a psychiatrist and a psychoanalyst (Paris and London). He is a member of the Société Psychanalytique de Paris and the International Psychoanalytical Association (IPA). He is also an anthropologist and an associate member of the American Anthropological Association. He was awarded the IPA's Prize for "Exceptional Contribution Made to Psychoanalytical Research" (2007). He is the author of several books, including *The Couple: A Pluridisciplinary Story* (Routledge).

THE ŒDIPUS COMPLEX

Focus of the Psychoanalysis-Anthropology Debate

Éric Smadja

Routledge
Taylor & Francis Group
LONDON AND NEW YORK

First published in French 2009
by Presses Universitaires de France

First published in English 2018
by Routledge
2 Park Square, Milton Park, Abingdon, Oxon OX14 4RN

and by Routledge
605 Third Avenue, New York, NY 10017

Routledge is an imprint of the Taylor & Francis Group, an informa business

Copyright © 2018 by Taylor & Francis*e complexe d'Oedipe, cristallisateur du débat psychoanalyse/anthropologie*

The right of Éric Smadja to be identified as author of this work has been asserted by him in accordance with sections 77 and 78 of the Copyright, Designs and Patents Act 1988.

All rights reserved. No part of this book may be reprinted or reproduced or utilised in any form or by any electronic, mechanical, or other means, now known or hereafter invented, including photocopying and recording, or in any information storage or retrieval system, without permission in writing from the publishers.

Trademark notice: Product or corporate names may be trademarks or registered trademarks, and are used only for identification and explanation without intent to infringe.

British Library Cataloguing in Publication Data
A catalogue record for this book is available from the British Library

Library of Congress Cataloging in Publication Data
A catalog record for this book has been requested

ISBN: 978-1-138-21317-3 (hbk)
ISBN: 978-1-138-21319-7 (pbk)
ISBN: 978-1-315-44888-6 (ebk)

Typeset in Bembo
by Swales & Willis Ltd, Exeter, Devon, UK

CONTENTS

BY WAY OF INTRODUCTION

Why choose such a title to tell a tale of the vicissitudes in the relations between these two disciplines born in the nineteenth century? I did so because it seemed to me that the Œdipus complex, a concept central to psychoanalysis, actually crystallises the body of misinterpretations, distortions, evasions, suspicions, and misunderstandings that, depending on the school of thought and the persons framing them, anthropologists have been able to express in different manners in opposition to psychoanalysis from the time of the first encounter between the fields up until the present day. So it is that the image of the Œdipus complex as constructed by anthropologists could assert itself as being paradigmatic of the one they were to develop about psychoanalysis.

What object or objects of conflict, even of rejection, within psychoanalysis could well hide and symbolise the Œdipus complex and its universality? Why such different and contrasting reactions? What would be the underlying reasons for these reactions? In terms of groupal psychoanalysis, what would be the underlying phantasising at work in the anthropologists and psychoanalysts? But also, what are the stakes involved? Are they genuinely scientific, or of another nature? What role could psychoanalysis well have played in this tale of conflict, in particular in its image and treatment of the sociocultural and historical reality?

Could an exploration of the methodological and epistemological characteristics of the two disciplines, such as an exploration of their differences and similarities, provide us with some insights, making this intelligible? Also, what about their respective histories and contributions to enriched understanding? Beyond this tale of conflict between these two human sciences, what does it tell us about the history of the ideas and their processes and modes of communication within the vast limited and boundless field of knowledge, ever in motion?

It is certain that, from the start, a plurality of factors at play complicated the conditions of the birth of this debate that would develop in several stages and in different places. I am proposing to contribute some responses to this multi-faceted inquiry and to suggest some lines of research, but also some principles for pluri- and interdisciplinary collaboration.

So, the first chapter will deal with the already complex question of the historical and epistemological conditions of the inauguration of this debate, particularly taking into consideration the context of the birth of these two disciplines and the characteristics of the beginning of their existence, the "creation" of the Œdipus complex, the status, role and impact of *Totem and Taboo*, both within the history of psychoanalysis and in the encounter with anthropology and its international context. Then I shall expand this debate along chronological lines and, for historical and epistemological reasons, I shall distinguish between two parts. Chapter 2 will deal with the historical debate and Chapter 3 with the contemporary debate. The historical debate, extending outward from the origins to the 1950s–1960s, will differentiate between three major cultural areas: Great Britain, the United States, then France, for the sake of greater intelligibility. The contemporary debate gives priority to France and the United States.

In fact, British social anthropology, with its great figures of the likes of Edward Evan Evans-Pritchard, Raymond Firth, Meyer Fortes, then Edmund Leach and Victor Turner, in particular, did not encourage any interest in psychoanalytical work or encounters with psychoanalysts. Yet, it is imaginable that Turner, for example, who worked extensively on the anthropology of ritual and symbolic activity, would have liked to have engaged in an exchange with psychoanalysts. It must be said that he left Great Britain to pursue his career in the United States as psychoanalytical anthropology was much more extensively developed there.

In France, I have chosen to present the thought of two anthropologists belonging to different currents of thought whose interest in psychoanalysis is obvious: Maurice Godelier and Bernard Juillerat. As concerns psychoanalysts, I begin with the very valuable contribution of groupal psychoanalysis with Didier Anzieu and René Kaës, then I look at the contribution of André Green, who worked out some conditions for exercising psychoanalytical thought in the sociocultural field, on myths and on many other cultural objects, but also suggested a model of the Œdipus complex of universal value.

In the United States, I have chosen to present the work of anthropologists close to psychoanalysis such as Melford Spiro and Gananath Obeyesekere, having, however, differences in their approaches. I have in fact wished to observe and analyse their relationship to psychoanalysis, how they perceive psychoanalytical theory, the conceptual tools that they take from it, the modalities of their use, and their field of application. And besides, which psychoanalysis is it a matter of, given the diversity and heterogeneity of the theories and practices? Consequently, Clifford Geertz or Marshall Sahlins, illustrious figures of contemporary American anthropology have not been included because they just simply have no place within the context of this debate. Quite obviously, certain American psychoanalysts have participated in this debate, such as Robert Paul, also an anthropologist, but I have preferred to limit myself to anthropologists. Finally, I have also decided not to discuss the Zurich

School of Ethno-psychoanalysis, a German-speaking approach created during the 1950s by three Swiss psychoanalysts Paul Parin, his wife Goldy Parin-Matthey, and Fritz Morgenthaler. This approach is rather less well known, and it will certainly have to be the object of a comparative investigation with the other new disciplines I deal with here.

After this extensive presentation of such rich and diverse writers and ideas, a general discussion proves indispensable from the perspective of ordering and giving shape to the facts collected, something which will put me in a position to develop a process of inquiry and to propose some responses. That will make up the content of Chapter 4. I shall thus make some remarks and commentaries about this tale of conflict, based on which I shall be able to outline some representations: that of the Œdipus complex as elaborated by anthropologists, to be compared with that of Freudian psychoanalysts; then that of psychoanalysis formulated by anthropologists; and vice versa, that of anthropologists elaborated by psychoanalysts. This will be followed by the stating of some hypotheses promoting greater intelligibility of this matter. Then epistemological and methodological reflexions will focus on the respective characteristics of anthropology and psychoanalysis, followed by an identification of their differences and similarities enabling us to reflect better on the latent determinant factors and motives involved in their conflict. Finally, I shall engage in a critical evaluation of the disciplines arising from the encounter between psychoanalysis and anthropology, but also sociology.

All that will, by way of conclusion, lead me to formulate some personal proposals regarding conditions conducive to fruitful scientific collaboration, as well as to extend an invitation to think about certain "events" in the history of the ideas and relations between the different fields of knowledge.

1

EPISTEMOLOGICAL AND HISTORICAL CONDITIONS OF THE DEBATE

I shall consider in succession: the epistemological and historical context of the emergence and development of these two disciplines; the elaboration of the central concept of the Œdipus complex; and the status, role, stakes and anthropological context of *Totem and Taboo*, at the heart of the debate of concern to us.

The birth of the human sciences

According to Michel Foucault, the nineteenth century made possible the conditions of the existence of the human sciences: psychology, sociology, the study of literatures and myths followed by the birth of ethnology, psychoanalysis, and linguistics. The object psychoanalysis and ethnology (anthropology) aimed at, the related position they occupy and the function they fulfil within the general area of the *episteme*, as well as their singular configurations, motivated him to inquire into their particular relationship. So it is that in *The Order of Things: an Archaeology of the Human Sciences* (1966), he talked of a "perpetual principle of dissatisfaction, of calling into question"[1] engendered by these two fields of knowledge. Indeed, by managing to decentre the subject, both in relationship to its own cultural references, confronting it with the strangeness of cultural diversity, and in relationship to the illusory omnipresence and omnipotence of its consciousness, making it then discover the unconscious depths of the psyche, these two disciplines proved fundamentally dangerous within human sciences and would thenceforth share that deep, destabilizing property.

The birth and beginnings of anthropology

The two principal founders of anthropology (as Tylor dubbed the field) are: the Briton Edward Burnett Tylor (1832–1917) and the American Lewis Henry Morgan

(1818–1881), who belonged to the first school of thought, evolutionism, which dominated the second half of the nineteenth century and the very beginning of the twentieth. However, the anthropologist Mondher Kilani[2] (1994), commenting on the work of his colleagues Jean Copans and Jean Jamin (1978–1979), reminded us that the Enlightenment in France also provided the conditions for the birth of this discipline with, in particular, Jean-Jacques Rousseau and the theoretical project of the Enlightenment philosophers, held by Claude Lévi-Strauss to be its great source of inspiration, establishing an imaginary direct line of descent from it, but especially from the Société des Observateurs de l'homme. This was a pluridisciplinary group, headed by Joseph-Marie de Gerando, inaugurating a collective approach based, on the one hand, on an elaborated theory, "the Ideology", rejecting metaphysics and laying claim to an ideology of facts, of experience that presaged positivism, and on the other hand, on a methodology oriented towards observation, its objects, and the manner of undertaking it. There would thus be another direct line of descent, that with field anthropology.

Lewis Henry Morgan was born in Aurora, New York, in 1818. An attorney by training, he very early on became interested in Indians, the Iroquois in particular. In 1851, he published *The League of Ho-de-no-sau-nee* in Iroquois, which is considered to be the first scientific treatise of North American Indian ethnography. This report revealed the existence of the social structure and political organisation of the Iroquois confederation. From the end of the 1850s, his principal preoccupation would become kinship. He then undertook a large scale comparative study of facts of kinship, whose findings would be recorded in his two major works, *Systems of Consanguinity and Affinity of the Human Family* (1871) and *Ancient Society* (1877).

He gave anthropology one of its objects, kinship, a field that has become classic, a method adapted to that object, the genealogical questionnaire, and some early scientific findings, namely, the discovery of some of the principles that non-European societies had chosen to organise the lineage and marriage ties among individuals and the groups making them up, the description of kinship systems. Morgan distinguished among societies in terms of kinship structure. He hypothesised that primitive societies were organised on the basis of kinship, in contrast to more modern societies organised on a political basis. According to the anthropologist Maurice Godelier, Morgan

> was motivated by the desire to answer a major question: How to show the cultural unity of all the American Indians and the Asiatic origin? In an attempt to reply, he had sent out hundreds of questionnaires, which were filled out by people working at the four corners of the earth; he carried out numerous structural analyses, and was ultimately able to lay the foundations of a veritable Mendelian table of kinship terminologies.[3]

Morgan started from the epistemological assumption of the evolutionism of his time, namely that evolution always proceeds from simple to complex. Thus, the simplest terminology called "Malayan" by him, then "Hawaiian" by George

Murdock, had to constitute the point of departure of the evolution of kinship systems. This terminology was in fact supposed to be marked by the time during which humanity lived in a stage of "savagery", practising "marriage by groups" and having partially brought an end to the sexual promiscuity of primitive animal hordes. Thus, in his estimation, the Polynesian societies became the living witnesses of the most ancient stage of the evolution of humanity. Later on, another segment of humanity went from the stage of barbarism, of clans, of "tribes", and that was the stage corresponding to "Iroquois" type terminologies (no distinction was yet made between the father and his brothers, the mother and her sisters). Finally, some societies in Europe and America moved on to the stage of civilisation corresponding to the modern terminology of the Europeans that Morgan called "Aryan" that was later christened "Eskimo". This terminology attested to the fact that, finally, the real, biological roles of the father and mother had been understood and that the human family had finally attained its ultimate, rational form based on monogamy.

Morgan died in Rochester in 1881, where he had taken up residence as a lawyer in 1844.

Edward Burnett Tylor was born in Camberwell, near London, in 1832. In 1871, he published *Primitive Culture*, which lent anthropology its status as an autonomous discipline. Concerned with exploring what culture was, he elaborated a schema of evolution saving the principal part for the development of the human mind, not by establishing a hierarchy of its accomplishments, but by highlighting a series of cognitive configurations. He believed in the uniqueness of human intellectual instrumentality. He distinguished and classified more than he ranked, even if his history of religion went through three stages: animism, polytheism, and the monotheism leading to Christianity. He is famous for his 1871 definition of culture:

> Culture or Civilization, taken in its wide ethnographic sense, is that complex whole which includes knowledge, belief, art, morals, law, customs and any other capabilities and habits acquired by man as a member of society.[4]

He was the "inventor" of animism, the religious conception by which human beings are plunged into a nature "animated" by supernatural beings or forces that they must appease by appropriate practices. This concept is based on dream life or on the interpretation that "primitive" people gave to dream life. He was also interested in the facts of kinship. With Morgan, he was at the origin of comparative analysis in anthropology. But, unlike him, he did not take an interest in the development of modes of social organisation.

Tylor's most valuable contribution was to have recognised the psychological motivations of cultural phenomena, but his psychologizing anthropology, centred around the classic notion of soul, relied on a crude psychology, with a predilection for rationalism and spiritualism.

The first anthropologists had been struck at a very early point by the similarities existing among customs and institutions of distinct and geographically distant cultures. In the nineteenth century, evolutionism gave a way of explaining those similarities through the thesis of convergence. All societies were to have been transformed by going through the same stages and by evolving in the same direction. It was therefore a matter of accounting for humanity's unique trajectory, the objective being to isolate the successive stages gone through and their laws of succession (cf. Morgan).

Anthropological evolutionism actually drew the essential part of its inspiration from the thought of the eighteenth-century Enlightenment philosophers. In particular, it uses the central assumption of a universal history embracing all of humanity in a single, focused, irreversible movement. The savages were then converted into primitives, and their cultures became incarnations or figurations of past "civilized" societies. The task of science would therefore be one of elucidating the mechanisms of passing from one state to the other, conceding uniformity of the human psyche. *The assumption underlying this linear evolutionism was in fact the universality of human mental processes.* But this nineteenth century evolutionism stands out by the significance it assigned to biological factors and by the considerable extension of the timeline it adopted concurrent with the discoveries of geology and palaeontology. If all of humanity is subject to the same historical movement, it is still necessary to explain why certain societies progressed, while others seem stuck in irremediable primitivism. This is the context in which the idea of race, of biologically given difference (meaning, of inequality) developed, a notion called upon to account for the cultural stagnation of non-western peoples. In this way, human nature itself was historicised, and no longer just society, as was the case in the eighteenth century.

The work of these anthropologists illustrates the split between strict parallelists, like Morgan, John Ferguson McLennan or James Frazer, for whom every society passes through a succession of distinctly defined unalterable stages, diffusionist evolutionists like Tylor, and German anthropo-geographers such as Adolf Bastian and Friedrich Ratzel, ready to accord a fairly large place to the borrowing of cultural elements.

This anthropological evolutionism constituted an essential period in the history of this discipline through the creation of its learning institutions (the first chair of anthropology in Great Britain for Tylor in 1896), the constitution of its terminology, such as that of kinship studies, and through the formulation of a certain number of problems which it continues to debate still today.

After the nineteenth century, this evolutionist frame of reference no longer seemed to account for the whole of ethnographic observations. Within this critical context, new interpretative models then emerged, among them the diffusionist school, which flourished at the beginning of the twentieth century. Friedrich Ratzel, Leo Frobenius and Fritz Graebner may be cited here. For these anthropo-geographers, the similarities obtainined among cultural traits of distinct societies had to be related to phenomena of contacts having occurred in the past among the geographically distant cultures concerned. In contrast to evolutionism, diffusionism sought to demonstrate the historicity of peoples presumed to be without history through the study of their distribution in space. They then attempted spatio-temporal reconstructions of cultural bodies. In Great Britain, this current of thought took a radical turn with what were called the hyper-diffusionist theses defended by Grafton Elliot-Smith and William James Perry, who saw ancient Egypt as being at the origin of all civilisations.

The birth of psychoanalysis

Sigmund Freud (1856–1939) created psychoanalysis at the end of the nineteenth century. In *On the History of the Psychoanalytical Movement* (1914), he wrote:

> psycho-analysis is my creation; for ten years I was the only person who concerned himself with it, and all the dissatisfaction which the new phenomenon aroused in my contemporaries has been poured out in the form of criticisms on my head. Although it is a long time now since I was the only psycho-analyst, I consider myself justified in maintaining that even to-day no one can know better than I do what psychoanalysis is, how it differs from other ways of investigating the life of the mind, and what would better be described by some other name.[5]

In his article "'Psychoanalysis' and 'The Libido Theory'" (1923), he defined his creation as follows:

> Psychoanalysis is the name: 1) of a procedure for the investigation of mental processes which are almost inaccessible in any other way; 2) of a method (based on that investigation) for treatment of neurotic disorders and 3) of a collection of psychological information obtained along those lines, which is gradually being accumulated into a new scientific discipline.[6]

Further on, he endeavoured to state both the "the principal subject matter" of his creation and the "foundations" of his theory in this way:

> The assumption that there are unconscious mental processes, the recognition of the theory of resistance and repression, the appreciation of the importance of sexuality and of the Œdipus complex – these constitute the principal subject matter of psycho-analysis and the foundations of its theory. No one who cannot accept them all should count himself as a psycho-analyst.[7]

From the beginning, Freud situated psychoanalysis in the family of the "natural sciences", sciences "in the strict sense of the word", adopting their "explanatory" rationality, in opposition to the family of the "sciences of the mind", to temptations of "totalizing worldviews", to which it would, nonetheless, make a contribution. Paul-Laurent Assoun considers that by summoning up this contrast between *Naturwissenschaften* and *Geisteswissenschaften*, Freud was appealing to a dichotomy that had developed in the course of a long epistemological debate, which is important to keep sight of in order to grasp how psychoanalysis is heir to it and how it is distinct from it.[8] He has in fact stated that this debate, known as the "battle of the methods" and particularly developed in Germany, would have precisely reached its apogee around the time of the birth of psychoanalysis. Moreover, he reminds us that it was Wilhelm Dilthey (1833–1911), founder of an epistemology of the human sciences, who proposed differentiating between these two scientific domains in terms of their objects, their methods – explanatory for the natural sciences, comprehensive and interpretative for the sciences of the mind – and in terms of the type of rationality involved.

For Freud, psychoanalysis was based on the interpretation that is an explanation. He rejected any idea of discontinuity between mind and nature, therefore of the dualism between these two categories of sciences. Thus, Assoun considers that he never strayed from the epistemological "monism" that at the same time proceeds from the will to respect the interplay between "nature" and "mind".[9] Consequently, the position of psychoanalysis is such that collaboration with the human sciences, "sciences of the mind", proves inevitable and necessary. One sees the twofold idea: the "human sciences" confirm the findings of psychoanalysis; they experience the "strangeness" of its discoveries and in this sense make them more "credible", acclimatizing them to an already constituted scientific universe. In return, psychoanalysis fructifies the fertile soil of the human sciences.[10]

In several texts, Freud in fact spoke of "the bridge" between psychoanalysis and the sciences of the mind and its mediating function, in particular. In *The Interpretation of Dreams*, for example, he had shown that the psychic processes at work in dream work are as active in pathological phenomena as in cultural products, through the universal symbolic. Apart from "'Psychoanalysis' and 'The Libido Theory'" (1923) and "Psycho-Analysis" (1926), he would come back to this in *New Introductory Lectures* (1932–1933).

Thus, for Freud, the unfolding of the essence of psychoanalysis implied a path leading to the medical sciences, but also to the sciences of the mind, consequently affirming its *dual epistemological affiliation*. It is this characteristic and its essential function as a link between the medical sciences and the cultural sciences established by Freud right from the beginning of the history of psychoanalysis and regularly recalled later on, that must be kept in mind for the intelligibility of the relationship between two disciplines under study here.

The birth of the Œdipus complex and its mythological analogy

Through first his self-analysis and then through his extensive clinical work, Freud would discover the Œdipus complex, which would become the central concept of the discipline of psychoanalysis. His studies required a considerable period of time (from 1897 to 1923, that is 26 years). The first mention of the existence of oedipal feelings in fact appears in Manuscript N accompanying the letter to Wilhelm Fliess dated May 31, 1897: "Hostile impulses against parents (a wish that they should die) are also an integral constituent of neuroses. . . . It seems as though this death-wish is directed in sons against their father and in daughters against their mother".[11] It was in the same year, in letter no. 71, of October 15, 1897, that he made a connection between the oedipal feelings and Sophocles' tragedy *Œdipus Rex*:

> To be completely honest with oneself is good practice. One single thought of general value has been revealed to me. I have found, in my own case too, falling in love with the mother and jealousy of the father, and I now regard it as a universal event of early childhood, even if not so early as in children who have been made hysterical. (Similarly with the romance of parentage in paranoia–heroes, founders of religions.) If that is so, we can understand the riveting power of *Œdipus Rex*, in spite of all the objections raised by reason against its presupposition of destiny; and we can understand why the later 'dramas of destiny' were bound to fail so miserably. Our feelings rise against any arbitrary, individual compulsion [of fate], such as is presupposed in [Grillparzer's], *Die Ahnfrau,* etc. But the Greek legend seizes on a compulsion which everyone recognises because he feels its existence within himself. Each member of the audience was once, in germ and in phantasy, just such an Œdipus, and each one recoils in horror from the dream-fulfilment here transplanted into reality, with the whole quota of repression which separates his infantile state from the present one.[12]

Organiser of the human psyche, Freud inquired into its universality independent of any historical and sociocultural variations· But, with this question of the universality of the Œdipus complex, he encountered the evolutionist assumption of the unity of the human psyche and humanity's unique historical trajectory, something which would prove detrimental to the conditions of the dialogue between psychoanalysis and anthropology from the beginning.

This major discovery marking the epistemic identity of psychoanalysis from the start also established a "primordial" link between psychoanalysis and mythology, science of the mind. Whence its structured evolution from the beginning through its dual link to the medical sciences, by belonging to the sciences of nature, and to the sciences of the mind, as mentioned above.

In his article "Freud et la mythologie"[13] (1970), Didier Anzieu made the pertinent observation that Freud's interest in mythology developed at the same time as his self-analysis progressed, that is between 1896 and 1899. Anzieu also underscored the fact that the mythological analogy only developed from the time of Freud's discovery of the Œdipus complex, which thus provided him with his original model. It was in his letter no. 78 to Wilhelm Fliess dated December 12, 1897 that he in fact stated the general principle of mythological analogy. There he asked Fliess whether he could imagine what endo-psychic myths might be and went on to tell him that they were the latest offspring of his mental labours. The vague inner perception of one's own psychic apparatus, he explained, stimulates illusions of thought that are naturally projected outward and characteristically into the future, into the world beyond. Immortality, retribution, the afterlife, he continued, are the conceptions of our inner psyche, are psycho-mythology.[14] While the Œdipus complex represents the originary model of the mythological analogy, it is permissible to think that right from the beginning the theoretical corpus of psychoanalysis was constituted by leaning on a science of the mind, mythology, thus confirming its dual epistemological affiliation. The terms "endo-psychic myths" or "psycho-mythology" patently attest to this. In addition, this letter expresses the idea, revolutionary for its time, that myths are psychology projected outward, an idea Freud would take up again in *Totem and Taboo* to define ethnology.

Keeping only to Freud's writings, Didier Anzieu has detected three main stages in the evolution of Freud's relationship to mythology – that of *The Interpretation of Dreams* (1900), that of *Totem and Taboo* (1912–1913), and that of *Moses and Monotheism* (1939) – and has extricated several fundamental ideas:

- Mythology and the other cultural facts, which he does not really differentiate, fulfil a "function of providing proof";
- The unconscious is not some "wild creation by Freud", since he finds it at work, with the same mechanisms, in domains other than his own dreams or his patients' symptoms;
- Mythology and the other cultural products do not only validate the psychoanalytic method of interpretation of dreams and symptoms;
- The universality of the same symbolic validates the Freudian hypothesis of the universality, atemporality, and indestructibility of the unconscious.

Totem and Taboo bursts onto the scene and the Œdipus complex's universal status

Freud was fifty-five years old when he undertook to write the four essays on the "resemblances between the psychic lives of savages and neurotics" beginning in August 1911 and collected together in 1913 under the title of *Totem and Taboo*. He then took the first major step in the psychoanalytical interpretation of ethnographic data leading him, in particular, to make the Œdipus complex the very basis of the first social institutions and to identify the action of unconscious processes in their development. From that point on, the Œdipus complex proved to be constitutive of the Freudian theory of culture.

In his preface, Freud cited two sources of inspiration and incitement: *The Elements of Folk Psychology* by Wilhelm Wundt (1912),[15] based on a non-analytical psychology; and *A Study of the Transformations and Symbolisms of the Libido* by Carl Gustav Jung (1911–1913),[16] exploring the problems of individual psychology using materials from folk psychology. In addition, he put forth his patent role of mediator between psychoanalysts and specialists of the sciences of the mind and the originality of his approach.

Assoun invites us to understand the Freudian project as falling, first of all, into the scholarly tradition of Wundt's "folk psychology", then into that of British anthropology. For Wundt, this collective psychology represented an "extension" of individual psychology, more than an "application", as it would be for Freud.

Within the evolutionist frame of reference of a theory of the evolution of the human mind, Wundt particularly tried to uncover the causes of the evolution of the collective psyche, of which the different cultures are but the diversification. And during the first half of the twentieth century, Freud pursued this approach by reaffirming the interest of a theory of the collective psyche. His paper on "The Interest of Psycho-Analysis from the Point of View of the History of Civilization" (1913) applies to the methodology of *Totem and Taboo* contemporaneous with it: "the psycho-analytic mode of thought acts like a new instrument of research. The application of its hypotheses to social psychology enables us both to raise fresh problems and to see old ones in a fresh light and contribute to their solution."[17] This application process is itself based on two principles. The first is that of the comparison of the childhood of the individual with the prehistory of peoples basing the transfer of one experience on the other. Thus,

> it seems quite possible to apply the psycho-analytic views derived from dreams to products of the ethnic imagination such as myths and legends.... A similar application of its points of view, its hypotheses and its findings has enabled psychoanalysis to shed light on the origins of our great cultural institutions–on religion, morality, justice and philosophy.[18]

The second principle consists of reading and interpreting sociocultural reality through the "individual" language of symptom and neurosis. We can, therefore, considerer with Assoun that *Totem and Taboo* falls into the same epistemological perspective as Wundt and his *Elements of Folk Psychology* does, but subverts it as well.

According to Geza Roheim, *Totem and Taboo* founded psychoanalytical anthropology.[19] In addition, it functioned as a unifying pole and frame of reference for the diverse endeavours of applied psychoanalysis, dispersed up until then, of Freud's disciples. From then on, it inaugurated and instituted a new, unified, homogenous field of psychoanalysis. Freud therefore accorded the Œdipus complex a central founding position in any psychoanalytical approach to cultural phenomena.

However, this Œdipus complex was yet to be fully worked out. In 1912–1913, it only concerned the positive component of the boy and his phylogenesis. Its negative component would only be revealed with the analysis of "Wolf-Man" (1914–1918)[20], and it would only be described in 1923 in its complete form in *The Ego and the Id*:

> Closer study usually discloses the more complete Œdipus complex, which is twofold, positive and negative, and is due to the bisexuality originally present in children: that is to say, a boy has not merely an ambivalent attitude towards his father and an affectionate object-choice towards his mother, but

> at the same time, he also behaves like a girl and displays an affectionate feminine attitude to his father and a corresponding jealousy and hostility towards his mother.... At the dissolution of the Œdipus complex the four trends of which it consists will group themselves in such a way as to produce a father-identification and a mother-identification....
>
> The relative intensity of the two identifications in any individual will reflect preponderance in him of one or other of the two sexual dispositions.[21]

The girl's Œdipus complex would be explored at a later stage in the texts on feminine sexuality, notably in "Female Sexuality" (1931),[22] then in "Femininity, Lecture XXXIII" (1933).[23]

In positing both the psychic and cultural universality of Œdipus complex (the boy's positive form), Freud therefore first broke his way into the anthropologists' field of investigation.

Totem and Taboo in Freud's opus

It would be befitting to integrate *Totem and Taboo* into the evolving dynamic of what it has produced theoretically, clinically and technically. This work in fact fits into the framework of the first topic of the psychic apparatus and the first theory of drives. But it also has a place in the domain of the "non-medical" extensions of psychoanalysis (to literature, painting, myths and religions, social problems).

In 1907, Freud wrote "Obsessive Actions and Religious Practices", the first article in which he tackled the question of religion. He established an initial analogy there between religion and obsessional neurosis, already conferring upon neurosis the role of interpreter and translator of the sociocultural fact. In 1908, he expressed his views on social problems in "'Civilized' Sexual Morality and Modern Nervous Illness" for the first time. This would in fact be psychoanalysis' entry into the question of Culture. He maintained that instinctual repression would be the founding principle of Culture, which is dealt with in economic terms. Freud located the essence of morality in instinctual limitation. Moreover, as Assoun suggests, this text should be considered to be the sociocultural counterpart of the *Three Essays*, forming a clinico-theoretical diptych, like *Totem and Taboo* and "The Interest of Psycho-Analysis". In 1910, he wrote "Leonard da Vinci and a Memory of his Childhood". Then, between 1911 and 1913, he wrote the four essays of *Totem and Taboo*.

Those years were also marked by a growing preoccupation on the part of psychoanalysts with symbolism and the forms of symbolisation. It is to be noted incidentally that among the additions Freud made to the original text of *The Interpretation of Dreams* (1900), the most important ones concerned symbolism in dreams. In that section, which only dates from 1914 (the year of the fourth edition), he presented the general symbolism of dreams as common to individual psychic formations (dreams, unconscious phantasies of neurotics) and to collective, social products, reflecting the existence of a universal symbolic language, a "basic language" belonging to humanity's phylogenetic archaic heritage. He wrote,

> this symbolism is not peculiar to dreams, but is characteristic of unconscious ideation, in particular among the people, and is to be found in folklore, and in popular myths, legends, linguistic idioms, proverbial wisdom and current jokes, to a more complete extent than in dreams.[24]

Extensive use is made of symbolism to represent the sexual material of dreams. The symbols would be there from the beginning of life, as evidenced in children's dreams and their symbolic. Thus, the symbolic poses problems of a phylogenetic and ontogenetic nature.

The number of symbols is infinite, but what is symbolised is very limited in scope: the body, sexuality (sexual organs, sexual acts, masturbation), birth, death, parents and blood relations, nudity. Later, other socio-anthropological writings would make their appearance among them: "Thoughts for the Times on War and Death" (1915), "Group Psychology and the Analysis of the Ego" (1921), *The Future of an Illusion* (1927), *Civilization and its Discontents* (1930), and *Moses and Monotheism* (1939).

The psychoanalytic movement and its vicissitudes

According to Freud, beginning in 1907, during the years following the establishment of relations between the Vienna and Zurich schools, psychoanalysis experienced extraordinarily rapid expansion. The First International Psychoanalytic Congress took place in Salzburg in the spring of 1908. This was in fact the first meeting of the friends of psychoanalysis who had come from Vienna, Zurich and elsewhere upon a suggestion made by Jung. Notably, it was decided that the journal *Jahrbuch für psychoanalytische und psychopathologische Forschung* would be created, published by Eugen Bleuler and Freud, with Jung as editor-in-chief, which would begin publication in 1909. In this way, close collaboration between Vienna and Zurich was established and developed. The Vienna Psychoanalytic Society was created in April 1908 and that of Berlin in August 1908. It was at the Second International Congress, held in Nuremberg in March 1910 on the suggestion of Sándor Ferenczi, that the International Psychoanalytical Association would be created, with Jung as its president.

Psychoanalysis, then undergoing full geographical expansion, and animated by a spirit of conquest, also broadened its content by establishing links between the clinical and psychopathological field and that of cultural products. Within this dynamic, the journal *Imago*, proposing texts on the application of psychoanalysis to social and cultural realities, was created in January 1912. Otto Rank would be the editor-in-chief, assisted by Hans Sachs. However, serious conflicts affecting relationships between "the founding Father and the collectivity of sons" already existed within the analytical movement. Alfred Adler left the Society in June 1911 and Wilhelm Stekel in October 1912, following disagreements on theoretical and technical matters. Moreover, Freud's and Jung's personal relations would deteriorate to a considerable degree with publication of the first part of *Transformations and Symbolisms of the Libido* in 1911, then the second part in 1913, leading to their break during the Munich congress held that same year.

That scholarly, but profuse, redundant, and confused book would have the dual function of demonstrating to Freud the scope of Jung's knowledge and of asserting his own thought. In addition, it founded a current of Jungian inspired psychoanalytical anthropology. One might in fact mention the neo-Jungian school from Gaston Bachelard to Gilbert Durand, going by way of the numerous historians of religions, among them Mircea Eliade.

Let us now take a look at some major points of divergence between Jung and Freud, both concerning the matter of understanding religions and mythology and regarding psychoanalytical theory, strictly speaking.

For Jung, the search for the processes of formation of collective representations could only be carried out by the comparative history of religions. He therefore rejected any notion of origin in drives and phantasy, as well as any process of sublimation and symbolisation in the Freudian sense. The Œdipus complex would no longer be at the basis of religions as Freud was maintaining. The comprehension of the individual psyche would be elucidated by the study of past mythologies, myth becoming the collective source from which dream and neurosis were drawn. He would argue for the primacy of phylogenesis over ontogenesis. Apart from this divergence about the relationship between the individual and collective, another one would concern the notion of Unconscious. The Jungian conception of the Unconscious is closely connected with the notion of archetype introduced in 1919. He distinguished between an "impersonal collective Unconscious" and a "personal Unconscious". The Unconscious common to all humanity has existed for all time, since it emanated directly from our animal antecedents. It is natural, innate, therefore, collective. It follows from this that the symbols constituting this impersonal unconscious themselves also exist for all time. In this sense, myth as supra-subjective symbolic elaboration is by definition atemporal. The "Personal Unconscious" has come from ontogenetic elements due in part to repression. Moreover, Jung would present an expanded definition of the libido leading to its radical desexualisation. By rejecting the Œdipus complex, he relegated the father to a marginal role and accorded major importance to the maternal archetype. Finally, in Jung, Freud's search for causality would be replaced by a mystical teleology.

On the History of the Psychoanalytical Movement in fact speaks of these two dissident movements, Adler's creating "individual psychology" and Jung's "analytical psychology".

What about the "applied psychoanalysis" Freud's disciples produced? It was the mythological work that predominated between 1906 and 1920. Let me cite some writings by Otto Rank, who became the recognised specialist in philosophy, literature and myth within the Psychoanalytical Society of Vienna (*The Myth of the Birth of the Hero*, 1908; *The Lohengrin Saga*, 1911; *The Incest Theme in Literature and Legend*, 1912); some writings by Karl Abraham ("Dreams and Myths: A Study in Folk-Psychology", 1909; "Giovanni Segantini: A Psychoanalytical Study", 1911; "Amenhotep IV. Psychoanalytical Contributions Towards the Understanding of his Personality and of the Monotheistic Cult of Aton", 1912); *The Significance of Psychoanalysis for the Human Sciences* (Otto Rank and Hans Sachs, 1913); as well as some texts by Ernest Jones that will be discussed later on.

Totem and Taboo and its incorporation into the international anthropological context

Totem and Taboo was published in New York in 1918 and in London in 1919. During those years, anthropology underwent profound changes simultaneously affecting its institutional, practical and theoretical orientations, as well as still being dominated by the great theoretical debate about totemism. Let us first deal with the latter.

This famous debate was initiated starting in the last decade of the nineteenth century by James Frazer's work *Totemism*, the veritable founding text, published in 1887. Incidentally, this concept had been introduced by John Ferguson McLennan in 1869 in an article entitled "The Worship of Animals and Plants". At a time when anthropology was undergoing deep transformations in different countries, the veritable hegemony of the totemic problem, which would last until the second or third decades of the twentieth century, resulted in frequent, and sometimes important, contacts between figures intellectually and geographically remote from one another, such as James Frazer, Andrew Lang, Franz Boas, Alexander Goldenweiser, Émile Durkheim, Arnold Van Gennep, Fritz Graebner, Wilhelm Schmidt, William Halse Rivers Rivers and Alfred Reginald Radcliffe-Brown, among others. The rivalry between the different interpretive approaches grew increasingly explicit right from the very beginning of the twentieth century, and the treatment of the totemic question was a privileged manner of gauging divergences among the evolutionists who had inaugurated the debate and the first representatives of the new methodological and theoretical orientations that were going to open the way to modern anthropology (European diffusionism and functionalism, American culturalism). Indeed, the concept of totemism has always remained "in the building stage", marked by successive attempts to delimit its definitive contours on both the social and the religious planes.

With *Totem and Taboo*, Freud intruded into this international anthropological confrontation by appropriating arguments essentially based on James Frazer's and Robertson Smith's theses, which enabled him to back up what he himself was proposing without inquiring into the appropriateness of his methodological approach, something which inevitably exposed him to vehement criticisms on the part of anthropologists.

Where did things stand with the profound reworking of the anthropological discipline? I shall look at this with insights drawn from the work of the anthropologist Bertrand Pulman.

On the theoretical plane, the unilinear evolutionism that had prevailed up until the beginning of the twentieth century was in distinct decline, while new schools of thought such as diffusionism and functionalism in Europe and culturalism in the United States were blossoming. At the same time, more and more specialised researchers (with degrees in sociology and anthropology) were leaving to work in the field. This movement would take place in two phases.

In an initial phase, researchers, who were not professional ethnographers, organised *Survey* type expeditions fairly rapidly covering a vast geographic area. William Halse Rivers Rivers and Charles Gabriel Seligman, both trained as physicians, were the dominant figures of this first phase. Alfred Cort Haddon organised an early Torres Straits expedition between 1898 and 1899. (I shall discuss the later voyages of these two masters of British anthropology at a later point.) Alfred Reginald Radcliffe-Brown (1881–1955), who graduated in 1905 from Cambridge, in moral sciences and sciences of the mind, first undertook fieldwork in the Andaman Islands from 1906 to 1908, thanks to the encouragement of Rivers and Haddon. He then lived in Western Australia from 1910 to 1913, subsequently publishing two monographs: *The Andaman Islanders* (1922) and *The Social Organization of Australian Tribes* (1931).

In a second phase, beginning in the 1920s, the need for intensive ethnographic experience, implying long stays in the field, language learning, and "participatory observation", in particular, became a necessary prerequisite for any legitimate elaboration of theories. Thus, the two monographs exemplifying this new regime of "ethnographic authority" appeared simultaneously: that of Radcliffe-Brown (1922) cited above and, especially, *The Argonauts of the Western Pacific* by Bronislaw Malinowski (1922), to which I shall return later on. Let me say right now that Malinowski in Great Britain and Franz Boas in the United States would be the initiators of the new anthropology imposing the model of ethnographic authority as one of principal foundations of the new "regime of truth" of contemporary anthropology.

It was therefore in this anthropological setting that *Totem and Taboo* was published in the United States and Great Britain. But I shall consider the reactions on the part of anthropologists, among them Alfred Kroeber's exemplary criticism (1920), at a later point, because, contrary to what one might imagine, this psychoanalysis-anthropology debate was introduced under different conditions and with different modalities and protagonists.

Notes

1 Michel Foucault, *The Order of Things: An Archaeology of the Human Sciences*, New York, Vintage Books, 1994 (1966), p. 36.
2 Mondher Kilani, *L'invention de l'autre*, Lausanne, Payot, 1994.
3 Maurice Godelier, *The Metamorphoses of Kinship*, London, Verso, 2011, p. 514.
4 Edward Burnett Tylor, *Primitive Culture: Researches into the Development of Mythology, Philosophy, Religion, Art, and Custom,* vol. 1, London: John Murray, Albemarle Street, 1871, p. 1.
5 Sigmund Freud (1914), *On the History of the Psychoanalytical Movement*, S.E., 14, London, Hogarth, p. 7.
6 Sigmund Freud (1923), "'Psycho-Analysis' and 'The Libido Theory'", S.E., 18, London, Hogarth, p. 235.

7 *Ibid.*, p. 247.
8 Paul-Laurent Assoun, *Freud et les sciences sociales*, Paris, Armand Colin, 1993, p. 13.
9 *Ibid.*, p. 16.
10 *Ibid.*, p. 22.
11 Sigmund Freud (1897), *Pre-Psycho-Analytic Publications and Unpublished Drafts (1886–1889),* S.E., 1, London, Hogarth, pp. 254–255.
12 *Ibid.*, p. 265.
13 Didier Anzieu, "Freud et la mythologie", *Nouvelle revue de psychanalyse*, Paris, Gallimard, 1970, No.1, pp. 114–145.
14 Jeffrey Masson (ed.), *The Complete Letters of Sigmund Freud to Wilhelm Fliess*, Cambridge, MA, Harvard University Press, 1985, pp. 285–286.
15 Wilhelm Wundt (1912), *The Elements of Folk Psychology, Outline of a Psychological History of the Development of Mankind*, London, Allen & Unwin Ltd., 1915.
16 Carl Gustav Jung (1911–1913), *Psychology of the Unconscious, A Study of the Transformations and Symbolisms of the Libido, A Contribution to the History of the Evolution of Thought*, New York, Moffat, Yard and Company, 1916.
17 Sigmund Freud (1913), "The Claims of Psycho-Analysis to Scientific Interest", S.E., 13, London, Hogarth, p. 185.
18 *Ibid.*
19 Cited by Roger Dadoun in his book *Geza Roheim et l'essor de l'anthropologie psychanalytique*, Paris, Payot, 1972.
20 Sigmund Freud (1918), "From the History of an Infantile Neurosis", S.E., 17, London, Hogarth.
21 Sigmund Freud (1923), "The Ego and the Id", S.E., 19, London, Hogarth, pp. 33–34.
22 Sigmund Freud (1931), "Female Sexuality", S.E., 21, London: Hogarth, pp. 225–245.
23 Sigmund Freud (1933), "Femininity, Lecture XXXIII", *New Introductory Lectures*, S.E., 22, London, Hogarth, pp. 112–135.
24 Sigmund Freud (1900), *The Interpretation of Dreams, Second Part,* S.E., 5. London, Hogarth, p. 351.

2
THE HISTORICAL DEBATE

In Great Britain

William Halse Rivers Rivers (1864–1922)

Born in Luton, Kent in 1864, Rivers first became a physician in London before undertaking research in the fields of experimental psychology, neurophysiology and psychopathology at St Bartholomew's Hospital in London. He specialised in the experimental study of sensorial systems, and especially of vision. He was appointed lecturer in physiological and experimental psychology at Cambridge University in 1897. In 1898, he participated as a psychologist in the Torres Straits Expedition led by his colleague Haddon, during which he met Seligman. For Rivers, it was a matter of using the methods of experimental psychology to study the behaviours of the islanders in their natural environment, then of comparing them with "civilised" peoples. This expedition was also the point of departure for specifically ethnologic interests. He would in fact conduct research in the field among the Toda in India (1902), then in Melanesia (1908 and 1914). His theoretical contributions bore on kinship and social organisation, in particular.

He took renewed interest in psychological questions when he was made a military physician during the First World War, which led him to treat traumatic neuroses of war. This was the context within which he discovered Freud's writings (*Studies on Hysteria* and *The Interpretation of Dreams*). After the war, he published *Instinct and the Unconscious* (1920), in which he presented his views on psychophysiology and their relationships to Freudian theses and sought as well to use certain Freudian concepts in his ethnologic analyses. The anthropologist Bertrand Pulman has noted that all throughout his life, Rivers was faced with a crucial problem, that of finding a satisfactory interrelationship, on both the personal and theoretical level, between psychophysiology and ethnology. His interest in psychoanalysis was precisely part of that quest for a principle of consistency between those two poles. The notion of traumatism would provide him with the conceptual framework enabling him to establish analogies between those two domains.[1]

In 1916, then 52 years old, Rivers in fact discovered the above-cited Freudian texts. It was at the end of his article "Sociology and Psychology" (1916) that he first alluded to psychoanalysis, which was, as Pulman has observed,[2] the first documented mention of it by a British ethnologist. The following is the passage in question:

> I should like now to draw attention to a recent movement in psychology, a movement which, in spite of all its faults, I am inclined to regard as one of the most important which has ever taken place in the history of the science. This movement, which is connected especially with the name of Freud, not merely gives to the subconscious or unconscious a far more important place in the ordering of human conduct than has generally been assigned to it, but it puts forward a definite mechanism of the processes by which the subconscious or unconscious takes effect, and by which its workings are disguised.[3]

Then, in a lecture entitled "Dreams and Primitive Culture" given in 1918 at the John Rylands Library, Rivers directly tackled the relationship between ethnology and psychoanalysis for the first time. He drew his colleagues' attention to the issue and devoted numerous publications to inquiring into the relevance of Freudian ideas and their possible impact on the field of ethnology, therefore playing the role of precursor in the blooming of the psychoanalysis/anthropology debate. He was even an associate member of the British Society of Psychoanalysis, founded by Ernest Jones.

Seeking above all to bring to light the neurophysiological bases of psychic life, his experimental psychology was theoretically very far removed from Freud's endeavours. His attentive reading of *The Interpretation of Dreams* and *Studies on Hysteria* had in fact left him with mixed feelings. He was both enticed by the distinction between latent and manifest content and sceptical about certain points, such as the role accorded to infantile sexuality. He would overestimate the influence of pathogenic external events in the aetiology of neurotic disorders, the importance of the notion of traumatism and, in particular, disregard all Freud's elaborations on psychic life and phantasy. Moreover, leaning on the very singular aetiology of the traumatic neuroses of war to refute the Freudian conception of the role played by unconscious factors, he brought to the fore the instinct of conservation, liable to correspond better to his biologising portrayal of the psyche. In his very perspicacious reading of Rivers' book *Instinct and the Unconscious* (1920) and other articles, Pulman has noted that Rivers did not seem to have understood the status and impact of the concept of the unconscious in Freudian theory, and that, moreover, his understanding of therapy seemed quite imprecise, as did his grasp of the notion of transference and resistance, in particular.

Moderately evolutionist in the beginning, starting in 1908, Rivers would side with the diffusionist, then hyper-diffusionist, positions of Grafton Elliot-Smith and William James Perry, for whom there was no independent development of cultures. For them, civilisation was to have appeared in the Nile Valley and then spread to distant lands. From the 1930s on, this hyper-diffusionism would become untenable.

Pulman considers that Rivers' approach to the psychoanalysis/ethnology debate was therefore flawed on two counts, since it was based, on the one hand, on an entirely personal and eminently debatable interpretation of the Freudian notion of trauma and, on the other hand, on a no less debatable implicit analogy between the life story of an individual and the history of a civilisation, the principle of which is connected with hyper-diffusionist positions.[4]

The reactions and misunderstandings running through Rivers' relationship with psychoanalysis would prefigure the future problems in this debate, and might be seen as constituting a sort of "primal paradigm" of it. Pulman has also noted that one of the very first attempts at dialogue between these two disciplines led ethnologists to make a mental association between Freud's works and hyper-diffusionist theses, something which probably influenced the judgement that other ethnologists who were opposed to diffusionism pronounced on psychoanalysis. Moreover, his work was one of the mediums through which Marcel Mauss in France, or Edward Sapir in the United States, apprehended psychoanalysis. So it was that Rivers' relationship to psychoanalysis was riddled with misunderstandings having two closely intertwined causes: on the one hand, a relative unfamiliarity with Freud's works, which he nonetheless meant to criticise; on the other hand, an ongoing desire to have Freudian discoveries coincide with the hyper-diffusionist assumptions he himself sided with at the end of his life.[5]

Charles Gabriel Seligman (1873–1940)

Born in London in 1873, Seligman studied medicine, then engaged in medical research. It was from this perspective that he participated in the expedition organised in 1898–1899 by Haddon in the Torres Straits, where he met Rivers. He would principally study pathology and the medical practices of indigenous peoples. It was after this experience that he discovered a new vocation for himself, driving him to orient his endeavours toward anthropology while pursuing his medical research. Thus, he returned to New Guinea in 1904, then undertook ethnographic investigations with his wife Brenda Zara Salaman on the Veda of Ceylon (1907–1908), then on the Nilotic peoples of Anglo-Egyptian Sudan, which he would visit on many occasions, the last time being in 1921–1922.

His monographs met with great success and earned him notoriety in academic circles and a central institutional position; he then became professor of ethnology at the London School of Economics beginning in 1910, and succeeded Rivers as president of the Royal Anthropological Institute. In particular, he trained Malinowski, Meyer Fortes, and Edward Evan Evans-Pritchard. He died in Oxford in 1940. Let us not forget that Seligman and Rivers were the preeminent anthropologists of their generation in Great Britain.

Seligman also devoted himself to work in physical anthropology and to the classification of racial types, history, and prehistorical archaeology, thus to the study of material culture. Finally, he was a remarkable teacher and research director. His works, however, did not have a determinant theoretical influence on the orientations of British anthropology.

He discovered Freud's work under the same circumstances Rivers did, as a military physician treating the traumatic neuroses of war. Starting in 1917, he was very impressed by Freud's writings, in particular, by his ideas about dreams, but he expressed significant reservations about the importance accorded to sexuality. Seligman then proposed to evaluate this new psychological theory by comparing it, not only with his hospital observations about traumatic neuroses, but also with his ethnographic material.

Pulman has given three major reasons for the influence of Seligman on the emergence and development of the psychoanalysis/anthropology debate. First of all, he considers that Seligman was right at the origin of the discussions about the universality of the Œdipus complex, since he was the one who drew Malinowski's attention to psychoanalysis. Next, Seligman's work was the point of departure for the abundant anthropological literature devoted to the dreams of primitive peoples in the Anglo-Saxon world. And, finally, Seligman was one of the very first to draw the question of the field into the anthropology/psychoanalysis debate.[6]

After the war, as soon as he resumed his work in anthropology, Seligman began reflecting on the relationships between psychoanalysis and anthropology and endeavoured to explore two problems in particular. What are the psychological determinants of the behaviours of primitive people? And, what do the dreams of primitive people mean?

Regarding the first problem, he appealed to the Jungian concept of introversion/extraversion, mixing it in with Freudian concepts. According to Seligman, the frequency of cases of dissociation among savages could be explained by the fact that they were extraverted, and this explanation showed the extent to which psychoanalytical concepts can be useful in shedding light on ethnographic data. As for the dream lives of primitive people, an important question in the British anthropological tradition since Tylor, Seligman would seek to discover in it the symbolic expression of their thoughts, desires, and emotions, then would inquire into the possible universality of dream symbolism and folklore. Unfortunately, he confused the meaning socially recognised or worked out by the dreamer and the latent content of the dream, as well as, like Rivers, denying the importance of sexuality, phantasy, repression, and the status of the unconscious in psychoanalytical theory. Appealing to an anti-diffusionist strategy in opposition to Rivers, he in fact wanted to demonstrate the existence of the universality of the contents of the unconscious through the existence of typical dreams and symbols with a fixed meaning, something which would enable him to explain cultural similarities without appealing to a diffusionist hypothesis, affirming rather the independent origin and the thesis of convergence.

From the late 1920s and early 1930s onwards, fieldwork prevailed. Indeed, intensive ethnography had just established itself as a preliminary stage indispensable to all anthropological theorisation. So, for Seligman, the main question relative to the Freudian hypotheses would be one of determining the extent to which they agreed or not with the discoveries of modern anthropology. Pulman has emphasised that for Seligman, as for many anthropologists, *Totem and Taboo* embodied this Freudian ambition to go ahead and theorise in the anthropological field while paying too little attention to ethnographic data. Freud did not seem to take into account the variability of cultural contexts. Under such circumstances, Seligman affirmed that no Freudian hypothesis should ever be accepted without further verification in the field. He therefore assigned field-workers a twofold mission. On the one hand, they were to have to verify the validity of the Freudian hypotheses on site and, on the other hand, make good use of ethnographic documentation to suggest necessary modifications of psychoanalytical theory.[7] This work of verification would be entrusted to his principal students, Malinowski, of course, but also Evans-Pritchard, Siegfried Nadel and Fortes, in particular.

Thus, Seligman also played a major role in establishing dialogue between anthropologists and psychoanalysts, especially in a context hostile to psychoanalysis. Nonetheless, his writings, like those of Rivers, also showed a profound lack of familiarity with Freud's ideas, in particular the conflictual, unconscious dimension of psychic functioning, and the concepts of drive, repression, phantasy, infantile sexuality, as well as the meaning of the processes at work in dream work. Moreover, the approach consisting of verifying the validity of Freudian theses "in the field" created a misunderstanding between these two disciplines, which differ from one another in terms of methodology and object. In particular, the observation of customs and behaviours involving external reality does not correlate with that of human psychic reality, which cannot be observed in the "field" and can be represented in a different manner and in a different "field". So it is that phantasy cannot be observed in the field. This type of misunderstanding would underlie this entire affair.

Bronislaw Malinowski (1884–1942)

Born in Cracow in 1884, Malinowski studied mathematics and physics, then philosophy of science at university. In 1908, he obtained his doctorate with a thesis entitled "On the Principle of the Economy of Thought".[8] In 1910, upon the initiative of his friend Annie Brunton, a pianist, he left for London, where he attended the sociology classes taught by Edvard Westermarck and the ethnology classes taught by Seligman at the London School of Economics. In 1913, he published his first book entitled *The Family among the Australian Aborigines: A Sociological Study*,[9] in which he set out methodological rules and studied kinship phenomena showing the quasi universal existence of the individual family in configurations varying profoundly depending on the social context. He also showed the great diversity of social representations relative to procreation, with the existence of societies in which there is ignorance of physiological paternity, as was the case among those Aborigines.

Spurred on by his mentor Seligman, he left Europe for Oceania in 1914, and would only return in the spring of 1920. Following the outbreak of the First World War, as he was an Austrian national, he was considered an enemy of the Australians and was therefore placed under house arrest in Australia, without having the right to return to Europe. It was initially agreed that he would undertake a detailed study of certain Melanesian populations that Seligman had only had the opportunity to observe very rapidly in 1904. But, this plan was modified because of the war, and Malinowski then spent time in the Trobriand Islands from June 1915 to March 1916, then from December 1917 to September 1918, a period of about twenty months, according to Pulman's sources.[10]

In 1922, his famous monograph *Argonauts of the Western Pacific* was published. In 1927, he held the first chair of Professor of Anthropology at the University of London and published *Sex and Repression in Savage Society*. Then, in 1929, a new work, *The Sexual Life of Savages in North-Western Melanesia*, was published. In 1938, he moved to the United States, where he gave seminars at Yale University. He died in New Haven in 1942. *A Scientific Theory of Culture and Other Essays*, a veritable manifesto of British functionalism, was published in 1944.

Field anthropology and the functionalist theory

Unlike Radcliffe-Brown (whose first monograph was also published in 1922), Malinowski was the first really to show in his scientific writings that he was theorising on the basis of previous experience in the field, thus inaugurating a new "regime of truth" in contemporary anthropological discourse. Along with his British colleague, he would be one of the founders of a functionalist theory of culture then emerging in the 1920s. Expanding upon the ideas of Auguste Comte, Herbert Spencer, and Émile Durkheim, this principle of functionalist explanation was anti-historical in inspiration. Human beings in society must be the object of a positivistic science modelled after the sciences of nature. This approach appeals massively to biological analogies to explain social phenomena and detect similarities of organisation obtaining between the two orders, social and biological, of phenomena. It develops a unitary conception of the social world. According to it, all societies obey identical laws of functioning. Finally, it accords ontological and explanatory primacy to the whole over its parts, in this case, to society over individuals.

The idea of an organic consistency of culture led Malinowski to bring out the importance of the notion of context and to conceive of the interdependence of social facts as an expression of their functional necessity (see his study of the Kula, 1922). His scientific theory of culture dealt with the functions of social facts such as institutions as responding to "derived", "elementary" needs and as being at the service of the survival of the community and the perpetuation of the culture.

Sex and Repression in Savage Society (1927)

It was during his second stay in the Trobriand Islands that Seligman asked Malinowski to test the validity of the Freudian theses among the Trobriands. Before leaving for Oceania, he had had no knowledge of psychoanalytical theory. It was only after the publication of his monograph, according to Pulman's research, that he would read *Three Essays on the Theory of Sexuality, Introductory Lectures on Psychoanalysis, Totem and Taboo* and *Group Psychology and the Analysis of the Ego*. He would also read works by Havelock Ellis and Alexander Shand, author of *The Foundations of Character*,[11] which he would find particularly enticing. He then started the debate with psychoanalysis in three texts: "Psycho-Analysis and Anthropology" (*Nature*, 1923), "Psycho-Analysis and Anthropology" (*Psyche*, 1924), translated and published in *Imago*, and "Complex and Myth in Mother-right" (*Psyche*, 1925).[12] These last two works would be republished in *Sex and Repression in Savage Society* (1927). He made three major assertions there:

- The Trobriands are ignorant of physiological paternity;
- They enjoy a very great deal of sexual freedom, and the child's psychosexual development does not take place in the stages described by Freud. In particular, there is neither anal erotism, nor latency phase;
- The Œdipus complex is not universal. It is not present among the Trobriands. However, a nuclear complex specific to matrilineal societies exists within the framework of which the boy's incestuous desires would be directed towards his sister, while his hostile impulses would be directed against his maternal uncle.

Before going over each one of these assertions, let us look at the problem as formulated by Malinowski in *Sex and Repression in Savage Society*, where he wrote:

> Psycho-analysis was born from medical practice, and its theories are mainly psychological, but it stands in close relation to two other branches of learning: biology and the science of society. It is perhaps one of its chief merits that it forges another link between these three subdivisions of the science of man. The psychological views of Freud – his theories of conflict, repression, the unconscious, the formation of complexes – form the best elaborated part of psycho-analysis, and they cover its proper field. The biological doctrine – the treatment of sexuality and of its relation to other instincts, the concept of the 'libido' and its various transformations – is a part of the theory which is much less finished, less free from contradictions and lacunae, and which receives more criticism, partly spurious and partly justified. The sociological aspect, which most interests us here, will deserve more attention. Curiously enough, though sociology and anthropology have contributed most evidence in favour of psycho-analysis, and though the doctrine of the Œdipus complex has obviously a sociological aspect, this aspect has received the least attention...

> The sociological nature of this doctrine is obvious – the whole Freudian drama is played out within a definite type of social organisation, in the narrow circle of the family, composed of father, mother, and children.[13]

Malinowski therefore maintained that the issues surrounding the Œdipus complex are not exclusively psychological, because two sociological aspects are involved: that of the sociological nature of family influences; and that of the impact of the complex on society. He considered that every family structure, varying in function of human societies, also presents a type of "nuclear complex", that is variable, and not universal, as the psychoanalysts had claimed without availing themselves of either ethnographic material or experience in the field.

Despite the now legendary criticism of the "sociological aspect" of psychoanalysis, researchers still focusing on this problem have unfortunately not picked up on an essential observation made by Malinowski on the subject of a principal characteristic of psychoanalysis, i.e., its links with biology and sociology, something which Freud had described. It was even "one of its chief merits" to have forged "another link between these three divisions of the science of man"!

Ignorance of physiological paternity

According to Malinowski, among the Trobriands, paternity is a purely social relation and "Real kinship, that is identity of substance", 'the same body', exists only through the mother. He explains that

> the husband is not regarded as the father of the children in the sense in which we use this word; physiologically he has nothing to do with their birth, according to the ideas of the natives, who are ignorant of physiological fatherhood. Children, in native belief, are inserted into the mother's womb as tiny spirits, generally by the agency of the spirit of a deceased kinswoman of the mother.[14]

Further on, Malinowski lists a father's "duty towards his wife's children". Thus, he is first a true "nurse", tender and conscientious, then would become a protective companion. While the "mother's brother represents the principle of discipline, authority, and executive authority within the family", the children will be only successors and heirs of their maternal uncle.[15]

On infantile sexuality and the phase of latency

All the while affirming that in Melanesia, the child's sexual development follows a different path than that of European children, especially characterised by the fact that there is "no repression, no censure, no moral reprobation of infantile sexuality of the genital type" and no period of what Freud supposedly called "pre-genital", "anal-erotic" interest, Malinowski also acknowledged that "the subject naturally presents certain difficulties of observation".[16]

Looking at the period extending from the age of six to puberty, he considered that the Freudian thesis of the latency period, observed among young Europeans, was not universally valid. It was not a matter of human nature, but of social factors. Thus, in Melanesia, this period of childhood is called the "stage of infantile independence", when boys and girls play together "in a sort of juvenile republic".[17] Among these games, he mentions the sexual pastimes initiating them into the future adult sexual practices. Their sexuality therefore undergoes gradual, continuous evolution up until puberty, while having strictly to respect one taboo, the very early one that governs relations between brother and sister born of the same mother and establishes strict measures for their separation. At a later point, Malinowski explained that this taboo extends to all the other women of the clan to which the boy belongs. So it is that "the sexual world is for the boy divided into two moieties: one of these, embracing the women of his own clan, is prohibited to him; the other, to which women of the remaining three clans belong, is lawful".[18]

Malinowski's text on the sexual freedom of the Melanesians is in fact strewn with contradictions. I find that their sexual practices are all the same restricted by rules, by prohibitions. What is more, confirmation of infantile sexuality is not simply based on observation of behaviours and attitudes as Malinowski might think and wish. Indeed, he himself recognises certain difficulties inherent in observation in his method and his essential principle. But, since he was primarily concerned with asserting sociological primacy over "human nature", which then created confusion between its psychic and biological components, the entire psychic dimension could not but have eluded him.

The Œdipus complex and the nuclear family complex

Drawing inspiration from the psychology of Alexander Shand, Malinowski defined these two complexes as being systems of the child's (the boy's) attitudes and feelings towards his father, mother, brother, sister and, among Trobriands, towards the maternal uncle. According to him

> the system of attitudes typical of our patriarchal society is formed in early Infancy... when the boy is about five or six years old, his attitudes are well formed, though perhaps not finally settled... In the matrilineal society at that stage, though the child has developed very definite sentiments towards its mother and father, nothing suppressed, nothing negative, no frustrated desire forms a part of them. Whence arises this difference? As we saw, the social arrangements of the Trobriand matriliny are in almost complete harmony with the biological course of development, while the institution of father-right found in our society crosses and represses a number of natural impulses and inclinations.[19]

He cites repression of the young boy's clinging to his mother, the distancing of the son from his father, therefore, the menacing rivalry. In contrast, Trobriands allow "the sensual clinging of the child to his mother . . . to take its natural course till it plays itself out".[20]

According to Malinowski, while in our culture the Œdipus complex solidifies and crystallises during this "early period of puberty", among the Trobriands, the "first complexes" are mainly formed during the "second epoch", during which the adolescent is submitted to two principal imperatives: the submission to matriarchal law inculcated and imposed by the maternal uncle, which then awakens in the adolescent ambivalent feelings composed of hate, jealousy, resentment, rivalry cloaked in veneration; and the taboo of incest with one's sister, which extends to all the maternal relations, then to women of the clan.[21] He wrote that:

> Applying to each society a terse, though somewhat crude formula, we might say that in the Œdipus complex there is a repressed desire to kill the father and marry the mother, while in the matrilineal society of the Trobriands the wish is to marry the sister and to kill the maternal uncle.[22]

So, Malinowski acknowledged that Freud and psychoanalysis had discovered a nuclear family complex specific to our patriarchal western society and had elucidated the causes of it, as well as laying claim to his own discovery, that of the nuclear complex existing in a family belonging to a matrilineal society such as the Trobriand society. But that is not all. He claimed to have made a second personal discovery:

> I have established a deep correlation between the type of society and the nuclear complex found there. While this is in a sense a confirmation of the main tenet of Freudian psychology, it might compel us to modify certain of its features, or rather to make some of its formulae more elastic. To put it concretely, it appears necessary to draw in more systematically the correlation between biological and social influences; not to assume the universal existence of the Œdipus complex, but in studying every type of civilization, to establish the special complex which pertains to it.[23]

It definitely seems that his basic lack of understanding of the Œdipus complex, as well as of infantile sexuality, is based as much on a denial of their phantasy, unconscious psychic dimension, scotomising the repression process, as on their behavioural, biological definition. Combining them with an assumption of sociological primacy and the enticing contributions of Shand's psychology led Malinowski to create a "nuclear family complex", a system of attitudes and sentiments of the child towards his close relations determined by the family structure inherent in the type of society.

Malinowski's discourse seems to me paradigmatic of the later discourse of the international community of anthropologists in the course of its history.

The Œdipus complex is in fact transformed into the nuclear family complex specific to our patriarchal society; a different type of complex exists in matriarchal societies. Consequently, he robs it of its universal value in order to replace it with the universality of the nuclear family complex that he had discovered. Malinowski therefore claimed his twofold discovery, that of the universal existence of the family complex, then of the type of complex prevalent in a matrilineal society, and that of the existence of a twofold correlation: on the one hand, between the type of society and type of family complex; on the other hand, between biological factors and social influences, since he also conceived of the nuclear complex as pertaining to biological factors, devoid of any properly psychic dimension.

In 1927, he would react to Ernest Jones' article entitled "Mother Right and the Sexual Ignorance of Savages", published in the *International Journal of Psychoanalysis* in 1925 and taken from a 1924 lecture given at the British Psycho-Analytical Society. Having already expressed a distinctly ambivalent attitude toward Freud's ideas in his articles of 1924 and 1925, he would confirm it and this would be accompanied by a surprising lack of comprehension of Jones' thesis, something that enabled him to maintain that his views were in accordance with Freud and would even confirm the universal scope of his discovery.

Let me point out that for Maurice Godelier, the fact that in a matrilineal society such as the Trobriand society "children are not engendered by the father but by the mother alone, the fact that they do not share any substantial or spiritual link with their father but are of the same blood as their mother and her brother and the fact that they re-embody one of their maternal ancestors, all correspond perfectly to the logic of their kinship system".[24]

Pulman has raised questions about the felicitous longevity of Malinowski's ideas in spite of his many contradictions proclaiming the reign of cultural relativism advocated by American anthropology. He considers that from both an ethnographic and a psychoanalytical point of view the longevity of Malinowski's contentions in the contemporary anthropological doxy, despite the pile of evidence to the contrary, is truly astounding. And it was Pulman who showed, in particular in his work *Anthropologie et psychanalyse* (2002), that Malinowski's discourse involves a certain number of contradictions internal to his argumentation, an obvious contrast between his general assertions and the careful examination of his ethnographic documentation. Moreover, Pulman mentions the paucity of Malinowski's knowledge of psychoanalysis and the lack of techniques for investigating the unconscious. Finally, he brings up the particular psychic circumstances in which the researcher found himself during his stay among the Trobriands, which unquestionably influenced his observations and analysis of the materials he collected.[25]

Ernest Jones (1879–1958)

Born on January 1, 1879 in Gowertown, Wales, Jones studied at the University College of South Wales in Cardiff, then at the University College of London. He obtained his physician's diploma in 1900, then turned to neurology and published works on hemiplegia, hysteria, and speech pathology. However, he was also drawn to surgery, psychopathology, and psychiatry. He held several posts in hospitals and engaged in many research projects. It was in 1903 that his friend and colleague, the surgeon Wilfred Trotter, spoke to him about Freud's works, his *Studies on Hysteria* in particular.

While continuing to practice as a neurologist, Jones learned German by reading *Fragments of an Analysis of a Case of Hysteria,* about the Dora case-history, and *The Interpretation of Dreams*. In 1905–1906, he was the first to practice psychoanalysis in England. He would meet Carl Gustav Jung at the congress in Amsterdam, then leave for one month to Munich to work in Emil Kraepelin's clinic. He participated in the first Psychoanalytical Congress held in April 1908 in Salzburg, where he presented his first psychoanalytical work entitled: "Rationalisation in Everyday Life". He met Freud there, but also other psychoanalysts, among them Abraham Brill, a young psychoanalyst living in the United States.

Serious difficulties encountered with his colleagues and public opinion would lead to the cessation of his hospital work in England. He was then offered a position as associate professor of psychiatry in Toronto, where he lived from September 1908 until the summer of 1913.

He and Brill would divide up areas of influence between them with the creation of an American Society affiliated with the international Association founded at the 1910 congress. Brill in fact created the New York Psychoanalytic Association (February 12, 1911) and Jones the American Psychoanalytic Association (May 9, 1911). During this Canadian period, Jones published his first writings on "applied psychoanalysis", which I shall come back to later on.

Having returned definitively to Europe, following Freud's advice, he went to Budapest in the summer of 1913 to undergo analysis with Ferenczi, which would last around two months. He would thus be the first analyst to have undergone personal psychoanalysis.

Upon his arrival in London, he founded the London Psychoanalytic Society on October 30, 1913, which was then dissolved in 1919 owing to disagreements with the members defending Jungian positions. So a new society, the British Psychoanalytical Society was created in February 1919, over which he would preside until 1944, just as he would preside over the International Psychoanalytical Association from 1920 to 1924 and from 1932 to 1949. He would give more and more lectures on psychoanalysis, working thus towards its progressive spread, both in the very reticent medical profession and in the general public. In 1920, he also founded the *International Journal of Psychoanalysis*, serving as its editor until 1939. He also coordinated the translation team composed of James and Alix Strachey, Joan Rivière, and John Rickman, who started work on the first systematic translation of Freud's works into English.

He fought to assure the scientific status of psychoanalysis in Great Britain and to establish a British psychoanalytical identity, in particular by defending Melanie Klein's ideas against the severe criticisms of Freud and his daughter Anna at the end of the 1930s. In the beginning of the 1940s, at the time of the "Controversies", he would play an important role as mediator between Anna Freud and Melanie Klein.

He devoted the last ten years of his life to writing the three volumes of Freud's biography (1953–1957) and his own autobiography, *Free Associations: Memories of a Psychoanalyst*, published in 1959. He died in 1958.

His work and its role in the psychoanalysis/anthropology debate

Jones' research work would be clinical and theoretical. His research on war neuroses would represent his most important clinical work. Theoretically speaking, there is his original research on psychoanalytical characterology "The God Complex: the Belief One is God and the Resulting Character Traits" (first published in German 1913), and "Anal-Erotic Character Traits" (1918), but also his contributions to the theory of affects (fear, hate, guilt), to the theory of instincts (aggressiveness and the death instinct), the introduction of the notion of *aphanisis* and his studies on feminine sexuality, in particular. I shall deal with his constant early interest in socio-cultural facts and his concern to apply the psychoanalytical method manifesting itself very early in his work on "applied" psychoanalysis. Indeed, from the time of his first psychoanalytical paper "Rationalisation in Everyday Life" (1908), he stressed the importance of psychoanalysis for the social sciences.

But Jones' first important works (1909–1916), which would lead to his masterful work on the theory of symbolism (1916), concerned dream activity (dreams and nightmares) and the interpretation of folklore themes and superstitions in terms of dream theory. His study *On the Nightmare* (1912)[26] was the model for his later writings on "applied" psychoanalysis and the point of departure of his research on symbolism and the forms of symbolisation. According to Jones, nightmares were a form of anxiety dreams expressing a psychic conflict regarding an incestuous desire. In this book he compared the particular characteristics and themes of nightmares with beliefs about incubuses, vampires, werewolves, the devil, and witches, which would be the product of the projection of repressed sexual material in which incestuous desires and forms of infantile sexuality dominate.

At the time *Totem and Taboo* was being written, Jones would produce papers exploring folkloric themes from legends, analysing their characteristics and their psychological meanings, as well as their symbolic relationship to different forms of infantile sexuality. So it was with "The Symbolic Significance of Salt in Folklore and Superstition", published in German in *Imago* in 1912, the first year of the journal, and "The Madonna's Conception through the Ear" published in German in 1914 in the *Jahrbuch der Psychoanalyse*.[27]

The ideas in these writings found fruition in the remarkable synthesis represented by "The Theory of Symbolism" (1916), a work bringing together the contributions of Freud, Rank, Sachs, and Ferenczi in order to pit them against Jungian theses.

According to Jones, true symbolism, in the strict sense of the word, must be distinguished from other forms of indirect representation. True symbolism, origin of symbols, differs from the symbolic equivalents that are products of symbols. Drawing inspiration from the writings of Rank and Sachs (1913), he saw symbols as a means of expression of repressed feelings and ideas and conceived of symbolism as a process by which an idea is used, usually unconsciously, as a substitute for an unconscious idea. As a product of substitution, it is linked to those other formations of compromise which are the symptoms. Symbolism would therefore proceed from repression. He thus detected a psychological source common to individual and cultural symbolisations. He concluded his study of the relationships of symbols to the unconscious in this manner:

> All psychoanalytical experience goes to shew that the primary ideas of life, the only ones that can be symbolised – those, namely, concerning the bodily self, the relation to the family, birth, love, and death – retain in the unconscious throughout life their original importance, and that from them is derived a very large part of the more secondary interests of the conscious mind. As energy flows from them, and never to them, and as they constitute the most repressed part of the mind, it is comprehensible that symbolism should take place in one direction only. Only what is repressed is symbolised; only what is repressed needs to be symbolised. This conclusion is the touchstone of the psychoanalytical theory of symbolism.[28]

He would pursue his work on the psychology of religion and of the Christian religion, notably with his essay "A Psycho-Analytic Study of the Holy Ghost Concept" (1922).[29]

But let us now look at his debate with Malinowski, mentioning to begin with the lecture entitled "Psychoanalysis and Anthropology" that he gave on February 19, 1924 to the Royal Anthropological Institute upon the invitation of its president, Professor Seligman.

"Mother Right and the Sexual Ignorance of Savages", published in *The International Journal of Psychoanalysis* in 1925, was initially a lecture read before the British Psychoanalytical Society on November 19, 1924.[30] For him, it was a matter of reacting to the propositions formulated by Malinowski in the three texts already mentioned and discussed above.

After referring to the writings of McLennan (*Primitive Marriage*, 1865) and Hartland (*Legend of Perseus and Primitive Paternity*, 1909), representing the mother-right as a relic of a time in which people were ignorant of the facts of procreation, and sexual ignorance having therefore played an important role in the development of social institutions and beliefs, he brought up Malinowski's valuable observations in the field and his final conclusion establishing the ignorance of paternity as being an original characteristic of primitive psychology. But Jones was clearly sceptical and not surprised by the Trobriand material. Indeed, his writings on the symbolism of salt, the conception of the Virgin Mary through her ear, his psychoanalytic study of the Holy Spirit, as well as Reik's research on initiation rites, would enable him to propose a solid psychoanalytical understanding of the presumed ignorance of physiological paternity in connection with the institution of mother-right.

As a preliminary, he made two critical remarks. In the first place, all the "savages" in the world, even those belonging to matrilineal societies, know the role played by the man in procreation. Moreover, as a good specialist in symbolism, he could not be surprised that the Trobriands' symbolic discourse on procreation expressed unconscious knowledge of the truth. So, he considered that these two phenomena (the ignorance of physiological paternity and the institution of mother-right) were determined by one and the same motivation, that of deflecting the hostility towards the father felt by the growing boy. The oedipal hatred of the father and its repression would have thus played the most important role according to Jones. He explained that "repudiation of the father's part in coitus and procreation, and consequently softening and deflection of the hatred against him, a consummation desired equally by son and father" is

> what has happened where the institution of mother-right is combined with the denial of paternal procreation...
>
> But the father is not so easily disposed of, a fact which might be used in support of Freud's suggestion... The father disappears from the scene only to reappear in a disguised form. The idea of the powerful and hated father is sacrificed in favour of an ancestral spirit, who in a supernatural manner impregnates the mother.[31]

Jones considers that "Malinowski's conclusion is doubtless correct on the purely descriptive plane, but he goes on to use it as the basis of an extremely doubtful hypothesis in which he attempts to modify Freud's theory of the nuclear family complex".[32]

Jones therefore defends the thesis of the defensive nature of the institution of the matrilineal system combined with its avuncular complex, where the "forbidden and unconsciously loved sister is only a substitute for the mother, as the uncle plainly is for the father". While Malinowski claimed that the Œdipus complex was but a "late product", Jones maintained that it was the "*fons et origo*".[33] And he concludes that

> The patriarchal system, as we know it, betokens acknowledging the supremacy of the father and yet the ability to accept this even with affection, without having to have recourse to a system either of mother-right or of complicated taboos. That means the taming of the man, the gradual assimilation of the Œdipus complex...
>
> Well might Freud say that the recognition of the father's place in the family signified the most important progress in cultural development.[34]

As I said above, Malinowski would respond to Jones in 1927 through his book *Sex and Repression in Savage Society*, which would be strenuously criticised.

In his article "Ernest Jones et l'anthropologie", Pulman has observed that in contesting Malinowski's conclusions, Jones profoundly called into question the model of ethnographic authority. If a psychoanalyst theorising in London was in a better position to interpret facts about the Trobriands than the ethnographer who had collected them, the field would lose at least a part of the credibility attributed to it in the discursive regime of contemporary anthropology.[35] He considers Jones' role in this debate to have been particularly underestimated both by anthropologists, which would be understandable, and by psychoanalysts, which is more worrisome – the latter, considering the major role played by Róheim. Pulman has said that it seems to him personally that, on this point, psychoanalysts have curiously, and too hastily, embraced the argument of ethnographic authority and that one need but note the litany of references that are both respectful and credit Róheim with having both genuine competence in psychoanalysis and direct ethnographic experience! Jones himself contributed to this image when, in the preface that he wrote for *The Riddle of the Sphinx* (Géza Róheim, 1934), he abundantly emphasised Róheim's "qualifications" and gave, so to speak, the impression of bowing to someone more competent than himself.[36]

Following Malinowski, at the beginning of the 1930s, the principal figures of British anthropology, especially Radcliffe-Brown and Evans-Pritchard, would express distinct distrust of psychoanalysis, due essentially to a reaction to Rivers' work, according to Pulman. Moreover, this debate was going to shift to the United States, animated then by the representatives of culturalism and of the school called "culture and personality". But, before going into the debate animated by these Americans, let us take a look at the major role played by Róheim.

Géza Róheim (1891–1953) and psychoanalytical anthropology

Born in Budapest on September 12, 1891, after finishing secondary school, Róheim attended the University of Budapest. However, owing to the lack of any regular teaching of anthropology there, he was obliged to pursue his studies in Leipzig, then in Berlin, in order to study human geography, of which anthropology was a branch in those days. It was during this period of his life that he was profoundly and lastingly influenced by the work of Adolf Bastian. He would obtain a doctorate in philosophy, section geography.

While pursuing his studies of anthropology, he discovered the works of Freud and his disciples, Sandor Ferenczi, Karl Abraham, Ernest Jones, and Carl Jung, in particular. He was immediately captivated by their ideas and fully subscribed to the Freudian doctrine, which he would never question. In 1911, at the age of twenty, he published a study in *Ethnographia*, the journal of the Hungarian Society of Ethnology, on "Dragons and Dragon Killers"[37] in which he appealed to psychoanalytical concepts.

During the years 1915 and 1916, he underwent analysis with Ferenczi, with whom he would remain bound by a close friendship. This psychoanalysis would be continued by Mrs Vilma Kovacs. He met Freud during the fifth Psychoanalytic Congress held in Budapest in September 1918. Over the course of the year 1921, the journal *Imago* accepted four of his successive studies on the self (*das Selbst*) which, along with his paper on "Australian Totemism", earned him the Freud Prize for applied psychoanalysis.

In 1925, he published his first major anthropological work, *Australian Totemism: A Pyscho-analytic Study in Anthropology*, in London.[38] Very interested in the problem of origins, he attached particular importance to the population that was considered to be the most primitive on the planet, and therefore closest to the origins: the Australians of the Central Desert Region. It was a matter of interdisciplinary research following directly from *Totem and Taboo*, the general thesis of which was that the great cultural and economic changes of the history of humanity – fire, agriculture, the domestication of animals, among others – would have their source in unconscious psychic motivations. Moreover, Róheim introduced phantasies associated with the mother figure into the model of the primal horde, as well as highlighting the essential bisexuality of cultural formations.

This book was published at the time Malinowski was casting doubt on the universality of the Œdipus complex and through this on the pertinence of psychoanalytical interpretations of ethnographic data. In addition, as discussed above, Jones was engaged in a debate with British anthropologists. So, the psychoanalytical community felt the need to send into the field an ethnologist who had received genuine psychoanalytical training. Róheim was the right choice, and plans for an expedition shaped up with the lively encouragement of Freud, Ferenczi, and Vilma Kovacs. At the beginning of 1928, Princess Marie Bonaparte proposed to finance an expedition that could extend over two or three years, and which Róheim was completely free to organise as he saw fit. Thus he left London with his wife at the end of 1928.

Róheim spent a month in Aden and Djibouti, then travelled to Australia, where he stayed from the end of February 1929 until the end of the year. Later, he left for Normanby Island for a nine-month stay lasting until November 1930. He then spent two months among the Yuma Indians, where Arizona, California, and Mexico meet. Finally, he would return to Europe. After giving many talks and lectures to psychoanalytic societies in Europe, he published "Psychoanalysis of Primitive Cultural Types" (1932). The International Psychoanalytical Association devoted two whole issues of *the International Journal of Psychoanalysis* to the publication of the text. For the first time, a psychoanalyst had actually directly studied "primitive" societies in the field by exclusively and systematically resorting to the methods of psychoanalysis. According to Róheim, these methods – which I shall describe below – would henceforth be used by every study in psychoanalytical anthropology. In 1934, he published *The Riddle of the Sphinx*.

Triply threatened, as a Jew, psychoanalyst, and democrat, he was obliged to choose the path of exile. He moved then to the United States in 1938. For nearly two years, he was attached to a psychiatric establishment, Worcester State Hospital, in Massachusetts. He devoted most of his time to practising psychoanalysis. Around the beginning of 1940, he moved to New York City, where he would remain until his death in 1953. There, he practised psychoanalysis, taught at the New York Psychoanalytic Institute, gave lectures and published one work after another. Among his important works are: *The Origin and Function of Culture* (1943), *War, Crime and the Covenant* (1945), *The Eternal Ones of the Dream* (1945), *Psychoanalysis and Anthropology* (1950), *The Gates of the Dream* (1953).

In 1947, thanks to a grant accorded by the Viking Fund Inc., he undertook a final field expedition, among the Navahos this time, and published "The Œdipus Complex of the Navaho" in his great synthetic work *Psychoanalysis and Anthropology* (1950). That same year, he founded an annual journal called *Psychoanalysis and the Social Sciences* so as to assure a wider impact for psychoanalytical anthropology, and provide it with a means of expressing and disseminating information and bringing people together. He died in 1953.

Sources of inspiration, influences

Apart from the major, decisive influence of Freudian thought, it can be said that Géza Róheim received and integrated a certain number of the notions and concepts of Ferenczi, Abraham, Klein, Herman, and the anthropologist Bastian, just as he would be vigorous in rejecting "two counter-models" represented by Malinowski and Abram Kardiner. Róheim's psychoanalytical anthropology was therefore developed as a faithful extension of Freudian thought. He would, however, rework certain fundamental concepts of psychoanalysis by introducing, notably, a brand new biological dimension with the theory of fœtalisation.

Sándor Ferenczi

Róheim had a conception similar to Ferenczi's when he proposed the idea of "genitalisation", of "libidinisation" of the milieu, of external reality, presented as a fundamental cultural process. Like Ferenczi, he would accord a primordial role to the mother–child relationship and show the extent to which the separation from the mother constitutes a fundamental traumatic situation. In addition, he would integrate the theory of seduction of the adult into his conception of ontogenetic trauma. He would also remain faithful to Ferenczi's biological inspiration and would be pleased to discover Louis Bolk's theory of fœtalisation, "bio-analysis" – substitute for that of Ferenczi – which he needed as an indispensable foundation for his construction. Finally, like Ferenczi, he would place the human body at the heart of his interests; and it would be both the point of departure and the point of convergence of his work in the discipline. For Róheim, there were no phantasies among the most archaic ones that do not find expression in the body and also concrete, physical realisation in acts and forms and cultural figurations.

Melanie Klein

With Klein and Róheim, Roger Dadoun has observed, it was a matter of radical, essential complementarity, something which has led him to say that there is nothing in the Kleinian "phantasy" not finding an anthropological equivalent in Róheim, and nothing in Róheim's descriptions and observations that some Kleinian discovery can fail to shed light on. In their work, Klein and Róheim, each from a different angle, viewed human reality as essentially being a place of phantasy, a phantasy universe.

Klein depicted its "inner side" in very young children; Róheim described its "external aspect" in cultural formations.[39] Róheim also made use of the paranoid position–depressive position succession as well as mechanisms of introjection and projection, essential components of the psychic structure and of culture. Finally, Róheim understood culture as a vast defence system against human anxiety. In his view, people always remained as anxious children; thus the link is established with the Kleinian conception of children's anxiety.

Adolf Bastian

Róheim apparently found in the German anthropologist Adolf Bastian a kind of academic, traditionalistic backing of his own conception of the universality of psychic structures through the differences of cultures. Bastian's theoretical vision, which presumes the psychic unity of humanity, places him outside evolutionism and diffusionism. According to him, out of essential and intrinsic necessity, humanity always spontaneously produces basic ideas, elementary universal mental forms that he called *Elementargedanken*, which are therefore at the origin of all human culture and will. At a second stage, these will be influenced by the milieu, leading to the constitution of cultural areas endowed with specific traits. At the same time, or at a third stage, these original cultural contexts would come into contact and influence one another reciprocally, thus initiating evolutions that again complexify and enrich their traits. According to Bastian, anthropologists must first extract these "elementary ideas" common to humanity, then study the modifications produced by the environment, and finally the transformations imposed by the historical evolution and cultural contacts. Ethnology's task would therefore essentially be that of an ethno-psychology.

That is the programme that Róheim translated into the language of psychoanalysis with the discovery of universal, abiding phantasies beneath the singularity of historical or external cultural traits.

Methods of psychoanalytical anthropology

Psychoanalytical anthropology as conceived by Róheim affirmed human unity, "the unity of the human race". It envisages the discovery and exploration of the multiple cultural and social expressions of the unconscious. The psychoanalyst-anthropologist would himself collect the ethnographic material in the field, which he would interpret at a later time. However, he would also have to remain a practising psychoanalyst. Roger Dadoun considers that this method of investigation enables one to eliminate a fundamental dichotomy. For him, it is not a figure of alterity and alienation that the psychoanalyst expects to find in the field in accordance with some typical phantasy of traditional ethnology, but rather the identity of the unconscious in diverse guises.[40] According to Róheim, the methods of psychoanalytical anthropology were nothing other than psychoanalysis itself in action in specific cultural contexts, the only differences lying in the norms and practical adjustments imposed by the field work.

The analysis of dreams

For Róheim, the dream material of men, women, and children, composed as it is of the account and associations, often indicates the unconscious meaning of an institution, a custom, a belief. He strenuously rejects the "culturalist" argument which considers it necessary to analyse dreams within their cultural contexts. The symbolism is universal, the psychic processes at work in dream work are universal, and the differences appearing in the secondary elaboration of the dreams of an Australian and a European can be elucidated with the help of associations. In "Dream Analysis and Field Work in Anthropology" (1947), he concluded his essay focused on the analysis of the dreams of two personalities of Melanesian culture named Ramoramo and Kauanamo by stating a valid universal methodological principle. He explained that

> The society in which Ramoramo and Kauanamo lived is matrilineal and matrilocal. Any anthropologist of the 'cultural' school would come to the conclusion that they have no Œdipus complex. The point is however that you cannot arrive at reliable conclusions regarding personality and the unconscious without analyzing dreams.[41]

Analysis of children at play

Róheim was the first to have applied the Kleinian technique of analysis of playing in the anthropological domain. In both Australia and Melanesia, he devoted very many sessions to observing the games of children of very different ages, sometimes supplying them with all the equipment for playing games of European origin, sometimes allowing them to express themselves spontaneously using objects chosen at random, or with their own body. He observed that, as everywhere in the world, children especially play at being papa and mama, at taking care of or punishing children, thus revealing the nature of the genuine parental relationships on the social level. Thus, for example, he observed that the games of the children of Normanby Island, a matrilineal society, would shed light on specific nuances of the Œdipus complex.

Detailed, precise investigation of sexual life

For Róheim, this was a question of indispensable research constituting an original approach to exploring the "psychic structure of a people". He considered, nonetheless, that because of the action of the repression at work in both them and the "civilised" researchers, it was not possible to keep, as Malinowski had done, purely and simply to the discourse of indigenous peoples.

Study of symbolism in myths

Róheim studied the symbolism in myths, stories, rituals, and customs, highlighting the pre-oedipal elements in particular, and taking into account a good deal of material that had generally been considered marginal and had been neglected: random remarks, slips of the tongue, jokes, insults, expletives, obscene anecdotes, and insignificant gestures, especially.

Some conceptual elaborations

The "ontogenetic theory" of culture occupies a central place in the theoretical work that I shall present before looking at certain of his concepts, his discourse on the Œdipus complex, and his response to Malinowski's criticism.

In opposition to Freud's phylogenetic conception, Róheim wished to identify the fundamental sources of culture in the existing mental structures. It was very young children who represented, who embodied, this living present in which cultural formations are rooted. It was the experiences they had and underwent that would serve as materials and a medium for all cultural work. Ontogenesis would therefore be the foundation of all culture. This is the principle behind Róheim's ontogenetic theory of culture.

For him, childhood was a traumatic experience opening onto two interdependent, parallel prospects. In the first place, there is a prospect that is phylogenetic in that it takes us back to the primal past of the human species, which is a fœtalised species, meaning that it has conserved and stabilised a fœtal status – according to the work of Bolk, a Dutch biologist who developed his theory of foetalisation, thus providing Róheim's psychoanalytical theory with a biological base. Indeed, born prematurely, before term – the term being defined by the complete evolution of a pre-human ancestor – unfinished, human beings do not in the beginning have at their disposal sufficient tools and means to face the world. They live in a situation of distress, dependency, and fear. That is why, as a fœtalised species, humanity lives in traumatic conditions.

The second prospect considered is ontogenetic. In every culture, individual human beings are subject, right from the beginning of their existence, to adults' actions. They are subject to pressures, conditioning, seduction, shocks, and "traumas" are solicited on all sides in every sense, and this transforms them, shapes them, makes them into cultural beings. Róheim called all these experiences, to the extent that they are organised and coordinated around a dominant form, "ontogenetic traumas". The dominant form is not the same in every culture. Each culture can be characterised by a specific trauma, and a particular dialectic relation takes place between trauma and culture. Culture imposes a trauma upon the children that acts as a primary cultural matrix, and the trauma governs the culture's specific forms and processes in a cycle that repeats itself in each generation. In *The Riddle of the Sphinx* (1934), Róheim wrote that "With the discovery that certain peoples have certain habits in their treatment of their children that produce traumata analogous to those discovered in analysis we have a new method of explaining the characteristic features of their sociology".[42]

But the phantasy dimension also plays a major role. Depending on the cultural areas in which parental intervention is exercised, it will awaken, mobilise, exacerbate and organise certain types of phantasies among themselves and invest them with an energy and power that one might call cultural in that they will later animate and nourish the typical formations of the cultural area in question. The ontogenetic trauma would therefore be a composite figure combining phantasy and reality, and the whole culture would be nothing other than a vast reactional formation constructed to respond to the ontogenetic trauma. Consequently, this ontogenetic theory of culture considers each culture's own trauma.

In his work *The Origin and Function of Culture* (1943), while reworking his ontogenetic theory of culture, Róheim depicted "civilization or culture as manifestation of the Eros", and showed that "human history is . . . based on Eros".[43] It is therefore the creative aspect of linking and unifying cultural formations that is highlighted there. However, for him, any view of the origin and function of culture would be incomplete without a theory of sublimation. Moreover, he established structural and fundamental identity between neurosis and culture through "analogies drawn between the institutions of primitive mankind on the one side and the 'individual institutions' of neurotics on the other".[44] Then he distinguished between neurosis and sublimation in this way: "A neurosis isolates; a sublimation unites. In a sublimation, something new is created–a house, or a community, or a tool–and it is created in a group or for the use of a group".[45]

By discovering an analogy between sublimation and cultural object, he introduced the notion of intermediate object halfway between the narcissistic position and the object position. This is in fact a matter of an object directed both toward the ego and toward an external reality. This would be the very definition of cultural objects according to Róheim. This concept can be compared to that of "transitional object" introduced and elaborated by Winnicott. But, if for Winnicott, the latter was initially essentially "an oral object",[46] for Róheim, the intermediate object, for example the Tjurunga (sacred object of the Central Australian tribes), was a phallic object figuring in a very sophisticated socio-cultural context.

In *The Gates of the Dream* (1952),[47] Róheim agreed with certain of Tylor's and Jones' major intuitions linking dream products to certain cultural products (animism for the former, and beliefs and popular superstitions for the latter). He would even go so far as to think that dreams were one of the major sources of human culture.

Let us now take a look at his criticism of Malinowski as regards the lack of any Œdipus complex in a matrilineal society. Róheim displayed an ambivalent attitude with regard to Malinowski. In addition, it was certainly because of Malinowski's endeavours that he would require that anthropologists have ongoing, complete, psychoanalytical training, in order to keep the unconscious in tune with cultural experiences.

On Normanby Island, a matrilineal society close to the Trobriands, he uncovered oedipal motions repressed in its members. His first findings would be published in 1932 in *The International Journal of Psychanalysis*:

> This society is based on a series of displacements of the Œdipus situation to the uncle-aunt-nephew situation and then to the brother-in-law-wife-husband situation.

Actually, the boy's teacher is not always the uncle. Some boys stay with their fathers. Or they may go to another relative in the mother's clan . . . In the manifest content of dreams, of course, the uncle will frequently be the enemy because the conflict with the uncle is frequently conscious or preconscious. Add to this the sister-incest myth of Tauhau and the fact that the girl-friend or mistress (rawerawe) is politely called nuhuna (sister) and we have the complete Malinowskian picture: no Œdipus complex but a man in love with his sister and ambivalent antagonism against the uncle! It was exactly on the basis of data like this that Malinowski made the same great discovery.

Now, of course, this is completely absurd. Since in the first five to ten years of his life the child has lived with the father and mother and it is only after this that he goes to his uncle, how can we assume that he starts with an avuncular complex instead of an Œdipus complex? Indeed, Malinowski himself states the facts clearly and in such a manner as to invalidate his own theory completely. . .

The child starts life in the Oedipal situation with an Œdipus complex. In the prepuberty phase society sets up another, more severe father for him to contend with. This is the maternal uncle. It is therefore possible to shift some of the hostility from the father to the uncle.[48]

His personal conception of the Œdipus complex

Róheim right away presented certain of his founding principles, phylogenetic ones especially, referring again to Bolk's theory, something which enabled him to reject the Freudian hypothesis that "it is evident that the Œdipus complex is a direct derivative of our partly premature, partly conservative (prolonged or retarded) rate of growing up."[49] He continues:

> Since man always wants a mother he must inevitably clash with his own offspring. The question is who owns the mother? We could also phrase it in this way: the adult is still oral, the oral child is already genital... Human sex-life is therefore influenced by a prolongation of infancy. But I think we have to do with a two-fold mechanism: the genitalization of the child is parallel to the infantilization of the adult....
>
> This double mechanism of the adult in the child and the child in the adult provides another background for the Œdipus complex.[50]

Then, Róheim alludes to some of the aspects of his transitional, intermediate position:

> One of the most general and indubitable findings of psychoanalysis is that the Libido progresses through gradual stages from the Ego to the Object, from narcissism to Object Love. The Oedipal object is a transition stage from Identification to Object Love, from childhood to adulthood. To say,

therefore, that a certain group or a certain individual has no Œdipus complex is just as meaningful as to say that they were never five years old, that from two they went straight to twenty.

Another transitional aspect of the Oedipal relationship is its position between phantasy and reality. For although there is plenty of unconscious aggression in the child-mother situation, hostility is much closer to consciousness and reality in the triangular situation.[51]

Finally, Róheim states a teleological function of the Œdipus complex, the father becoming, besides an ideal figure, the precursor of all the enemies of the boy's adult life and the mother, the prototype of all desirable women. We thus discover an original conception of the Œdipus complex, enriching the Freudian view.

His legacy

Dadoun has written that the fight Róheim fought for a psychoanalytical anthropology was for a long time, to a large extent, a solitary one, but by founding the journal *Psychoanalysis and the Social Sciences* he succeeded in gathering a whole research movement.[52] He in fact particularly influenced the researchers of the "culture and personality" school, among them Edward Sapir, but also anthropologists such as Ruth Benedict, Margaret Mead, Clyde Kluckhohn. Others engaged in fruitful exchanges with Róheim. This was the case with Werner Muensterberger, Georges Devereux and Weston La Barre. A certain number of anthropologists would attack Róheim, both for his way of disregarding the overall organisation of the societies that he visited and for his way of flitting about collecting the materials he needed – principally the indications of the Œdipus complex. However, his radical challenging of Freud's phylogenetic viewpoint in favour of the major, founding role of ontogenesis in culture would be acknowledged.

In the United States

The debate in the United States began in 1920 in a relatively conflictual manner with the two major figures in anthropology, Boas and Kroeber.

Franz Boas (1858–1942)

Franz Boas shaped all of American anthropology.

He was born in Minden, Westphalia in 1858. After studying mathematics and physics at various different German universities, he wrote a doctoral thesis on the variations in the colour of water (1881). Interested in geography and curious to see the world, he left for Baffin Island in northern Canada, where he planned to study the influence of the environment on the way indigenous people live and think. In 1883–1884, he travelled through that region and lived with the central Eskimos, convincing himself while among them that the role played by history, language, and culture was greater than that played by natural conditions. Returning to Germany, he became a *Privatdozent* at Berlin University. He worked with Ratzel and at the Ethnographical Museum with Bastian. A group of Bella Coola Indians brought to Berlin in 1885 awakened his interest in the cultures of the Pacific Northwest, which he was able to visit in 1886 with funds provided by the museum. The reception he received in New York after this first expedition, which would be followed by several others, prompted Boas to settle in the United States and to acquire American nationality. He then taught at Clark University, and later became a professor of anthropology at Columbia University in 1899. At the same time he worked as a curator at the American Museum of Natural History where he designed and arranged the ethnographic wings. Between 1919 and 1922 he worked in the Southwest among the Pueblo Indians. He died in New York in 1942.

Boas authored an impressive series of works covering all the domains of anthropology. His interest in the problems of physical anthropology was thus continuous and steady. Against traditional anthropology, he would demonstrate the impossibility of defining a "racial" or "biological type", which resulted in a radical criticism of the notion of race and of the contrast between "primitive" and "civilised". For him, language and culture played as important a role in the differences between peoples as biological heredity. He was one of the very first to understand that language mastery was an essential tool in ethnological investigation, that each language possessed its own structure that it was proper to bring out. Thus, what we know about the languages of the American Northwest (Chinook, Kwakiutl, Tsimshian, for example) essentially comes from Boas, and he is the one who began the linguistic study of the Pueblo Indians.

When it came to ethnology, Boas was first of all a meticulous observer of all the aspects of indigenous life. One must describe, then understand. Alongside the historical causes, he also sought to determine the psychic processes enabling each people to realise an original synthesis. Each culture has a style that is expressed in different manners. According to him, the ultimate goal of ethnological investigation was to know and understand the life of the individual as it is fashioned by social life and the way society itself is modified by the action of the individuals making it up. This logic internal to Boas' thought is the key to discovering the multiple nuances of American anthropology as it unfolded during the first half of the twentieth century. In particular, to be found there are the sources of the idea of "cultural pattern" and of the questions asked by the "culture and personality" school.

In *Structural Anthropology*, Lévi-Strauss wrote that "Boas must be given credit for defining the unconscious nature of cultural phenomena with admirable lucidity. By comparing cultural phenomena to language from this point of view, he anticipated both the subsequent development of linguistic theory and a future for anthropology, whose rich promise we are just beginning to perceive."[53] According to Lévi-Strauss's formulation Boas would have thus made language study a sort of paradigm for the study of other symbolic systems.

In his article entitled "Methods of Ethnology" (1920), Boas argued against two dominant conceptions of cultural history: evolutionist and diffusionist. He in fact rejected arbitrary classifications and pseudo-historical speculation. For him, it was above all a matter of reconstituting demonstrable or plausible contacts for recent periods in limited areas. As he wrote,

> the history of human civilisation does not appear to us as determined entirely by psychological necessity that leads to a uniform evolution the world over. We rather see that each cultural group has its own unique history, dependent partly upon the peculiar inner development of the social group, and partly upon the foreign influences to which it has been subjected...
>
> While on the whole the unique historical character of cultural growth in each area stands out as a salient element in the history of cultural development, we may recognise at the same time that certain typical parallelisms do occur. We are, however, not much inclined to look for these similarities in detailed customs but rather in certain dynamic conditions which are due to social or psychological causes that are liable to lead to similar results.[54]

Expressing his opinion about the importance of psychoanalysis for ethnology, in the same paper he wrote,

> While, therefore, we may welcome the application of every advance in the method of psychological investigation, we cannot accept as an advance in ethnological method the crude transfer of a novel, one-sided method of psychological investigation of the individual to social phenomena the origin of which can be shown to be historically determined and to be subject to influences that are not at all comparable to those that control the psychology of the individual.[55]

So, he saw psychoanalysis as favouring a regression back to the vast comparative syntheses of unilinear evolutionism making universalist psychological claims. He was also wary of the idea of a universal symbolism or folklore.

In his foreword to Margaret Mead's *Coming of Age in Samoa* (1928), Boas observed that individuals and their personal lives, in the manner in which they experience their cultures, their own experiences, are left out of systematic presentations of the cultural life of a society. Moreover, he established a distinction between certain universal cultural categories such as "courtesy", "good manners", "conformity to definite ethical standards", and their singular and variable contents, in the function of societies. Then he would contrast the relativity of cultural traits to the universality of fundamental traits of human nature, in this way establishing and characterising the contrast between anthropology and psychoanalysis:

> In our own civilisation the individual is beset with difficulties which we are likely to ascribe to fundamental human traits. When we speak about the difficulties of childhood and of adolescence, we are thinking of them as

> unavoidable periods of adjustment through which everyone has to pass. The whole psycho-analytic approach is largely based on this supposition.
>
> The anthropologist doubts the correctness of these views...[56]

So it was that he acknowledged that Mead's investigation had had the merit of invalidating the theses of psychoanalysis and confirming anthropology's relativist assumption. In his words, "The results of her painstaking investigation confirm the suspicion long held by anthropologists, that much of what we ascribe to human nature is no more than a reaction to the restraints put upon us by our civilisation".[57]

Alfred Louis Kroeber (1876–1960)

Kroeber was born in New Jersey in 1876 into a Protestant family of German origin which remained German-speaking. Entering Columbia University as early as 1892, he discovered anthropology by attending Boas' courses on language. In 1902, he defended the first thesis in anthropology at his university and the second in all of the United States. His career was essentially spent at the University of California, Berkeley. He became one of the masters of North American Indian studies and the person most knowledgeable about the Californian Indians. His research covered a very large domain embracing physical anthropology, linguistics, archaeology, and especially ethnology (the Yurok, Mohave, Zuni tribes, etc.).

Kroeber was particularly interested in the question of the nature of culture. He considered culture to be a universal manifestation, each particular culture being the matter of a certain conformity to a pattern. The relations between the cultures could consequently be expressed in terms of relations between patterns. The dividing of the North American Indian space into "cultural areas" finds its justification in this, and it is to him that we owe a systematic presentation of it. The study of cultures first consists of an identification of "cultural units", parameters of which cultures, as local totalisations, are specific arrangements. This study would have to involve a twofold, synchronic and diachronic, approach.

Having undergone analysis in 1917, he worked as a psychoanalyst in San Francisco from 1918 to 1920 and maintained a very ambivalent relationship to psychoanalysis throughout his entire life. He exercised considerable influence, both through his teaching and through his writings. He died in Paris in 1960.

In his first article, published in 1920 in the same issue of the *American Anthropologist* as the article by Boas cited above, Kroeber acted as the spokesman for the anthropological criticisms of *Totem and Taboo*.[58] From the start he asserted himself as a representative of historical ethnology. His criticisms bore on the content in a ten point "formal examination" of Freud's hypothesis, on the method and construction of his argumentation, on his sources relative to "speculative" evolutionist anthropology represented by "armchair" anthropologists of the likes of Frazer, as opposed to the new field researchers. Kroeber noted "the essential failure of its finally avowed purpose", but nevertheless acknowledged the significance of the problems Freud had raised and that, however "precipitate his entry into anthropology" had been, he had brought "to bear keen insight, a fecund imagination".[59] Kroeber wrote,

> But, with all the essential failure of its finally avowed purpose, the book is an important and valuable contribution. However much cultural anthropology may come to lean more on the historical method instead of the psychological method, it can never ultimately free itself, nor should it wish to, from the psychology that underlies it. To this psychology the psychoanalytic movement initiated by Freud has made an indubitably significant contribution, which every ethnologist must sooner or later take into consideration. For instance, the correspondences between taboo customs and "compulsion neuroses"... are unquestionable, as also the parallelism between the two aspects of taboo and the ambivalence of emotions under an accepted prohibition... Again the strange combination of mourning for the dead with the fear of them and taboos against them is certainly illumined if not explained by this theory of ambivalence....
>
> It is even possible to extend Freud's point of view.[60]

Moreover, he singled out one of Freud's major intuitions concerning the notion of "social compromise formations", which he expressed in terms of the institutionalisation of psychic impulses:

> primitive societies have institutionalized such impulses as with us lead to neuroses. The individual of neurotic tendency finds an approved and therefore harmless outlet in taboo, magic, myth, and the like, whereas the non-neurotic, who at heart remains attached to reality, accepts these activities as forms which do not seriously disturb him.[61]

He thus shed light on one of the essential differences between individual, psychic reality, and collective, socio-cultural reality finding expression in the difference between the psychic disposition, the symptom, and the institution.

In his second article of 1939, "Totem and Taboo in Retrospect",[62] he saw "no reason to waver over" his critical analysis of 1920, but harshened his judgement of psychoanalysis and psychoanalysts. He described Freud's thought as constantly vacillating between two poles, historical and psychological, between two truths, historical and abstract. "A historical finding", he wrote, "calls for some specification of place and time and order; instead of which, he offers a finding of unique cardinality, such as history feels it cannot deal with."[63]

Refusing, therefore, to confer any historical legitimacy upon the event of the father-slaying by the primitive horde, he asked "whether Freud's theory contains any possibility of being a generic, timeless explanation of the psychology that underlies certain recurrent historic phenomena or institutions like totemism and taboo" and suggested that there we would "obviously be on better ground".[64] He further challenged the universalist claim of Freud's ideas, writing that "Freud's thesis would reduce to the proposition that certain psychic processes tend always to be operative and to find expression in widespread human institutions. Among these processes would be the incest drive and incest repression, filial ambivalence, and the like; in short, if one like, the kernel of the Œdipus situation."[65]

Pondering the obstacles standing in the way of a fruitful re-evaluation of Freud's hypothesis, potentially heuristic as concerns the intelligibility of cultural facts, Kroeber additionally detected resistances in Freud himself and his disciples, among them Jones, in his dispute with Malinowski, then Róheim:

> They insist on operating within a closed system. At any rate, if not wholly closed, it grows only from within; it is not open to influence from without. A classical example is Ernest Jones's resistance to Malinowski's finding that among the matrilineal Melanesians the effects directed toward the father in our civilization are largely displaced upon the mother's brother, the relation of father and children being rather one of simple and relatively univalent affection. Therewith Malinowski had really vindicated the mechanism of the Œdipus relation. He showed that the mechanism remained operative even in a changed family situation; a minor modification of it, in its direction, conforming to the change in given condition. Jones, however, could not see this, and resisted tooth and nail.[66]

He considered the existence of two sets of fundamental concepts formulated by Freud.

Those of the first set, among them repression, regression and infantile persistences, sense of guilt, "the effects toward members of the family" and dream symbolism, had gradually become an integral part of general science, while those of the second set, the censor, the superego, the castration complex, the explanation of cultural specific phenomena, had not in the main found their way into science. However, psychoanalysts had accorded much the same heuristic value to both sets, interweaving them into a single theoretical system. On the basis of indications of a lack of openness of an ideological nature and a confusion between external reality and phantasy, Kroeber set up an analogy between the psychoanalytical movement and religious systems:

> In this quality of non-differentiation between what the scientific world accepts as reality and rejects as fantasy, between what is essential and what is incidental, the orthodox psychoanalytical movement reveals itself as partaking of the nature of a religion–a system of mysticism; even, it might be said, it shows certain of the qualities of a delusional system. It has appropriated to itself such of the data of science–the cumulative representative of reality–as were digestible to it and has ignored the larger remainder. It has sought little integration with the totality of science, and only on its own terms. By contrast, science, while also of course a system, has shown itself a relatively open one: it has accepted and already largely absorbed a considerable part of the concepts of psychoanalysis.[67]

Nevertheless, he would spare Freud these virulent attacks and esteem him for his largeness of mind and for that matter as "one of the great minds of our day!"[68]

Kroeber's critical discourse with regard to *Totem and Taboo* and, beyond that, to psychoanalytical thought and psychoanalysts, would long remain representative of that of the international anthropological community as a whole. I shall return to this in my general discussion.

Ruth Fulton Benedict (1887–1948)

Benedict was born in New York in 1887. After studying literature, she studied anthropology at the New School for Social Research in New York City from 1919 to 1922, where she was the student of Alexander Goldenweiser and Elsie Clews Parsons. In 1922–1923, she became Boas' assistant at Barnard College. Under the influence of Robert Lowie, she grew interested in the vision quest among the Plains Indians. In 1922, upon Kroeber's instigation, she had her first field experience among the Serrano Indians of southern California, then engaged in research among the Pima and Pueblo Indians of the southwestern United States (the Zuni). She directed research on the Apaches of that region (1930) and on the Blackfoot of the North Plains (1938).

From the start, her thought fit into the culturalist ideological frame of reference, marked as it was then by the influence of American psychoanalysis. In *Patterns of Culture* (1934), she in fact proposed a typology of cultures based on categories borrowed from psychopathology and the Nietzschean distinction between the Apollonian and the Dionysian. This work was born out of reflexions on the contrast between the culture of Pueblo Indians and that of the Pima.

I shall not discuss this book, but wish to underscore the radical aspect of the images of anthropology and cultures elaborated by Benedict along the lines of Boas' thought, but also that of Malinowski. So it is that she considered that it was the primary vocation of anthropology to stress the diversity of cultural configurations and to have the unique qualities of each of them acknowledged. Anthropologists were also to have to combat the ethnocentrism prevalent in our contemporary western societies so as to bring people to view all cultures as being equal.

Margaret Mead (1901–1978)

Mead was born in 1901 in Philadelphia into a milieu well acquainted with the social sciences – her father being an economist, a professor at the University of Pennsylvania, her mother holding a degree in sociology. In 1921, she began studying anthropology and psychology at Columbia University where she later held the position of associate professor. Trained by Boas and his assistant Benedict, she decided to leave for Samoa in 1925, then spent time in the Admiralty Islands with Reo F. Fortune in 1928–1929. She used her first experiences to write two books that marked milestones: *Coming of Age in Samoa* (1928) and *Growing up in New Guinea* (1930).

Endeavouring to connect the psychological characteristics of individuals with the conditions and expressions distinctive of the Oceanian cultures that she had studied, to their methods and to the context of their upbringing, she questioned – contemporaneous with Lévy-Bruhl's notion of pre-logical mentality and Freud's comparison between primitive mentality and infantile mentality – the universality of the critical difficulties characterising the years of adolescence.

The comparison then made between three societies of New Guinea (where she had gone with Fortune) having very different cultural orientations (Arapesh, Mundugumor, Chambri), enabled her to tackle the fundamental question of biological differences relative to sex in an innovative fashion and to shed light on the impact of cultural determinism on the women's and men's personalities. From Mead's point of view, methods of upbringing, adult personality structure, and fundamental cultural orientations formed an organised, connected whole whose exploration had to lead to a rethinking of the status of "human nature" within each culture. This is also what she undertook in the work I shall present.

Coming of Age in Samoa

In her introduction to *Coming of Age in Samoa* Mead wrote,

> The anthropologist, as he pondered his growing body of material upon the customs of primitive people, grew to realise the tremendous role played in an individual's life by the social environment in which each is born and reared. One by one, aspects of behaviour which we had been accustomed to consider invariable complements of our humanity were found to be merely a result of civilisation... He learned that neither race nor common humanity can be held responsible for many of the forms which even such basic human emotions as love and fear and anger take under different social conditions.
>
> So the anthropologist, arguing from his observations of the behaviour of adult human beings in other civilisations, reaches many of the same conclusions which the behaviourist reaches in his work upon human babies who have as yet no civilisation to shape their malleable humanity.
>
> With such an attitude towards human nature the anthropologist listened to the current comment upon adolescence. He heard attitudes which seemed to him dependent upon social environment – such as rebellion against authority, philosophical perplexities, the flowering of idealism, conflict and struggle – ascribed to a period of physical development. And on the basis of his knowledge of the determinism of culture, of the plasticity of human beings, he doubted. Were these difficulties due to being adolescent or being adolescent in America?...
>
> But for the student of the adolescent there is no such simplicity of working conditions. What we wish to test is no less than the effect of civilisation upon a developing human being at the age of puberty.[69]

This introductory passage brings several thoughts to mind. First of all, one sees that Mead's approach is in line with the spirit of the research of Boas, the founder of American anthropology, in orienting ethnological investigation toward the influence of society and of its institutions on the life of individuals and their personal experiences; and, therefore, on their moulding by the culture and on the unique qualities of every cultural configuration.

Moreover, a methodological and ideological convergence is established from the outset between behaviourist psychology, very influential in the United States, and American culturalist anthropology, the one basing itself on the other. It is a question of the observation and interpretation of specific behaviours conditioned by the social environment from the time of every individual's childhood. Consequently, their unconscious psychic dimension would be systematically denied, something which is at the basis of the radical separation between Freudian psychoanalysis and culturalist anthropology. What is more, what is a matter of "human nature" would necessarily be biological in nature. So would there have been a confusion in Mead's mind between biological reality and the unconscious psychic reality discovered by psychoanalysis, but also a pure and simple dismissal of the "psychic"? This is what comes out of this programmatic, theoretically oriented introductory text and would be confirmed afterward.

Finally, this 1928 text was published one year after *Sex and Repression in Savage Society* by Malinowski and seems to me to fit in perfectly with the spirit of "discovery" and Malinowski's relativist approach, consisting, as I have already explained, of rejecting the universality of the Œdipus complex (in the boy), transformed into family complex specific to patriarchal societies, this complex being a matter, by the way, of biological factors. Mead pursued this approach by exploring female adolescence, a period of physiological transformation, pertaining therefore to human nature, but whose forms of expression are determined by the family environment, shaped by the social organisation and the distinctive features of the culture.

By travelling to Samoa, she had therefore envisaged answering the following question: "Are the disturbances which vex our adolescents due to the nature of adolescence or to the civilisation? Under different conditions does adolescence present a different picture?"[70] This was a revolutionary question because it was without precedent at a time when anthropologists were still according priority to the exploration of customs, beliefs and social institutions, kinship, mythology, social organisation, and material culture, in particular.

After having described the Samoan family, children's upbringing, the social and sexual life of girls, their place in the community, then the personal experience of adolescence, Mead came to the conclusion that adolescence in Samoa is not generally a time of crisis and tension but rather of "painless development from childhood to womanhood"[71]: "To live as a girl with many lovers, as long as possible and then to marry in one's own village, near one's own relatives and to have many children, these were uniform and satisfying ambitions."[72] On the other hand, she asked what it was that "accounts for the presence of storm and stress in American adolescents?" What differences could be detected between these two civilisations?[73]

Mead proceeded to engage in a comparative study of certain traits characteristic of Samoan and American social life. In the first place, she noted a "lack of deep feeling", "the general casualness of the whole society", which permitted the avoidance of conflicts and poignant situations in Samoa, something which according to her contrasted strongly with America and with most primitive civilisations. Then she noted the existence of a limited "number of choices which are permitted to each individual" in Samoa, as opposed to young Americans who face numerous groups whose ideas and standards of conduct are often different and contradictory, which is a source of disturbance.[74]

She thus made reference to the fundamental difference between a slowly evolving, simple, homogenous primitive culture, and a heterogeneous, diverse, disparate, modern culture. The third element taken into consideration concerned the existence of neuroses that were unknown because they are not present in Samoa, but are very frequent among us. She therefore asked about the role and characteristics of the "early education of Samoan children which have fitted them for a normal, unneurotic development" and, to this end, referred to her privileged interlocutors, the behaviourists and psychoanalysts who, according to her, had discovered the enormous influence of the family environment on the psychological development of children.[75]

So, she "logically" came to examine the fundamental differences between Samoan and American family organisations mainly finding expression, in the case of the former, in the lack of close relationships between parents and children, therefore, of "specialised feeling which results from the diffusion of affection in the household", something standing in contrast to the influence of those so strong, lasting ties on members of American families.[76] Then she asked about their possible advantages:

> What are the rewards of the tiny, ingrown, biological family opposing its closed circle of affection to a forbidding world, of the strong ties between parents and children, ties which imply an active personal relation from birth to death?
>
> Specialisation of affection, it is true, but at the price of many individuals' preserving through life the attitudes of dependent children... And with such a question in our minds it is interesting to note that a larger family community, in which there are several adult men and women, seems to ensure the child against the development of the crippling attitudes which have been labelled Œdipus complexes, Electra complexes, and so on.[77]

Mead then transformed the Œdipus complex into a pathological affection specific to western families, American families in particular. Thus, on the one hand, confirming Malinowski's thesis, she told readers that she had not found any objective existence either of an Œdipus complex or of an Electra complex among Samoans; on the other hand, she implicitly affirmed that the presence of these pathological, neurotic complexes in childhood condition and determine the emergence of a critical form of adolescence. She therefore found a culturally determined link between the type of childhood family complex and the future form adolescence might take.

> Let us now look at her conclusion, which strikes me as surprising, to say the very least: adolescence is not necessarily a period of stress and strain, but... cultural conditions make it so...
>
> Given these cultural attitudes, adolescence, regarded now not as a period of physiological change, for we know that physiological puberty need not produce conflict, but as the beginning of mental and emotional maturity, is bound to be filled with conflicts and difficulties.[78]

There seems to have been some confusion in Mead's mind between physiological puberty, considered as a time of physiological change, and adolescence considered as a psychic maturational process, therefore critical. So, we might in fact understand that the socio-cultural milieu may come into play in the ways of dealing with this critical period that the young members of every society go through. Psychic and physiological processes intertwine and the community takes charge of them. In Samoa there is probably an avoidance of conflicts and critical situations, which represents one social solution among others, therefore corroborating their existence.

Abram Kardiner (1891–1981), his psychoanalytical anthropology and school of "culture and personality"

The researchers of the culture and personality school began reflecting on the processes of cultural acquisition by individuals during their childhood and then entered into an often conflictual dialogue with psychoanalysis. They used both somewhat distorted psychoanalytical concepts and behaviourist concepts to describe the interactions between the child, the family environment, and the culture, thus affirming variability of the processes of the children's socialisation and challenging Freud's main concepts, among them the universality of the Œdipus complex.

Abram Kardiner, psychiatrist, psychoanalyst, and anthropologist, underwent analysis with Freud in 1921, then entered the New York Psychoanalytic Society and Institute in 1922, where he worked until 1944. Around the beginning of the 1930s, he began to grow interested in the relationships between culture and personality and in 1936 he created a seminar at the New York Institute, thus playing a decisive role in the constitution of this anthropological current attentive to the dialogue between the two disciplines. In 1937, the sessions were held at Columbia University and had as participants Edward Sapir, Ruth Fulton Benedict, Cora du Bois, and especially Ralph Linton, with whom he wrote a first work: *The Individual and his Society: The Psychodynamics of Primitive Social Organization* (1939). In 1945, he published a collective work, *The Psychological Frontiers of Society*. In 1961, he left New York for Atlanta where he taught at Emory University until 1968. He died in Connecticut in 1981.

His first work already contained everything he taught, everything undergirding his thought: the concept of basic personality; the distinction established between primary and secondary institutions; the refutation of some of the major Freudian hypotheses; the constitution of a psychology focused on the ego and its adaptive mechanisms.

Fundamental theoretical principles and concepts

According to Kardiner, individuals stand halfway between the institutions that shape and direct their adaptation to the external world, and their fundamental biological needs (hunger, sex, and dependence, in particular) that try hard to obtain satisfaction. He defined institution as *"any fixed mode of thought or behavior held by a group of individuals (i.e., a society) which can be communicated, which enjoys common acceptance, and infringement of, or deviation from which creates some disturbance in the individual or in the group"*.[79] He then reduced every culture to a catalogue of institutions, the regularity of which confer upon it its singular configuration:

> In this way culture can be seen molding, directing, and controlling biological and social needs, and at the same time determining the conditions under which they can be satisfied. But institutions have another function, to offer placebos and compensations for feelings, arising from the inability to satisfy these biological needs and needs created or accentuated by the culture.[80]

He distinguished between two principal categories of institutions, primary and secondary. Among the "primary institutions" figure the family, the "Us", basic disciplines including breast-feeding the children and weaning, sphincter control associated with disciplines pertaining to cleanliness and order, sexual disciplines, among them incest taboos, and subsistence techniques. They would create certain "psychic constellations" in the individual's ego, the set of which form the basic personality, which would produce the secondary institutions destined to appease the needs and tensions aroused by the primary institutions. It is to be emphasised that the basic disciplines would be a good example of the pressures imposed on the individual by the primary institutions. Forces are concealed in them, obliging the individual to repress a given drive. According to Kardiner, institution and repression interact.

Among the "secondary institutions" figure taboo systems, religion, rituals, folktales, and techniques of thinking. All changes in the primary institution are accompanied by changes in the secondary institution. The "basic personality" is therefore situated halfway between primary and secondary institutions. Kardiner explains that,

> The adjustment required by different environmental realities and those created by the mores that govern human relationships must in each culture produce different end results in the personality... The basic constellations in the individual created by these conditions are his ego structure, subjectively considered, or his basic personality structure, objectively considered.[81]

Kardiner explained that this psychic constellation is formed through the interaction of needs, drives, affects, and perceptions. He included the following elements in the basic personality:

- Techniques of thinking or idea constellations;
- The individual's security system defined as "that system of adaptations which insures the individual acceptance, approval, support when necessary, esteem, and maintenance of status";[82]
- The superego formed through the individual's contact with the institutions. For Kardiner, it became a function of the ego in adaptive maneuvers. A superego based on obedience to the discipline would differ from that formed in a society in which the child is not the object of any punishment. In this latter case, it would take the form of feelings of shame, without guilt;
- The attitudes toward supernatural beings (religion).

Thus, this basic personality varies from society to society.

Elements of a critical discussion of Freudian sociology and personal conception of the Œdipus complex

Kardiner criticised two "parallelisms" established by Freud based on the evolutionist hypothesis. The first concerned ontogenesis as a repetition of the phylogenetic model. The second was about the Œdipus complex, which

> was not only the nuclear phenomenon in neurosis, but the nuclear complex about which all other factors in social organization and culture became concentrically arranged. This proposition made the character of the analogy final; processes in the individual and processes in society were similar, nay, identical. The individual has an Œdipus complex, society has an Œdipus complex...[83]

The libido theory as a tool for understanding social phenomena led to failure, according to Kardiner. Being predisposed toward the individual in our society, Freud formulated hypotheses on the types of human reaction attributed to instincts and not to the interaction of institutions and human needs. Freud considered the basic personality to be identical in all human beings, independently of the culture to which they belonged. The differences evident in the indigenous populations were to be evaluated in terms of the stage of evolution they had reached. He neglected, then, the distinctive character of the institutions and their role in the formation of the basic personality.

Finally, Freud claimed that the Œdipus complex had created the social organisation, but Kardiner maintained that it was the opposite that had occurred. Indeed, according to him, the Œdipus complex represented the fusion of needs for dependency and sexual desire concentrated on the same object. He considered that from the cultural point of view, it was only found to exist in societies where the aspirations to dependency and their consequences were exaggerated by the sexual taboos. In a society which did not prescribe them, the sexual phase of ego development unfolds freely, preventing the fusion of aims of dependence and sexual desires. For him, appealing to the survival of something remote to explain the

Œdipus complex amounts to robbing institutions of all their dynamic significance, because it was not a matter of the survival of a phylogenetic complex, but that of the institutions that brought it about, as can be verified by the study of societies in which the disciplines differ from ours. Why, for example, he asked, was this not found in Marquesan and Trobriand cultures, which know no restriction of the sexual aim? This is a fact inclining one to think that, instead of slowing the individual's development, engaging in sexual activity compatible with early childhood promoted it. And he concluded that the Œdipus complex that Freud saw as proof of the existence of a universal personality structure was but the expression of a specific set of primary institutions.

It seems to me that Kardiner's principal concepts (basic personality, primary and secondary institutions) yield a very mechanical view of individual/society relations. Cut off from their phantasy, instinctual, conflictual, unconscious dimension, individuals seem to me to be reduced to a list of basic biological needs and a system of adaptation to the outer world, in this case, to the institutions also conditioning them, while society is seen rather as a homogenous and undifferentiated whole – the abundance and hierarchy of the groups, as well as the conflictuality of social relationships, being scotomised.

It could be said that, through a reconsideration-reinterpretation of the relations between individuals and their societies, his project to combine psychoanalysis and anthropology (his work having been called an essay in psychoanalytical anthropology) led him within the evolving context of American psychoanalysis and of the reign of the "relativist" model – combining with the determinant influence of behaviourist psychology – to distort Freudian concepts and to simplify socio-anthropological concepts.

With regard to the Œdipus complex, he adopted a "relativist" position characteristic of that generation of psychoanalysts – influenced and convinced by the anthropological theses and ethnographic authority – to which Erich Fromm and Karen Horney belonged. Moreover, in contesting Freudian "biologism", of which the Œdipus complex is a part, there was a pressing need to counter it with "culturalist" thought grounded in experience in the "field". This once again resulted in a denial of instinctual, unconscious psychic reality in Kardiner's thought, i.e., a rejection of the very foundations of psychoanalysis as it had been defined by its creator, Freud.

The psychoanalysts Erich Fromm and Karen Horney

Belonging to the new American psychoanalysis and subscribing to culturalist viewpoints, Fromm and Horney attached considerable importance to socio-cultural factors in both the aetiology and treatment of mental illnesses, seriously distorting Freudian theory. So it is that they contested, in particular, the universality of Œdipus complex considered as a product of modern civilisation and only characteristic of the middle class. This major refutation on the part of psychoanalysts was a phenomenon unprecedented both in the recent history of psychoanalysis and in that of the conflictual relations with the anthropologists. I am alluding neither to

Jung nor to Kardiner. It is as if the taking into consideration of the socio-cultural factors and unique features of each culture by psychoanalysts was to cause the abandonment of the assumption of the psychic unity of humanity, of which the universality of the Œdipus complex was paradigmatic.

Erich Fromm (1900–1980) and the creation of an analytical psychosociology

Fromm was born into a German Jewish family in Frankfurt am Main on March 23, 1900. His grandfather and two great grandfathers on his father's side were rabbis. Alongside five to six years of study of the Talmud with his mentor Salman Baruch Rabinkow, Fromm studied law at the University of Frankfurt, then interrupted his study of law in order to study sociology and psychology at Frankfurt, then at the University of Heidelberg. Alfred Weber, the brother of Max Weber, was his sociology professor. He then took Professor Emil Kraepelin's psychiatry courses at the University of Munich. His doctoral thesis under the direction of Professor Weber was on Talmudic law in three Jewish communities.

He underwent analysis three times, the third time with Hanns Sachs in Berlin in 1927. After his training at the Berlin Psychoanalytic Institute, he became a member of the Berlin Psychoanalytical Society, beginning in this way his life as a psychoanalyst. As a member of the Frankfurt School headed by Max Horkheimer, he represented psychoanalysis within this pluridisciplinary group striving fully to understand society. In the course of his pluridisciplinary training, certain figures inspired him and profoundly influenced his thought, among them Freud, Ferenczi and Georg Groddeck in psychoanalysis, Karl Marx, Alfred Weber and Johann Jakob Bachofen in the social sciences. Very early, he endeavoured to connect Marxism and psychoanalysis, or more precisely to establish interconnections between historical materialism and Freudian thought.

As early as 1933–1934, he fled Nazi Germany for the United States, where he settled in New York and, along with Harry Stack Sullivan, Clara Thompson and Karen Horney founded the William Alanson White Institute, a psychoanalytic institute. He would be an analyst, supervisor and leader of seminars there. He met anthropologists of the likes of Mead, Benedict and Linton and participated in the "Neo-Freudian Movement" or "Culturalist School". Of this, he wrote,

> Although Horney, Sullivan, and I are usually classified together as a "culturalist" or "Neo-Freudian" school, this classification hardly seems justified. In spite of the fact that we were friends, worked together, and had certain views in common – particularly a critical attitude toward the libido theory – the differences between us were greater than the similarities, especially in the "cultural" viewpoint. Horney and Sullivan thought of cultural patterns in the traditional anthropological sense, while my approach looked toward a dynamic analysis of the economic, political, and psychological forces that form the basis of society.[84]

Since the International Psychoanalytical Association no longer wanted him as a direct member, he later became the clinical director of the William Alanson White Institute in New York from 1946 to 1950. In 1949, he founded the Mexican Society of Psychoanalysis in Mexico City. He died in Muralto, Switzerland on March 18, 1980.

Criticism of Freud and Freudian thought

Fromm very early developed a critical approach toward Freudian thought, situating it within its historico-social context, that is to say within the framework of the bourgeois middle class of nineteenth-century Europe, but also as an heir to the rationalism of the philosophers of the Enlightenment. Very ambivalent with respect to Freud and Freudian psychoanalysis, he devoted many works to the subject, among them: *Sigmund Freud's Mission, an Analysis of his Personality and Influence* (1959); *The Crisis of Psychoanalysis, Essays on Freud, Marx, and Social Psychology* (1970), and *Greatness and Limitation of Freud's Thought* (1979).

One of Fromm's major contributions seems to me to have been that he attempted to elaborate an analytical psychosociology connecting Freudian theory and Marx's historical materialism, thus introducing the creation of new notions.

As early as 1929, in his three-page article entitled "Psychoanalysis and Sociology"[85] Fromm inquired into the relationship between psychoanalysis and sociology which, according to him, has two sides: one being the application of psychoanalysis to sociology; the other being the application of sociology to psychoanalysis. In that paper, he warned that the "application of psychoanalysis to sociology must definitely guard against the mistake of wanting to give psychoanalytic answers where economic, technical, or political facts provide the real and sufficient explanation of sociological questions."[86] He considered that psychoanalysis could bring to sociology knowledge of the human psychic apparatus, assess the role of the instinctual, of the unconscious in human beings in the organisation and development of society and the different social phenomena. He believed that however "important it may be to point out to sociologists the banal fact that society consists of living people and that psychology is one of the factors affecting social development, it is equally important that psychology not underestimate the fact that the individual person in reality exists only as a socialized person."[87] He also saw the importance of a "series of further important problems",

> for instance, the question of to what extent the family is itself the product of a particular social system, and how a socially conditioned change in the family as such might influence the development of the psychic apparatus of the individual. Or there is the question of what influence the growth of technology – i.e, an ever increasing gratification, or a decreasing deprivation, of the instincts – has on the psyche of the individual?[88]

An additional problem pertaining to the most important psychosociological questions then arises, namely, "What connections exist between the social, especially the economic-technical, development of humanity, and the development of the psychic apparatus, especially the ego-organisation of the human being?"[89]

He then tried to lay the foundations of an analytical psycho-sociology, set out in his work *The Crisis of Psychoanalysis* (1970). This is a collection of articles written between 1932 and 1969, in which he said, "Up to now, the vast majority of psychoanalytic works, which have tried to apply psychoanalysis to social problems, have not met the requirements incumbent on any analytical social psychology".[90] He sharply criticised the writings of Reik and Róheim, especially, but acknowledged the value of those of Reich, to whom he felt rather close. He considered that a fundamental error committed by psychoanalysts consisted of a lack of assessment of the function of the family. They had "almost completely overlooked the fact that the family itself . . . is the product of a specific social and (in a narrower sense) class structure; that it is simply the psychological agency of the society and class from which it comes".

According to him,

> They had found the correct starting point for explaining the psychological influence of society on the child, but failed to take notice of it. How was that possible? The psychoanalytic investigators were simply duped by a prejudice that they shared with every bourgeois investigator – even those who were progressive. They had turned bourgeois, capitalist society into an absolute; and they more or less consciously believed that it was the "normal" society, that its conditions and psychic factors were typical for "society" in general.[91]

The affirmation of the universality of the Œdipus complex seemed to him to be particularly paradigmatic. He considered that the "absolutization of the Œdipus complex led Freud to base the whole development of mankind on the mechanism of father-hatred and the resultant reactions, without any regard for the material living conditions of the group under study."[92] As I have already emphasised, Fromm would belong to this group and to this generation of psychoanalysts who contested the universality of the Œdipus complex because of their twofold approach, both psychoanalytical and socio-anthropological, which probably fuelled a need to revolt against the founding Father.

For Fromm, socio-economic conditions represented the major, primary factor in the moulding of the instinctual apparatus and the psyche of the members of a society, which acts through the intermediary of the family. This yields a "libidinal structure", specific to a given society, a notion that he would later call social in nature in his work *Escape from Freedom* (1941). But, for him, this "libidinal structure" would in turn play an important role in the affective evolution of diverse layers of society and in the nature of "ideological superstructures". Thus, social psychology would have to explore the unconscious foundations of "psychological attitudes" and "socially significant ideologies" by demonstrating the action of socio-economic conditions on libidinal forces.

In 1932, he began to develop a whole psychoanalytical characterology that was both individual and social in nature. In "Psychoanalytic Characterology and Its Relevance for Social Psychology",[93] he explained that by disengaging the libidinal basis of character traits, psychoanalytic characterology enabled one to understand their dynamic function as productive forces in society. But on the other hand, psychoanalytic characterology could serve as the point of departure for a social psychology that would show how the character traits common to most of the members of a society were conditioned by the distinctive nature of that society. This social influence on the formation of character works first, and above all, through the family. In what way and up to what point a child's pregenital tendencies are repressed or reinforced, in what way sublimations or reaction formations are stimulated, all essentially depend on the educational process, which in turn is an expression of the society's overall psychic structure. Certain character traits prove more useful within the framework of a social or economic structure, or within the framework of a given class structure (and they enable individuals to progress with respect to that property).

Fromm then proposed to apply the principles of his characterology to the psycho-sociological problem of the spirit of capitalism or of bourgeois society conceived as being the sum total of the character traits typical of the human beings of that society, with the emphasis placed on the dynamic function of the character. He quite obviously detected connections between those character traits and those typical of the anal character, from which he concluded that the "typical libidinal structure of bourgeois man is characterized by an intensification of the anal libido";[94] this underlying anal eroticism having acted as a "productive force" in the development of the capitalist economy. He was quite obviously pondering the meaning and significance of such an analytical social psychology for sociology. His principal interest would then lie in the fact that the libidinal forces finding expression through character traits were factors that stimulated or slowed the evolution of a society and its productive forces. And the notion of the "spirit" of an era, of a society, could also be elucidated by the set of these character traits typical of the members of a specific society.

The Revision of Psychoanalysis presents Fromm's personal approach to psychoanalysis, which he considered socio-biological, and dual in nature. Pursuing a "dialectic revision" of Freudian theory in this work, Fromm introduced new notions, such as that of the "social filter" specific to each culture and forming the "social unconscious", but also the notion of social repression dialectically interconnecting with individual repression. The social filter

> determines *which* experiences are permitted to arrive at consciousness. This "filter", consisting of language, logic, and mores (prohibited or permitted ideas and impulses), is of a social nature. It is specific to every culture and determines the "social unconscious," which in turn is rigidly prevented from reaching awareness because the repression of certain impulses and ideas has a very real and important function for the functioning of the society. Hence all of the cultural apparatus serves the purpose of keeping the social unconscious intact.[95]

He also explained that there will be social repression of certain experiences that do not adapt to the structures of a given society.

We have now come to the end of my brief survey of the ideas of Fromm who, by creating an analytical psycho-sociology, attempted to establish fruitful interconnections between Marxist sociology – especially stressing the importance of the economic factors, productive forces of a society – and an interpretation of Freudian thought. He used it to develop a social characterology enabling him to link individual libidinal forces to social productive forces through the intermediary of character traits. For him, the principal factor linking sociology and psychoanalysis founding his psycho-sociology was in fact the libidinal economy and its social ends. I shall also note a certain kinship with Malinowski's thought and the cultural relativism dominating American anthropology, focusing in particular on a relativist conception of the Œdipus complex which, as I have mentioned, Fromm fully embraced and defended.

Karen Danielsen Horney (1885–1952)

Born in a suburb of Hamburg in 1885 to a Norwegian father and a mother of Dutch-German origin, Karen Horney studied medicine at the University of Freiburg and then at the Universities of Göttingen and Berlin. She married Oskar Horney in 1909. In 1910, she underwent analysis with Karl Abraham and in 1920 became one of the founding members of the Berlin Psychoanalytic Institute. In 1932, she immigrated to the United States, where Franz Alexander offered her the position of Associate Director of the newly established Chicago Psychoanalytic Institute. In 1934, she settled in New York and joined the New York Institute. In 1941, she organised the American Institute of Psychoanalysis, of which she would be the dean until her death, and founded, in addition, the *American Journal of Psychoanalysis*, of which she was the editor-in-chief. She died on December 4, 1952 in New York.

Her thought is traditionally divided into three phases. The 1920s and the beginning of the 1930s were marked by her work on feminine psychology, in disagreement with Freud on certain points, such as the psychological development of women, penis envy, and feminine masochism. The 1930s were characterised by her move to the United States and her relations with the representatives of American culturalist anthropology. She distanced herself from the "biologism" of Freudian thought and tried to develop a conception of psychoanalysis taking into account the role played by culture and interpersonal relations. Just as in her model of neurosis, she proposed to focus on the "current" constellation of inner conflicts and defences rather than on infantile origins. Two works are characteristic of this period of her thought: *The Neurotic Personality of our Time* (1937) and *New Ways in Psychoanalysis* (1939). Finally, in the 1940s, she produced her mature theory expounded in her two last books: *Our Inner Conflicts* (1945) and *Neurosis and Human Growth* (1950).

The Neurotic Personality of our Time

In *The Neurotic Personality of our Time*, marked by the influence of American anthropologists such as Mead, Benedict, and Sapir, Karen Horney presented a conception of neurosis that deviated from that of Freud and his disciples. She related its genesis, structure, and symptomatology to the historico-cultural context, thus presupposing a cultural relativism of normality and abnormality; she rejected any assumption of the universality of human nature which, according to her, betrayed a mistaken biological orientation. This would be so for both neurosis and the Œdipus complex and for Freud's conception of masochism.

Right from the introduction to the book, she felt the need to justify the emphasis she had placed upon the "current" component in neurosis, something which enabled her to include intervention of socio-cultural factors that in the final analysis determine the particular form of individual experiences, therefore rejecting the "biological" conditions so dear to Freud.

In the first chapter entitled "Cultural and Psychological Implications of Neuroses", she attributed to both neurosis and the notion of normality a status of cultural relativity that led her to contest the idea of the universality of human nature. But she also brought up the difficulty she had in defining neurosis, given the combination of socio-cultural and psychological elements. Nevertheless, she attempted to describe it as "a psychic disturbance brought about by fears and defenses against these fears, and by attempts to find compromise solutions for conflicting tendencies. For practical reasons," she said, "it is advisable to call this disturbance a neurosis only if it deviates from the pattern common to the particular culture".[96]

Her criticism of the Freudian conception of the Œdipus complex, as well as her personal views

In *The Neurotic Personality of our Time*, Horney wrote,

> Freud's observations concerning the Œdipus complex were made on neurotic persons. In them he found that high-pitched jealousy reactions concerning one of the parents were sufficiently destructive in kind to arouse fear and likely to exert lasting disturbing influences on character formation and personal relations. Observing this phenomenon frequently in neurotic persons of our time, he assumed it to be universal. Not only did he assume the Œdipus complex to be the very kernel of neuroses, but also he tried to understand complex phenomena in other cultures on this basis. It is this generalization that is doubtful. Some jealousy reactions do arise easily in our culture in the relations between siblings as well as in those between parents and children, as they occur in every group living closely together.
>
> But there is no evidence that destructive and lasting jealousy reactions – and it is these we think of when talking of the Œdipus complex or of sibling

> rivalry – are in our culture, not to speak of other cultures, so common as Freud assumes. They are in general human reactions but are artificially generated through the atmosphere in which a child grows up.[97]

And she added a particularly interesting footnote:

> These remarks, presented from a general point of view in disagreement with Freud's conception of the Œdipus complex presuppose that it is not a biologically given phenomenon, but is culturally conditioned. Since this point of view has been discussed by several authors – Malinowski, Boehm, Fromm, Reich – I confine myself to a mere mention of the factors which may generate the Œdipus complex in our culture: lack of harmony in marriage, as a result of conflicting relations between the sexes; unlimited authoritative power of the parents; taboos on every sexual outlet for a child; tendencies to keep a child infantile and emotionally dependent on the parents and otherwise isolating it.[98]

Horney in fact notably adhered to the point of view expressed by Malinowski, a figure of ethnographic authority, but also to that of Mead, and appropriated this "biological" representation of the Œdipus complex characteristic of Freudian biologism, which made it one of the components of "human nature", therefore universal. The "biological nature" of the Œdipus complex must be counterbalanced by the "cultural conditioning" necessarily subject to variations. It is therefore a matter of transforming the Œdipus complex, not only into a cultural formation, but also into western neurotic formation. This is what Mead managed to do and what is suggested to us by Horney in her personal conception:

> I believe that the Œdipus complex is, instead of a primary process, the outcome of several processes which are different in kind. It may be a rather uncomplicated response of the child, provoked by the parents giving sexually tinged caresses, by the child witnessing sexual scenes, by one of the parents making the child the target of blind devotion. It may, on the other hand, be the outcome of a much more complicated process. As I have already said, in those family situations which provide fertile soil for the growth of an Œdipus complex, there is usually much fear and hostility aroused in the child and their repression results in his developing anxiety. It seems probable to me that in these cases the Œdipus complex is brought about by the child clinging to one parent for the sake of reassurance. In fact a fully developed Œdipus complex, as Freud has described it, shows all the trends – such as excessive demands for unconditional love, jealousy, possessiveness, hatred because of rejection – that are characteristic of the neurotic need for affection. The Œdipus complex in these cases is not then the origin of the neurosis, but is itself a neurotic formation.[99]

Thus, Karen Horney seems to me to be a fine example of a "successful" encounter between psychoanalysts and anthropologists, at the expense of sacrificing the integrity of the psychoanalytical concepts constituting the very foundations of psychoanalysis and its epistemic identity. Her arrival in the United States following the first controversies roiling the European analytical movement is not without significance.

Georges Devereux (1908–1985) and ethnopsychiatry

Georges Devereux was born György Dobo into a Jewish family in Lugos, Transylvania in the year 1908. In 1926, he went to Paris to study physics and chemistry with Marie Curie and Jean Perrin. In 1929, he learned Malay at the Ecole des langues orientales and took the courses taught by Mauss, Levy-Bruhl and Rivet at the Institut d'ethnologie de Paris. He then decided to orient himself toward anthropology. In 1932, he obtained the right to change his name to Gheorghe (i.e., Georges) Devereux. He left for the United States where he became the student of Alfred Kroeber, and in 1933 he undertook fieldwork for the first time in Arizona among the Hopi, Yuma, and Cocopa Indians, then among the Mohaves of the Colorado River. In 1934, he left for Indochina where he lived among the Sedang Moi. In 1935, he defended his doctoral thesis, written under Kroeber's direction, entitled *The Sexual Life of Mohave Indians*. In 1939, he met Róheim, worked with Pitirim Sorokin, and published an innovative article entitled "A Sociological Theory of Schizophrenia".[100] In it, he in fact heralded the creation of a new discipline, that of ethnopsychiatry. In 1944, he taught French at Columbia University, then sociology in Port-au-Prince, Haiti. In 1946, he arrived in Paris and took a research position at the Centre National de la Recherche Scientifique. In addition, he underwent analysis with Marc Schlumberger of the Société Psychanalytique de Paris. In 1947, Karl Menninger brought him to work at the Winter General Hospital in Topeka, Kansas. He underwent analysis for a second time with Hans Jokl. In 1950, he treated a Blackfoot Indian. In 1951, he published *Reality and Dream: Psychotherapy of a Plains Indian*. In 1952, he became an associate member of the Topeka Institute for Psychoanalysis and joined the Philadelphia Psychoanalytic Society. Between 1955 and 1961, he published numerous articles, among them "Mohave Ethnopsychiatry and Suicide: The Psychiatric Knowledge and the Psychic Disturbances of an Indian Tribe" (1961).[101] During this period he was accepted as a member of the American Psychoanalytic Association. In 1963, with the support of Claude Lévi-Strauss, Roger Bastide, and Fernand Braudel he became a member of the Ecole Pratique des Hautes Etudes in Paris. He therefore settled in France, learned Ancient Greek and oriented himself toward the psychoanalysis of Greek myths. In 1964, he became a member of the Société Psychanalytique de Paris. His important publications after 1967 were: *From Anxiety to Method in the Behavioral Sciences* (1967); *Basic Problems of Ethnopsychiatry* (1980) (first published in French in 1970 with a preface by Roger Bastide); *Ethnopsychoanalysis: Psychoanalysis and*

Anthropology as Complementary Frames of Reference (1972); *Tragédie et poésie grecques. Etudes ethnopsychoanalytiques* (1975); *Femme et Mythe* (1982). He died in Paris in 1985.

Devereux became an anthropologist before becoming an analyst, in the United States then in France. Immersed in the American culturalist tradition and in the blossoming "culture and personality" school, he would stand out by producing original ideas inspired by his multifaceted training and the great breadth of his culture. He radically opposed cultural relativism, against which he never ceased to protest.

The relationship between psychoanalysis and anthropology, between psyche and culture

Devereux viewed the relationship between psychoanalysis and anthropology in an innovative manner, establishing a relationship of complementarity between them. In his *Basic Problems of Ethnopsychiatry* (1970), he explained that psychoanalysis and ethnology study what is specifically human in human beings, meaning what distinguishes human beings as cultural beings from *homo sapiens* conceived of in biological terms. Psychoanalysis attaches particular importance to what is specifically human in the human psyche, and ethnology to what is characteristic of human beings and of them exclusively, in culture and society. Then he talked about the human characteristics of differentiation and individualisation. He considered, additionally, that culture and the human psyche were inseparable concepts, from the methodological as well as from the functional point of view, and that the uniformity of the human psyche also implied the uniformity of human culture with a capital 'C'. He maintained that cultures, like individuals, differ essentially in the manner in which their constitutive elements are juxtaposed and organised into structures and patterns. He then proposed a formulation he had worked out of the precise nature of the logical connection between culture and the human psyche according to which they are historically "coemergents", reciprocally presupposing one another. They could not therefore "genetically" follow one from the other. Moreover, he differentiated the process of humanisation, or the process of culture acquisition in itself, enabling the realisation of human potentialities, from that of ethnicisation or the process of acquiring a specific culture which provides a set of specific means for realising these potentialites.

In an article entitled "Culture and the Unconscious" (1955),[102] Devereux stated three postulates and a conclusion of great significance for this study: 1) the psychic unity of mankind – unity involving the capability of extreme changeability; 2) the principle of limited possibilities; and 3) the fact that something existing openly in one society, and even culturally actualised there, is often repressed in another society. From these three postulates he drew the ineluctable conclusion that if all psychoanalysts were to make a complete list of all the drives, desires, and phantasies surfacing in the clinical setting, this list would correspond point by point to a list of all the beliefs and all the known cultural procedures established by ethnologists. He considered this conclusion to be necessarily valid since all phantasies and all cultural phenomena are the products of human mind, and therefore, in the final analysis, of the unconscious.

We find there an observation and a general conclusion that had already been established by Róheim and that constitute the very foundation of the existence of a psychoanalytical anthropology, or the presence of psychoanalysis in the socio-cultural field.

Thus, the connections between anthropology and psychoanalysis could therefore be based on the dual uniformity of their key concept and of their object, culture, and the psyche, on their logical connection and their "co-emergence", as well as on the correspondences of their products, cultural phenomena and phantasies, for example. However, no simple exteriority–interiority relationship obtains between culture and psyche, because culture is internalised, is integrated into the psyche, is introjected, and is also lived as an inner experience while preserving its external status, just as the psyche is externalised, projects itself onto external reality, and is symbolised individually and collectively, notably through institutions.

In addition, Devereux introduced the valuable notion of latent and manifest cultural patterns, writing in *From Anxiety to Method in the Behavioral Sciences* that each "culture contains also the negation of its manifest pattern and nuclear values, through a tacit affirmation of contrary latent patterns and marginal values. *The complete real pattern of a culture is a product of a functional interplay between officially affirmed and officially negated patterns. . .*"[103]

Inquiring into the utility of psychoanalysis as a specialised ethnological technique of investigation, Devereux deemed that it could not supply the elements necessary for an exhaustive ethnography of a given society, but that it would be an extremely effective means of highlighting the matrix of values and meanings to which a cultural phenomenon belonged. Ethnologists, he considered, find this type of information to be of the greatest interest, because an act, an attitude, or a material object is only a cultural phenomenon to the extent that it has its place in a matrix of values and significations. He then synthesised his conception of the relationships between these two disciplines explaining that psychoanalysis and ethnology yield not additional, but complementary, understandings, that there in fact exists a Heisenberg-Bohr kind of indeterminacy relationship between the ethnological comprehension and psychoanalytical comprehension of human behaviour. Only concern for convenience and economy would therefore determine when or at what point it becomes preferable to abandon an analytical investigation for an ethnological one and vice versa.

Where does the psychoanalyst stand with regard to culture?

Devereux considered that it was the psychoanalyst's duty to understand perfectly the nature and function of the culture in itself, and considered in itself, not only because it represents a universal human phenomenon, but also because its general categories – not to be confused with their possible content in some specific culture – are universal phenomena. No matter what the cultural diversity, the simple fact of having a culture is a properly universal experience, and human beings function as creators, creatures, manipulators, and mediators of culture in any place and in the same manner.

The creation of ethnopsychiatry

Devereux defined ethnopsychiatry as an interdisciplinary science endeavouring to compare and coordinate the concept of "culture" (a key concept of anthropology) with the "normality–abnormality" conceptual pair specific to psychiatry, but that it was its duty to determine the exact locus of the boundary between normality and abnormality. He considered that

> From a psychiatric viewpoint, the valid criteria of normality are absolute, that is, they are independent of the norms of any given culture or society but are identical with the criteria for Culture as a universally human phenomenon. Emotional maturity, a sense of reality, rationality, and the ability to sublimate can certainly contribute to the individual's adjustment in a healthy society and insure survival in a pathological one; they are nevertheless logically independent of adjustment itself.[104]

He therefore opposed relativist theses relating pathological criteria to the norms of each culture, thus ruling out the existence of absolute criteria. He defined culture as being above all a standardised system of defences, and consequently integral with functions of the ego. However, as experience, it would, according to him, be related to the superego and to the ego ideal.

In the course of his theoretical elaboration resulting from his experience as both an ethnologist and a psychoanalyst, Devereux was led to propose and to distinguish – on the basis of unconscious repressed material and the cultural standpoint – between two types of unconscious: the cultural or ethnic unconscious and the idiosyncratic unconscious. According to him, the individual's ethnic or cultural unconscious was that portion of his or her total unconscious that he or she shared with most members of his or her cultural community. Each culture allows certain phantasies, drives, and psychic manifestations to reach consciousness and to remain conscious and requires others to be repressed, maintained unconscious by certain defence mechanisms and often reinforced by cultural pressures, something which explains why all the members of a culture have a certain number of unconscious conflicts in common. The idiosyncratic unconscious is composed of elements that individuals have been forced to repress as a result of specific unique forms of stress and that they have had to undergo.[105]

According to Devereux, human beings live with and manipulate cultural materials in five specific ways: normally, immaturely, neurotically, psychotically, and psychopathically. He established a typology of personality disorders and identified four types of ethnopsychiatric categories: type disorders, ethnic disorders, "sacred disorders" of the shamanistic type, and finally, idiosyncratic disorders.

He used the term **type disorder** to designate the illnesses peculiar to the type of society that produces them. For him, the aetiology of "any" non-idiosyncratic disorder was essentially determined by the type of social structure in which this disorder appeared, while its clinical description was especially structured by the ethnic cultural pattern. Thus, the short psychotic episode (*bouffée délirante*) was one of the type psychoses of relatively simple societies which, when aggressive and self-destructive impulses are superimposed, it takes the form of an amok attack among the Malay, or a Crazy Dog quasi-psychosis among the Crow. In modern society, there are schizophrenias, psychopathic states, and obsessive–compulsive and character neuroses.[106]

Ethnic disorders. Each cultural area, and perhaps even each culture, has at least one, and often several, disorders of this kind. They are structured and arranged culturally and generally have a name, for example, the Malay's *amok* and *latah,* the *imu* of the Ainus, the *windigo* of the Canadian Algonquians, the heartbreak syndrome of the Mohaves. Devereux considered that in situations of "stress", the culture itself provides the individual with "patterns of misconduct", to borrow Ralph Linton's expression. Everything transpires as if the group was saying to the individual: "Don't do this but if you must, do it this way". Ethnic disorders precisely constitute patterns of misconduct *par excellence.*[107] In a lecture on the relationship between psychology and sociology, that I shall discuss later on, Marcel Mauss, who was one of Devereux's mentors, rightly brought up the notion of collective symbolisation in connection with these "ethnic disorders".

"Sacred" disorders of the shamanistic type. Devereux held that shamans were seriously neurotic or even psychotic people in a state of temporary remission. For him, their dominant conflicts were rooted in their ethnic unconscious. Shamans were only "adapted" to a relatively marginal sector of their societies and cultures. Although their situations were institutionalised, they remained "dystonic" with regard to their own egos and sometimes even with regard to their cultures in general. He considered that ethnic disorders resembled shamanistic disorders in that they both used the defences and symptoms provided them by the culture and specifically developed for that purpose. Nonetheless, ethnic disorders took their means of defence from one segment of the culture and shamanistic disorders from another. They differed as to the origin of their basic conflicts, which were rooted, not in the ethnic unconscious, but in idiosyncratic traumatisms sufficiently current in a given culture to compel that culture to take note of this as soon as their frequency or intensity exceeded a certain threshold.

Devereux believed that in **idiosyncratic disorders**, the symptoms and means of defence were not provided by the culture, but were improvised by individuals. In this case it would be a matter of individual and no longer of cultural symbolisation.

He came to *affirm the existence, unheard of up until then because unimaginable, of sick societies, which he distinguished from healthy societies*, thus rejecting the classic theory of adjustment. For him, the theory of adjustment refused to admit the existence of societies that were so "sick" that one had to be quite "sick" oneself to be able to adjust to them. He considered that it went without saying that in speaking of sick cultures, he was not following the questionable example of Ruth Benedict who had claimed to have made a psychiatric diagnosis of diverse cultures. For Devereux, in the theory of making adjustment the criterion of sanity also proved indefensible in light of the important distinction Erich Fromm had formulated between healthy adjustment and sadomasochistic conformism. In short, there was good reason to establish a fairly simple distinction between external (overt) adjustment and internal adjustment, some degree of overt adjustment being necessary for the survival of the individual in any society.[108]

This discourse was in total opposition to, on the one hand, that of his colleagues who were culturalist anthropologists and, on the other hand, to that of his other colleagues who were psychoanalysts, Fromm and Horney, for example. Devereux was proposing a certain type of distinction based on social realisation or not, through sublimation, between properly human characteristics, individualisation and differentiation. Thus, a healthy society would rather foster individualising sublimations in its members to the detriment of de-individualising repressions and "suppressions"; while a sick society would principally stir up repression, reaction formation, and other de-individualising regressive processes.

The Œdipus complex

Devereux situated the Œdipus complex both within the framework of this dual uniformity, as a psycho-sociological phenomenon, but also detected there a physiological dimension linked to human feminine sexuality, in particular that connected with maternity. He said that what was important to him was that "the sexualisation of maternity is at the root of the Œdipus complex" that the mother's unconscious "seductiveness" triggers.[109] Elsewhere, in a paper published in *Basic Problems of Ethnopsychiatry*, he suggested that the parents' counter-oedipal drives were prior to the child's oedipal drives. He explained that while it was often a question of parental seduction in clinical observations, the same people who reported this on the level of observation hastened to regain the terra firma of the Œdipus complex, a phenomenon presented as being spontaneous when they came to generalise or conceptualise it. And when an explanation is required, instead of relating the Œdipus complex and the behaviour it arouses to an overt "counter-oedipal" incentive, they took refuge in the ice age myth imagined by Freud in one of his rare questionable moments. Devereux professed to believe in the universality of the Œdipus complex, not because it was biologically determined in children, but because the Laius or Jocasta complex was biologically determined in adults, and subsequently induced by the adult in each child born and to be born for all time.[110]

It is rather surprising to find that, while appealing to a certain Freudian orthodoxy, Devereux had a "biological" view of the Œdipus complex after the fashion of his American colleagues who were anthropologists and psychoanalysts. The child's Œdipus complex is structured upon that of its parents, without needing to be biologically determined in them. He scotomised the "primal" phantasy dimension, something which I find singularly astonishing!

Researchers, their objects, and their fields

To conclude, I shall note Devereux's major innovative intuitions concerning researchers' relationships to the objects they observe and to their fields, characterised by a primordial anxiety leading them to employ diverse defence mechanisms, all fitting into the framework of transfero-counter-transferential processes. The discovery of this counter-transferential dimension of researchers with respect to their ethnographic fields proves particularly fruitful when it comes to elucidating certain forms of anthropologists' theoretical elaboration, in particular, that of Malinowski. I expand upon these reflexions in the final chapter.

It does not seem to me that justice has been done to the originality of Devereux' ideas, both within the cultural and historical context in which they were produced and nowadays. Yet, he clearly established and expanded upon epistemologically pertinent, theoretical and empirical bases the conditions of a finally fruitful encounter between psychoanalysis and anthropology, which has certain heuristic value, including the exemplary creation of ethnopsychiatry.

In France

The French school of sociology founded by Émile Durkheim left a lasting mark on a certain tradition of French thought, but also exercised considerable influence on the British functionalist school (Malinowski and Radcliffe-Brown, in particular). The prospect of a dialogue, even of any interest in psychology, even less in psychoanalysis, seems to have been ruled out with Durkheimian sociology, although contemporaneous with the latter. The sources of this French socio-anthropological thought can be located principally in the eighteenth century among the Enlightenment philosophers, Montesquieu and Rousseau in particular, but also in the Society of the Observers of Man, a pluridisciplinary group interested in the observation of facts and the elaboration of a methodology heralding positivism, and then in one of the founders of sociology, Auguste Comte (1798–1857), some of whose fundamental ideas can be found in Durkheim.

Émile Durkheim (1858–1917)

Belonging to a family of rabbis and a philosopher by training, Durkheim is considered to have been the founder of the French school of sociology. In 1896 he founded *L'Année sociologique*, a major journal for this new French sociology.

Durkheim would rectify Comte's "west-centred" evolutionism and claim the existence of a plurality of societies having different "morphologies", "physiologies", and histories, as well as upholding the unity of the human mind. He had initially thought of developing sociology mainly on the basis of history. But upon discovering the British anthropological school, he came to understand that ethnology must also be integrated into sociology. Thus, this steady dialogue between sociology, ethnology, and history would be a source of richness for this school of sociology. Nonetheless, in extending Comte's thought, he would rule out any possible relationship with psychology and, though he was Freud's contemporary, he would misjudge his ideas. For all that, certain notions dealing with collective life led him to resort to psychological language, all the while distancing himself from psychological science as a complementary tool for the interpretation of social facts.

The main idea that he used to define sociology was that of the priority of the whole over the parts, the irreducibility of the social whole to the sum of its elements and the explanation of the elements by the whole. This was one of Comte's fundamental principles. When the phenomenon to be explained was social in nature, according to the principle of the homogeneity of cause and effect, the cause had to be social too; whence a fundamental rule of the sociological method, that of the explanation of a social phenomenon by another social phenomenon and the explanation of a comprehensive phenomenon by another comprehensive phenomenon.

According to Durkheim, it is the society that gives birth to the individual and not the individuals that give birth to society. Consequently, he established the primacy of society over the individual, who was but an expression of it. It was necessary to explain individual phenomena by the state of the collectivity and not the latter by the former.

The central theme of his thought was that of the relationship between individuals and the collectivity. How can a collection of individuals constitute a society? How can they arrive at that condition of social existence which is a consensus?

This is the subject of his first book, *The Division of Labour in Society* (1893). He responded to this fundamental question by appealing to a distinction between two forms of solidarity: what he called mechanical solidarity with interchangeability of individuals, specific to societies said to be archaic; and what he called organic solidarity with the differentiation of individuals, characteristic of modern western society. In this same work, he introduced the concept of collective consciousness, of particular interest to psychoanalysts because it is analogous to the notion of group psyche postulated by Freud in the last pages of *Totem and Taboo*. He defined it as the "totality of beliefs and sentiments common to the average man of a society".[111] It would be the "psychic type" of the society that does not change with each generation and rather links successive generations to one another. This collective consciousness would involve greater or lesser extension or force depending on the societies, being greater in societies having mechanical solidarity than in those having organic solidarity.

In *The Rules of Sociological Method* (1895), he considered social facts to be things, everything that is given presenting itself or being obvious to observation. Another characteristic, as he saw it, of social facts is that they put pressure on individuals. He reminded us that every social fact was caused by another social fact and never by a fact of individual psychology. However, a passage from this work cannot but raise questions for psychoanalysts, and group analysts in particular. It reads:

> [S]ociety is not the mere sum of individuals, but the system formed by their association represents a specific reality which has its own characteristics.
>
> Undoubtedly no collective entity can be produced if there are no individual consciousnesses: this is a necessary but not a sufficient condition.

> In addition, these consciousnesses must be associated and combined in a certain way. It is from this combination that social life arises and consequently it is this combination which explains it. By aggregating together, by interpenetrating, by fusing together, individuals give birth to a being, psychical if you will, but one which constitutes a psychical individuality of a new kind. Thus it is in the nature of this individuality and not in that of its component elements that we must search for the proximate and determining causes of the facts produced in it. The group thinks, feels and acts entirely differently from the way its members would if they were isolated. If therefore we begin by studying these members separately, we will understand nothing about what is taking place in the group. In a word, there is between psychology and sociology the same break in continuity as there is between biology and the physical and chemical sciences. Consequently every time a social phenomenon is directly explained by a psychological phenomenon, we may rest assured that the explanation is false.[112]

A social fact is therefore singular. That is the sense of Durkheim's methodological thought. Nonetheless, the group thinks, feels, acts, and the combination of individual souls produces a psychic individuality. His references to psychology are, however, undeniable.

Durkheim's study of *Suicide* (1897), written in collaboration with Marcel Mauss, deals with a pathological aspect of modern societies and with a phenomenon in which the relationship between the individual and the collectivity is found in the most striking way. He wished to demonstrate the extent to which individuals are determined by the collective reality.

He considered the sociologist's job to be that of studying correlations between the circumstances and the variations in the rate of suicide, which are social phenomena. He thus distinguished between suicide, an individual phenomenon, and the rate of suicide, a social phenomenon; there was a psychological predisposition to suicide, but the force determining suicide was not psychological, but social. Whence Durkheim's theory that suicides are individual phenomena whose causes are essentially social. There are "suicidogenic" currents running through society, having their origin in the collectivity, and being the real or determinant cause of suicides. The same social circumstances that create "suicidogenic" currents create those psychological predispositions because the individuals living in the conditions of modern society have definite, and consequently vulnerable sensibilities. Thus, the real causes of suicide are social forces that vary from society to society, from group to group, from religion to religion, emanating from the group and not from individuals. Too much integration and submission can in fact determine it (fatalistic suicide and especially altruistic suicide, typical of traditional societies, are very rare), just as lack of socialisation and integration (anomic suicide and egoistic suicides, typical of modern societies) can. Durkheim observed that individualism weakens our contemporary society, as well as weakening individuals themselves, something which boosts the increase in anomic and egoistic suicides in our societies.

It is therefore a matter of a social fact linked to the social organisation and the hazards of socialisation, and the social integration of the individual.

His religious sociology, expressed fully in *The Elementary Forms of Religious Life* (1912), divides the world into sacred and profane phenomena. His work raises a major question, which he formulated in this way: "We must ask ourselves, then, what compelled man to see the world as two heterogeneous and incompatible worlds, though nothing in palpable experience seems to have suggested the idea of such radical duality".[113] He posited the idea of religion as the primary social institution, a thesis still combatted today, and the sacred as being the criterion of the religious. The notion of divinity is interpreted as being a symbol, that of "transfigured" society; it would represent a "principle of grouping and unification". His definition of religion is exemplary and opens up vast vistas for reflexion. According to Durkheim, *"a religion is a unified system of beliefs and practices relative to sacred things, that is to say, things set apart and surrounded by prohibitions – beliefs and practices that unite its adherents in a single moral community called a church"*.[114]

This definition eliminates those involving notions of the supernatural or of divinity. Moreover, as the sociologist Camille Tarot has observed, its force lies in the fact that it would respond to demands of objectivity and formalisation posited in advance. For him, in a sense, it foreshadowed structuralism, because it introduced the notion of system – that very notion of system that Ferdinand de Saussure introduced into language – and which is the key concept of the structural approach.[115]

The Durkheimian view of the sacred, complex whole, changing from one society to another and from one era to another, combines two elements, affective and intellectual. It is a universal category, represents a communicative, contagious force. It also appears ambivalent, torn between pure and impure.

According to Durkheim, religion is part of social "morphology" and "physiology". It has functions, integrates and regulates individual behaviours, as well as attaching collective goals to individual desires. A reflexion on the conditions of the emergence of the "religious idea" must raise questions for us as psychoanalysts: "It is in these effervescent social settings, and from this very effervescence, that the religious idea seems to be born".[116] The fundamentally libidinal dimension of groups that Freud had identified could in fact connect up with this Durkheimian discourse on the emergence of the sacred.

Camille Tarot has underscored the considerable place that *The Elementary Forms of Religious Life* accorded to the problem of the symbol and symbolisation.[117] Indeed, in that work, Durkheim succeeded in formulating the essential idea that no society can exist without symbols and all social life is based on symbolism:

> Social life, then, in every aspect and throughout its history, is possible only thanks to a vast body of symbolism. The material emblems, the embodied representations with which we are especially concerned in the present study, are a particular form of that symbolism. But there are many others. Collective feelings can be embodied equally in personalities or formulas: some formulas are flags; some personalities, real or mythic, are symbols.[118]

He developed a sociological theory of symbolisation regarding the totem, the "clan's flag",[119] the place of projection of collective force, then concerning rites, assemblies, and effervescent groups. Totemism therefore represented a symbolic fact, and religion became a system of symbols.

Durkheim's thought is rich and opened up new avenues of research for his successors, Mauss, Lévi-Strauss, and Bastide in particular. Nevertheless, the notions of collective consciousness, of psychic individuality of a new kind qualifying the group as the introduction of symbols, of symbolism, and of symbolisation could constitute themes for reflexion common to psychoanalysts, as well as representing connections between the two orders of reality: psychic and socio-cultural.

Marcel Mauss (1872–1950)

Nephew of Durkheim, after an *agrégation* in philosophy, Mauss studied Sanskrit, Indology, and the history of religions. As the sociologist Tarot has observed,[120] he would be a collaborator, a team player, and a faithful, but free, heir. He always remained a Durkheimian sociologist, but with an empirical, pragmatic orientation first of all, preferring monographs and complementing the objectivism of the Durkheimian method with attention paid to experience and practices. Persuaded of the extreme complexity of social facts, he vigorously criticised British evolutionism, which he believed misjudged the complexity and discontinuities among cultures and the plurality of choices they made. Considering himself compelled to renounce sociogenesis, he settled into synchrony out of an initial concern for methodological rigour, favouring problems of nature and function and foreshadowing functionalism, then structuralism. It was also a matter of applying the sociological method in order to understand the differences and to rethink – on the basis of them and not without them – the unity of the human race, which is the mission of anthropology. In many respects, he showed himself to be very close to his colleague and friend Boas.

In Tarot's opinion,[121] he was therefore indebted to Durkheim for the sociological method for dealing with social facts, the project of integrating sociology and ethnology and that of creating a sociology of religion. But, he was also convinced that sociology always had to remain close to history and historical criticism, that it had to give back its full place to the psychology that Comte's and Durkheim's thought had banned, as well as to philology and to the nascent linguistics, of which it had been ignorant.

He was instrumental in having anthropology accorded an autonomous status in France. This relatively late emancipation and institutionalisation of anthropology moreover intersected with that of psychoanalysis in France, since the Société psychanalytique de Paris was founded in 1926. Beginning in 1925, he, Lucien Lévy-Bruhl, and Pierre Rivet founded and organised the Institut d'ethnologie of the University of Paris. From 1926 to 1940, he taught a course called "Instructions d'ethnographie descriptive" there, something which enabled him to define the rules of the ethnographic method and to divide anthropology into social morphology and social physiology, form and function (involving representations and practices). It was through this teaching that the first generation of French field ethnologists (among them, Marcel Griaule, Michel Leiris, Alfred Métraux and Jacques Soustelle, especially) would receive their training.

He introduced the idea of *total social fact*, which entails the search for connections among the economic, political, social, and ideological orders. A social fact can in fact only be understood in reference to the whole of society in which it figures and the latter in reference to the human being that it both develops and realises, whence the closely related idea of *L'Homme total* (Karsenti, 1997).[122]

In his famous work *The Gift* (1923–1924)[123] Mauss laid down the gift as a socio-anthropological problem central to every theory of exchange and the idea that gifts are a form of symbolism; gifts are symbols of the social bond and exchange, but also play an operative role in the bond and lend objectivity to the otherwise invisible reality.

But, as Tarot has emphasised, one of Mauss' fundamental contributions lay in introducing an elaboration of a symbolic theory of society and in identifying the symbolic nature of social facts. He had a semiotic and linguistic conception of symbols, producers of networks of meanings functioning by referring back and forth among themselves. It was in *A General Theory of Magic*,[124] a book about the controversial theory of *mana* written in collaboration with Henri Hubert (1902–1903), that he drew attention to the problems of symbolism in a systematic manner for the first time. Tarot has remarked that starting from force to arrive at logics of meaning, Mauss highlighted the role of symbols, associating force and representation, meaning and power,[125] something which could not but raise questions for psychoanalysts confronting the force of drives and the meaning of representations. Let us not forget that Ernest Jones' theory of symbolism is close to this Maussian view of symbols.

In 1924, Mauss gave a lecture on the "Real and Practical Relationships between Psychology and Sociology",[126] which Tarot considers marked the birth of the anthropology of the symbolic, or the explicit shift from Durkheimian sociology in the direction of the problems surrounding the symbolic. Tarot has maintained that Mauss was aware of the need to replace the issues surrounding representation and mental states that had dominated philosophy and psychology by issues involving signs, which he refused to distinguish from symbols.[127]

This lecture is of interest to us for several reasons: on the one hand, as concerns the development of his conception of symbol, symbolism, and symbolisation; on the other hand, with respect to his innovative manner of viewing collaboration with psychologists, which could in certain respects inspire that between anthropologists and psychoanalysts. In addition, he cursorily voiced his negative opinion of *Totem and Taboo*, something I shall look at. As concerns his stand toward psychoanalysis, he did not seem to have had any direct contact with it through reading, but rather knew it through the intermediary of his friend the British anthropologist Rivers. That is what Bertrand Pulman has already encouraged us to believe.

But let us go back to this lecture in which Mauss otherwise clearly formulated his aspiration to realise a study of the "complete man" considered in terms of the multiple relationships established between his or her body, mind, and socio-cultural setting.

Mauss began his talk by speaking of the existence of "two specialized realms: the realm of consciousness on the one hand", object of psychology, and the "realm of the *conscience collective* and collectivity", object of sociology.

He considered that sociology had to appeal to psychology for the exploration of the vast field of collective representations, an essential part of that discipline. Nonetheless, he also considered that the share of collective representations, including ideas, concepts, collective feelings, motives for traditional practices, especially, was considerable, even in the individual consciousness, whence the risk of sociology's intruding into the field of psychology. He then looked at the services psychology had rendered to sociology, saying that the whole theory of collective representations and collective practices, that whole psychological part of his studies, depended exclusively on three sciences in addition to his own – on statistics and history, which teach the facts and their circumstances, and finally on a third science, psychology, which enables one to understand, that is, to interpret, them, whatever they may be, in precise, intelligent, scientific terms. But, he said, since he had already spoken of representations and collective practices, that is to say, of acts and habitual ideas, he had necessarily been speaking a psychological language; his analysis of the facts of collective consciousness could not in fact speak any other language than that of psychologists. He explained that,

> That is why Durkheim, pupil of Wundt and Ribot, Espinas, Ribot's friend, and the rest of us, the followers of these teachers, have always been ready to accept the advances of psychology. For only the latter, besides our own elaborations, provides us with the necessary concepts, the useful words which denote the most numerous facts and connote the clearest and most essential ideas.[128]

That was therefore a manner of speaking unprecedented in the history of French socio-anthropological thought, Comte and Durkheim, as I have already mentioned, having already ruled out any collaboration with psychology. It is nothing less than surprising that Mauss included Durkheim in his project of listening and openness to the discourse of the masters of the psychology of the time. In addition, we learn that his uncle was also the student of Wundt, founder of a psychology of the peoples.

He chose four notions: that of vigour and of mental or nervous weakness, the notion of psychosis, that of symbol, and finally, that of instinct.

It was in connection with the notion of psychosis that Mauss referred to Freud's *Totem and Taboo*, which makes a particularly interesting analogy. He noted that a second advance had been made when psychologists – and French neurologists and German psychiatrists – had replaced the notion of obsession by the notion of psychosis. The latter having proven fruitful for him and his colleagues, he said that he and they were following their work closely. He believed that the hypothesis of the state of the whole consciousness, of a state having its own force of development, proliferation, deviation, multiplication, and ramification, of a state that takes hold of the whole psychological being, must become common to him and psychologists. However, he made it clear that he would *of course not indulge in the excesses of psychoanalysis*. He considered *Totem and Taboo*, only to mention Freud's last book, to be something quite different from psychoses and called it the last of the key, system books, which he saw no reason to have to multiply endlessly.[129]

When it came to the notion of symbol and of symbolic activity of the mind, he expressed innovative ideas in comparison to Durkheim and positioned himself as a precursor of Lévi-Strauss, saying that it had already been agreed that most mental states were not isolated phenomena. But the fact that most were something more than what was meant by the word "mental state", that they were signs, symbols of the general state and of a host of activities and images, and especially the fact that they were used as such by the deepest mechanisms of the consciousness was something new. For, was not the notion of symbol entirely ours, derived from religion and law? He pointed out that he and Durkheim had long taught that people could only be in communion and communicate through symbols, through enduring, common signs, external to individual mental states, which just simply follow one after the other, through signs for groups of states then taken to be realities. He said that he had long thought that *one of the characteristics of the social fact was precisely its symbolic aspect*. In most collective representations, he explained, it is not a matter of a single representation of a single thing, but of a representation arbitrarily, or more or less arbitrarily, chosen to signify others and to exercise control over practices. He said that he had come to be sure of his theory by the very fact of his agreement with psychologists. If what they were telling him and his colleagues about the individual consciousness was true, it was all the more true of the collective consciousness. The activity of the collective mind was even more symbolic than that of the individual mind, but it was so in exactly the same sense. From that point of view, there was no difference of intensity, of kind, no difference of type. That idea of symbol could be used concurrently with its predecessors and combined all together they could explain important elements of myths, rites, beliefs, of faith in their efficacy, of illusion, of religious hallucination, aesthetics, lies, and collective delirium and its rectifications. In this masterful text of 1924, Mauss was already introducing a programme for collaboration between anthropologists and psychoanalysts around the process of symbolisation, its fields of individual and collective production, and of their interactions, that is still pertinent nowadays.

Mauss built a chronological bridge between the nineteenth and the twentieth century. The theoretical legacy of the nineteenth century in fact died in his work, and all the original contributions of the twentieth century in the domain of the human sciences took shape or had their seeds in it, according to Tarot. Along with him we can cite field ethnography's wresting of ethnology away from history, linguistics' aiming to take over from philology, the synchronic approach's replacing the diachronic approach, long term orientation's replacing an event by event approach, the equality of cultures, the importance of the notion of system, precursor of that of structure, and of the symbolic in particular.

Claude Lévi-Strauss

Lévi-Strauss was born in Brussels in 1908. He obtained a law degree, then an *agrégation* in philosophy in 1931 in Paris. He then taught philosophy in the secondary schools in Mont-de-Marsan, then Laon from 1932 to 1934. A member of the French cultural mission in Brazil, he served as a professor at the University of Sao Paulo from 1935 to 1938. During this period, he undertook ethnographic missions in the Mato Grosso, then in the Amazon Rain Forest. He returned to France, then, after the defeat in 1940, left France again for New York City, where he taught at the New School for Social Research from 1941 to 1945, and at the Ecole Libre des Hautes Etudes. Upon returning to France, he defended his doctoral thesis entitled *The Elementary Structures of Kinship* in 1948, thus becoming Docteur ès-Lettres. In 1949, he served as assistant director of the Musée de l'Homme and director of studies at the Ecole Pratique des Hautes Etudes, where he held the chair of Comparative Religion of Non-Literate Peoples. From 1959 to 1982, he was a professor at the Collège de France, where he held the chair of social anthropology. In 1960, he founded the Laboratory of Social Anthropology. He was elected to the Académie Française in 1973.

At odds with the British functionalist school, and although close to Boas' and Kroeber's thought, Lévi-Strauss also found a place in the Durkheimo-Maussian tradition. He would in fact pursue Mauss' work on the symbolic and speech acts. According to Tarot (2007), however, he imposed an interpretation of Mauss consisting of separating him from Durkheim, then imposed a partly imaginary genealogy upon his own structuralism.[130] For Lévi-Strauss, it was therefore a matter of showing that structuralist reflexion on signs and symbols first originated in linguistics, which had its sources in Saussure as reinterpreted by the Russian formalists Jakobson and Trubetskoy, while Tarot maintains that structuralism emerged from the work of Durkheim and Mauss in the field of sociology of religion. Lévi-Strauss then pointed to several consequences of this "substitution of genealogy": the abandonment of the concept of society in favour of that of culture; the idea that society and religion can only be explained in terms of the symbolic; a scatter-brained, vague conception of religion; disposing of the notion of the sacred and an attempt at substitution by the symbolic.

Tarot has identified two means of access to structuralism: 1) sociological, through the gift, the symbol of exchange; 2) linguistic, with the notion of sign as equivalent to symbol.[131] In a most pertinent extension of this reflexion, the anthropologist Patrice Bidou observed in Lévi-Strauss, from the time of *The Elementary Structures of Kinship* to the *Mythologiques*, via *Totemism*, a constant concern to banish every individual component, through affects, attitudes, from his "object", in order to stress formal constructions and systems of classification. He considers that *Totemism* occupied a central position in this process. Indeed, according to him, the subject was left out of consideration, changing the vertical – emotional – relationship between the individual and his or her totem into a horizontal system of relationships among clans. The only thing that would then be left would be to extend the field of application of the classificatory undertaking to mythology by viewing myths as systems of horizontal relationships – myths among one another and, within myths, constitutive elements among one another – without troubling themselves with the vertical link that the members of a society maintain with their myths.[132] And this verticality of the link to the totem and to myths pertains to the sacred and to the religious eliminated by Lévi-Strauss, something which connects up with Tarot's views.

Bidou further notes that in retaining the totem, meaning, the system of classifications, and by dropping the taboo which individuals' attitudes and emotions are hooked onto, Lévi-Strauss thus placed totemism and mythology on the same level as kinship, that of a whole made up of separate units whose internal logic, systemic nature which structuralists confuse with all meaning.[133] He elaborated a new theory of culture based on language and gifts as a set of symbolic systems and of systems of communication.

But, fundamentally, it was his plan to explore the life of the human mind and what conditions this life, "unconscious thought" and its laws, understood through the study of symbolic systems –language and kinship systems, for example – the task of the ethnologist being to explore the unconscious elements of social life, in the sense defined by Boas, and not by Freud. This is why, as he wrote in *The Savage Mind*, "ethnology is first of all psychology",[134] but a cognitive, non-affective psychology, affects and drives having no place there. For him, the psychological was subordinated to the sociological. As he wrote in "Introduction to the Work of Marcel Mauss" (1950) "the psychological formulation is only a translation, on the level of the individual psychical, of what is strictly speaking a sociological structure".[135] The unconscious was at the origin of all the symbolic systems, but this "structuralist" unconscious was distanced from the Freudian unconscious, something to which I shall return.

In "Introduction to the Work of Marcel Mauss", Lévi-Strauss emphasised Mauss' modernism to the point of making him into a structuralist. Commenting on his talk on the relationship between psychology and sociology, he took up the definition of social life as "a world of symbolic relationships" and maintained that,

> It is natural for society to express itself symbolically in its customs and its institutions; normal modes of individual behaviour are, on the contrary, *never symbolic in themselves*: they are elements out of which a symbolic system, which can only be collective, builds itself. It is only abnormal modes of behaviour which, because desocialised and in some way left to their own devices, realise the illusion of an autonomous symbolism on the level of the individual.[136]

Would not symptomatic formations be individual symbolisations, without necessarily being illusory? Further on, he presented his famous definition of culture:

> Any culture can be considered as a combination of symbolic systems headed by language, the matrimonial rules, the economic relations, art, science and religion. All the systems seek to express certain aspects of physical reality and social reality, and even more, to express the links that those two types of reality have with each other and those that occur among the symbolic systems themselves.[137]

In addition, according to Lévi-Strauss,

> Individual psychical processes do not reflect the group; even less do they pre-form the group... That *complementarity* of the individual psychical structure and social structure is the basis of the fruitful collaboration, called for by Mauss, which has come to pass between ethnology and psychology. But that collaboration will only remain valid if ethnology continues to claim a leading place for the description and objective analysis of customs and institutions, for the psychological study in depth of their subjective aspects can consolidate the leading position of objective analysis, but can never relegate it to the background.[138]

He wrote of a subordination of the psychological to sociological to which Mauss had in fact drawn attention.

These few quotes enable us immediately to detect, as early as 1950 in the continuation of *The Elementary Structures of Kinship* (1949), Lévi-Strauss' principal theoretical orientations, but above all a deep ambivalence with regard to the impact of the psyche and of its polymorphic manifestations in the sociocultural field.

This conflictual relation that he would maintain with psychoanalysis began, as early as 1949, with the conclusion of the *Elementary Structures*. He in fact had already criticised *Totem and Taboo* and Freud's thought there. Those criticisms would be pursued, here and there, in particular in *Totemism* (1962), the end of *The Naked Man* (1972), and especially in *The Jealous Potter* (1986). However, he also showed a concern to make a comparison between ethnology and psychoanalysis, particularly in some chapters (notably in "The Effectiveness of Symbols") of his work *Structural Anthropology* (1958), where he drew a comparison between the training of ethnologists and that of psychoanalysts, as well as between the field and the couch.

Thus, in "The Effectiveness of Symbols" (1949), he gave his own definition of the unconscious, the "structuralist" unconscious so different from the Freudian unconscious, and went on to compare shamanistic therapy and psychoanalytical therapy, suggesting an interest in and the lingering presence of psychoanalysis in his mind. His theory of therapy seems to revolve around the symbolic distinguishing of shamanistic therapy from medical therapy, which brings the former closer to psychoanalytical therapy. Western medical treatment would in fact separate the universe of the objective cause of illnesses from the subjective world of the patient, Lévi-Strauss observed, while this type of split would be foreign to shamanistic therapy. And this is what would enable it to be successful, because in the shamanistic paradigm, the cause of the illness (the monster) is still part of the "symbolic material" as well as the sick person's world of subjective representations. Thus, symbolic practice has a hold over the cause.

The relationship between "monster and illness" internal to the same mind would be a relationship of symbol to thing symbolised, or, in linguistic terms, of signifier to signified. The shaman provides the sick person with a language in which unexpressed states can be expressed; Lévi-Strauss therefore makes explicit the logic of the shamanistic interpretation as inducing a reorganisation of the patient's symbolic universe. Found in this text are the notions of language, resistance, transference, conflict and interpretation. Enough to make any psychoanalyst happy! In addition, in 1949, he had already referred to the work of linguists in order to situate this interpretation within the context of signifiers. But let us pursue the analogy proposed:

> In this respect, the shamanistic cure lies on the borderline between our contemporary physical medicine and such psychological therapies as psychoanalysis. Its originality stems from the application to an organic condition of a method related to psychotherapy. How is this possible? A closer comparison between shamanism and psychoanalysis – which in our view involves no slight to psychoanalysis – will enable us to clarify this point... The patient suffering from neurosis eliminates an individual myth by facing a "real" psychoanalyst; the native woman in childbed overcomes a true organic disorder by identifying with a "mythically transmuted" shaman.
>
> This parallelism does not exclude certain differences, which are not surprising if we note the character – psychological in one case and organic in the other – of the ailment to be cured. Actually the shamanistic cure seems to be the exact counterpart to the psychoanalytic cure, but with an inversion of all the elements. Both cures aim at inducing an experience, and both succeed by recreating a myth which the patient has to live or relive. But, in one case, the patient constructs an individual myth with elements drawn from his past; in the other case, the patient receives from the outside a social myth which does not correspond to the former personal state. To prepare for the abreaction, which then becomes an "adreaction", the psychoanalyst listens whereas the shaman speaks. Better still: when a transference is established, the patient puts words into the mouth of the psychoanalyst by attributing to him alleged feelings and intentions; in the incantation, on the contrary, the shaman speaks for his patient. He questions her and puts into her mouth answers that correspond to the interpretation of her condition, with which she must become imbued... The comparison with psychoanalysis has allowed us to shed light

> on some aspects of shamanistic curing. Conversely, it is not improbable that the study of shamanism may one day serve to elucidate obscure points of Freudian theory. We are thinking specifically of the concepts of myth and the unconscious.[139]

We shall see later on that this notion of "individual myth" of neurosis, along with the importance of language and of signifying interpretation, would be taken up by Lacan in 1953. But that is not all, because Lévi-Strauss, reader of Freud's texts, went on to engage in a radical criticism of the psychological definition of the Freudian unconscious in order to make a new one out of it, structuralist in nature, constituting one of the theoretical foundations of his anthropology, which would particularly inspire Lacan in his "return to Freud":

> The unconscious ceases to be the ultimate haven of individual particularities – the repository of a unique history which makes each of us an irreplaceable being. It is reducible to a function – the symbolic function, which no doubt is specifically human, and which is carried out according to the same laws among all men, and actually corresponds to the aggregate of these laws. If this view is correct, it will probably be necessary to reestablish a more marked distinction between the unconscious and subconscious than has been customary in psychology. For the subconscious, as a reservoir of recollections and images amassed in the course of a lifetime is merely an aspect of memory...
>
> The unconscious, on the other hand, is always empty – or, more accurately, it is as alien to mental images as is the stomach to the foods which pass through it. As the organ of a specific function, merely imposes structural laws upon inarticulated elements which originate elsewhere – impulses, emotions, representations, and memories.[140]

It is curious to observe the establishment of a distinction between unconscious and subconscious in the work of Lévi-Strauss who, as an attentive reader of Freud had not been able to detect it in his work, but possibly confused it with the Jungian distinction between individual unconscious and collective unconscious, the individual unconscious corresponding to Lévi-Strauss' subconscious. Nonetheless, he could have also found inspiration in Pierre Janet's ideas. According to Lévi-Strauss, the unconscious prevails over the life story of the individual and its products. He suggested analysing the particularities of the subject's symptoms in accordance with the laws of the unconscious that had organised the events of the subject's life into a discourse or made these events into symptoms.

Moreover, the predominance already accorded to the structure over the content, to laws over the individual vocabulary, that he never ceased to take up in diverse writings, in particular those on myths, refers back to the primacy of the symbolic function, meaning of the unconscious over the subconscious, which is individual in nature.

In "The Structural Study of Myths" (1955), Lévi-Strauss particularly wrote of the structural method's enabling him to rid himself of the obstacle that the search for a primitive version of a myth had long represented and to propose his innovative approach consisting of defining each myth "as consisting of all its versions". Thus the Freudian interpretation of the Œdipus myth, or rather of Sophocles' *Œdipus Rex*, would represent one of the numerous versions of it. According to him, "not only Sophocles, but Freud himself, should be included among the recorded versions of the Œdipus myth on a par with earlier or seemingly more 'authentic versions'".[141]

Let us continue tracking down increasingly violent criticisms, remarks, allusions, and analogies toward psychoanalysis, in particular in *Totemism* (1962), then in *The Jealous Potter* (1985).

In *Totemism*, Lévi-Strauss comes back to *Totem and Taboo* and Freud's thesis, explaining that unlike Kroeber his attitude had rather hardened over the years. He wrote there,

> Contrary to what Freud maintained, social constraints, whether positive or negative, cannot be explained, either in their origin or in their persistence, as the effects of impulses or emotions which appear again and again, with the same characteristics and during the course of centuries and millennia, in different individuals. For if the recurrence of the sentiments explained the persistence of customs, the origin of the customs ought to coincide with the origin of the appearance of the sentiments, and Freud's thesis would be unchanged even if the patricidal impulse corresponded to a typical situation instead of to a historical event.
>
> We do not know, and never shall know, anything about the first origin of beliefs and customs the roots of which plunge into a distant past.[142]

Seeming to agree with Durkheim, he observed that in the final analysis he too had derived social phenomena from affectivity, bringing him in an unexpected way nearer to Freud. It was a matter of Durkheim's theory of totemism starting from need and finishing with an appeal to feelings:

> Durkheim's theory of the collective origin of the sacred... rests on a *petitio principii*: it is not present emotions, felt at gatherings and ceremonies, which engender or perpetuate the rites, but ritual activity which arouses the emotions. Far from the religious idea being born of "effervescent social surroundings, and of this very effervescence," they presuppose it. Actually, impulses and emotions explain nothing: they are always *results*: either of the power of the body or of the impotence of the mind.
>
> In both cases they are consequences, never causes. The latter can only be sought in the organism, which is the exclusive concern of biology, or in the intellect, which is the sole way offered to psychology, and to anthropology as well.[143]

In *The Jealous Potter* (1985), Lévi-Strauss unleashed all the virulence of his attitude toward Freudian psychoanalysis, already present, but restrained since the time of *The Elementary Structures*, resorting, among other means, to humoristic attacks. Would the death of his friend Jacques Lacan have been a condition favouring this free expression of his hostility?

Lévi-Strauss went back on several characteristics of mythic thought, especially on the use of several codes, and reproached Freud for only considering the "psycho-organic" code systematically, to the exclusion of all others, as well as imposing its constant presence, therefore not envisaging its possible absence.

He criticised the Freudian theory of symbolism and called his thought mythic, justifying this analogy by means of examples. He wrote,

> His greatness lies partly in a gift he possesses in the highest degree: he can think the way myths do. Considering that the snake can take on a male or female connotation, he wrote: "This does not, however, mean that the symbol has two significations; it is simply employed in the inverse sense"... He also wrote that in dreams we often find "the procedure of reversal, of turning into the opposite, of inverting relationships"...
>
> Still, working in an indirect way, Freud here reaches a key notion: that of transformation, which is at the root of all his analyses.[144]

Freud could have responded to Lévi-Strauss that his mythic thought was just simply the expression of unconscious thought through its so singular processes.

Lévi-Strauss would express his scathing humour by establishing an analogy, surprising on the strictly formal level, between Sophocles' *Œdipus Rex* and Labiche's *The Italian Straw Hat*. He contended that, "The interest we take in Sophocles' tragedy and Labiche's comedy comes, despite their different contents, from the specific properties of the armature they share. In a sense, one could say that *Œdipus Rex* and *The Italian Straw Hat* are expanded metaphors of each other."[145] He was in fact reminding us that the pleasure generated by these plays was due more to their formal qualities than to their content. But, even so, why compare these two works? He answered in this way:

> I was therefore following the example of these myths, faithful to the lessons of mythic thought, when I confronted comedy with tragedy, legendary heroes with vaudeville characters: for each of these genres provides a grid that allows us to decipher messages – a task that neither, alone, could accomplish. Is this not always the case when it comes to questions of signification?[146]

Finally, he once more defended himself from the reproach repeatedly made that he was denying the existence of a psychic reality by challenging the primacy accorded to psychic forces which simply "irrupt upon a structure already in place, formed by the architecture of the mind".[147]

We have now reached the end of this study of Lévi-Strauss' thought and its so conflictual relationship to Freudian psychoanalysis.

Jacques Lacan (1901–1981)

Lacan was born in Paris on April 13, 1901. He studied medicine, then undertook his internship in psychiatry at Sainte-Anne's psychiatric hospital in the ward of Doctors Henri Claude, Gaëtan de Clerambault, and Georges Heuyer. Greatly interested in literature and philosophy, he frequented the surrealist group during the 1920s. Beginning in 1928, he participated in the "Evolution psychiatrique" group, a centre of renewal in psychiatry. He established ties with the philosophical research group in 1933–1934 and participated in the activities of the Collège de Sociologie founded by Georges Bataille, Michel Leiris, and Roger Caillois in 1937, which would carry on its activities until 1939. He attended Alexandre Kojève's seminar from 1934 to 1936 at the Ecole Pratique des Hautes Etudes, where he was initiated to Hegel's thought.

In 1932, he published his dissertation in medicine entitled *De la psychose paranoïaque dans ses rapports avec la personnalité*. It focused on a case of criminal paranoia that he had worked on at Sainte-Anne's, the "Aimée case" (Marguerite Anzieu). That same year, he began engaged in "didactic analysis" with Rudolph Loewenstein, something he would pursue up until 1938–1939.

In 1934, he became a member of the Société Psychanalytique de Paris (SPP) and participated in the XIVth International Congress of Psychoanalysis in Marienbad in 1936, where he presented a report on the "Mirror Stage", which he would take up again in 1949.

He was elected a titular member, therefore training analyst, of the SPP in 1938. That same year, he wrote the article on family complexes for *Encyclopédie Française*, which I shall come back to at a later point.

The year 1949 was particularly important for Lacan's work. It was the year in which he met Claude Lévi-Strauss, who would have a major influence on the evolution of his thought. In addition, he gave his talk on "The Mirror Stage as Formative of the *I* Function"[148] at the XVIth International Congress of Psychoanalysis held in Zurich.

He participated actively in this phase of the reconstruction of his Society and in 1951 started up his Seminar, which would be held there until 1953. He would also give his talk on "Intervention on Transference" to the Congress of Psychoanalysts of Romance Languages, which heralded a mutation in his thought. This was the beginning of his "return to Freud".

The year 1953 was crucial. It began with his election to the presidency of the SPP and the opening of the Institute under the direction of Sacha Nacht. However, discontent was growing among students of the SPP for numerous reasons, and conflicts were becoming more intense between the analysts having a medical orientation – such as Nacht – and those with a more liberal, academic orientation – Daniel Lagache, Juliette Favez-Boutonier, Françoise Dolto, especially.

The question of the training of analysts and of the length of the sessions would be at stake. After having rejected before the SPP the idea that the group's dissatisfaction was "entirely connected with the ideas and personal action of the Society's sitting president, Doctor Lacan",[149] the latter group of credentialed analysts resigned on June 16, 1953 and announced the creation of the Société Française de Psychanalyse (SFP), which would be presided over by Lagache. Lacan then decided to abandon, not only his functions as president, but also the SPP to join his colleagues who had resigned. The issue at stake in this rift in 1953 would have very probably been the theory of the unconscious and/or the very principle of the practice.

On July 8, 1953, Lacan inaugurated the new Society with a lecture entitled "The Symbolic, the Imaginary, and the Real", initiating thus a new stage of his thought in a process of mutation, marked from then on by the prevalence of the symbolic and of the order of language over the imaginary introduced in 1936 with the imago of the mirror stage.

On September 26, 1953, he pronounced his "Rome Discourse" entitled "The Function and Field of Speech in the Analytical Experience and Relation of the Field of Psychoanalysis to Language", more often presented as "Function and Field of Speech and Language in Psychoanalysis".[150] It was initially a matter of his Report for the Congress of Psychoanalysts of Romance Languages, but it became that of the first Congress of the SFP. This paper is often presented as having been the manifesto of Lacan's return to Freud, profoundly influenced as Lacan was by the thought of Lévi-Strauss, as we shall see later on. His seminar, now public, opened on November 18, 1953 at Sainte-Anne's, in the ward of his friend Professor Jean Delay. It would remain there until 1963. Having debuted with a rereading of Freud's "Papers on Technique",[151] he pursued this and took up the main clinical cases.

The year 1963 was that of his "excommunication", that is to say, of his exclusion from the International Psychoanalytical Association and the loss of his position of training analyst. His seminar at Sainte-Anne's was discontinued on November 20. With the support of Louis Althusser, it would be transferred to the Ecole Normale Supérieure in January 1964 and would continue until June 1969. During this period, he abandoned his "return to Freud" in order to develop his own thought and the foundations of psychoanalysis with the Seminar "The Four Fundamental Concepts of Psychoanalysis" (Book XI).[152] He would formalise his own concepts, such as "the barred subject", the object *a*, and the Other, especially.

During the year 1964, he founded the Ecole Française de Psychanalyse, which would become the Ecole Freudienne de Paris (EFP). The year 1966 was marked by the publication of his *Ecrits* by Seuil.[153]

From 1969 to 1979, the Seminar migrated to the law school. The 1970s were characterised by the Seminar's great "topological turn", with the encounter with the mathematician Pierre Soury as a new source of inspiration. This was the period of the "mathemes" and "Borromean knots".

There were political and theoretical conflicts within the EFP and rivalry between the School and the Department of Psychoanalysis of the University of

Paris VIII-Vincennes directed by Jacques-Alain Miller. Lacan dissolved the School at the beginning of 1980 and shortly afterward created the "Cause Freudienne", then adopted the "Ecole de la Cause Freudienne" toward the end of that same year. He died in Neuilly on September 9, 1981.

Before addressing my aim of discovering and analysing Lacan's relations with the social sciences, I shall look at some characteristics of his teachings and publications.

Paul-Laurent Assoun has pointed out that apart from the publication of his doctoral thesis in 1932, Lacan did not, strictly speaking, put his name to any book.[154] However, his thought found expression through the *Ecrits*, on the one hand, and the Seminar, on the other. Published on November 15, 1966, the *Ecrits* anthologised thirty-four of his articles written between 1946 and 1965 (out of fifty writings). Since 2001, upon the initiative of Jacques-Alain Miller, an additional anthology of his writings for the period 1938–1980 entitled *Autres Ecrits* has been published. The Seminar was the living place of Lacan's thought, recounts Assoun, an ongoing endeavour from 1951 to 1979–1980 that reflected the oral side of "Lacan's thought", in other words, his *speech*. It was a veritable workshop in which Lacan was the principal worker – but in which, it must not be forgotten, his disciples and interlocutors participated.[155] It was a matter of twenty-six years of teaching and, as Assoun has remarked, while the work was disjointed, it promised to be a powerful factor of unity. How could his work be unified, or rather recaptured? Whence the catchphrase around which the project organised, namely, the "return to Freud".[156]

I have chosen to explore Lacan's relationship to the social sciences based on two books by Markos Zafiropoulos, his *Lacan et les sciences sociales*[157] and his *Lacan and Lévi-Strauss, or the Return to Freud 1951–1957*.[158]

Lacan and the social sciences

Considering that it had been insufficiently studied – or even *not* studied – up until the time of his writing, the sociologist and psychoanalyst, Markos Zafiropoulos has explored and analysed the major impact of the social sciences on Lacan's thought from 1938 on. Yet, very early on, especially from the time of his 1938 article on family complexes, Lacan mentioned Durkheim on two occasions as well as the work of Malinowski. Zafiropoulos, then, distinguished between two periods of Lacan's thought: the first, from 1938 to 1950, marked by the major reference to Durkheim, and the second, from 1951 to 1957–1960, permeated with Lévi-Strauss' structuralist thought, which he encountered in 1949, but also, and to a much lesser degree, by certain of Mauss' writings. The following text, *Family Complexes in the Formation of the Individual* (1938),[159] is particularly representative of that early period.

"Family Complexes in the Formation of the Individual"

To begin with, I should be more specific regarding Lacan's position vis-à-vis Freudian theory in 1938.

Lacan rejected the theory of primary narcissism and the theory of Freud's successors including the ego Ideal, and also the thesis of primal parricide, and the death instinct. We shall see where he stood with respect to the Œdipus complex. Moreover, he differed from Freud in that he used Durkheim's work. While Freud took an interest in Durkheim's writings on religious sociology, but also in the fundamental text "The Prohibition of Incest and its Origins", Lacan turned particularly to the "law of family contraction", apt to account for the "conjugal anomie", his use of which we shall discover.

The original title of the manuscript of this article was "Situation de la réalité familiale". It was first published as "La Famille" in the *Encyclopédie Française* upon the request of Henri Wallon and Lucien Febvre.[160] It would be republished in 1984 with the title *Complexes familiaux dans la formation de l'individu.*

As a social institution, the family has some major functions, among them early education and the transmission of culture, of structures of behaviour and representation, thus establishing psychic continuity between the generations. In addition, it presides over the fundamental processes of psychic development.

According to Lacan, this research into the facts of the family, "as a psychical object and occurrence", never objectifies instincts, but always complexes whose essential characteristic is its conditioning by cultural factors at the expense of natural factors. This discourse presents a striking analogy with that of Malinowski. These complexes play the role of organisers in psychic development. He identified three types:

- the weaning complex polarised by the "maternal imago" required for the child's survival dominates the first six months;
- the complex of intrusion, from six to eighteen months of age, dominated by imago of a fellow human (imago of siblings), provides subjects the unifying image of their own bodies – which therefore comes to them from others and in the mirror to ground an ideal image of themselves – and constitutes the solution to the weaning complex;
- the Œdipus complex, dominated by the paternal imago presumed finally to introduce the subject to alterity, to socialisation and to the ego Ideal.

Quite clearly drawing inspiration from Malinowski's writings, Lacan introduced the socio-cultural variable of the Œdipus complex. He said,

> Even though psychological analysis has shown that the Œdipus complex has to be understood in terms of its narcissistic antecedents, this does not mean that the complex can be grounded independently of sociological relativity. The most decisive source of its psychic effects results from the fact that the imago of the father concentrates in itself the functions of repression and sublimation. But this in turn is socially determined by the existence of the paternalistic family.[161]

Lacan subscribed to Malinowski's analysis, for which the separation of the functions of the father and of the maternal uncle brought about a different balance in the psyche, as attested to by the absence of neurosis in this type of matrilineal society. *He therefore defended the thesis of the social relativity of Œdipus complex, and thus rejected the universal nature of the Œdipus complex* so "epistemologically" essential for Freud and psychoanalysis.

In addition, he referred to Durkheim's law of contraction of the family institution, which takes into account the history of the paternal family institution evolving from its large primitive forms organised in accordance with the model of lineage answering to paternal sovereignty, toward its present reduced, conjugal form dominated by matrimonial interests managed by the figure of a father having progressively reduced power and authority, especially in 1938. So, the diagnosis made was one of the decline in the value of the paternal imago due to this evolution of the family. Lacan located the moment triggering this devaluation of the paternal imago in the reversal effected by the Church in the fifteenth century of the social supremacy of the family institution in favour of marriage, something contemporaneous with the economic revolution that engendered bourgeois society and modern human beings.

Lacan observed that a great number of psychological consequences seem to come in the train of the social decline of the paternal imago, a decline therefore causing a psychological crisis to which he linked the emergence of psychoanalysis itself.

Thus, relying on the socio-anthropological authority of well-known figures, he challenged the idea of the universality of the Œdipus complex relative to socio-historical conditions and observed a downgrading of the paternal imago connected with an evolution of the institution of the family from its largest primitive forms toward the contemporary conjugal family. Lacan therefore adopted Durkheim's thesis.

Nonetheless, Zafiropoulos has indicated that, starting in the 1960s–1970s, historical, sociological and demographic research had invalidated this law of contraction of the family institution. Everywhere and in every age, the presence of the conjugal form of the family has, in fact, been preponderant by a wide margin all throughout the history of mankind. So, this law and its consequences as deduced by Lacan had been robbed of all their scientific worth. Indeed, the downgrading of the Œdipus complex subsequent to a generalised decrease in the value of the father in the family was no longer a condition of the Freudian discovery, any more than this decline in the paternal imago may have brought about the contemporary neurosis mentioned by Lacan in 1938, or the proliferation of the neurotic nature of psychopaths diagnosed in the 1950s, or, finally, the discovery of originary formations of the superego.

According to Zafiropoulos, referring to the sociological authority of the time, which inaugurated a scientific "regime of truth", Lacan was to have insisted for nearly fifteen years on taking into consideration the morbidity of paternal deficiency. He could therefore not have known that the Durkheimian thesis was wrong. In Zafiropoulos' estimation, lack of familiarity with Lacan's Durkheim period has kept people from clearly realising that when it came to the family question it was definitely Lacan's choice of Lévi-Strauss that in 1953 enabled him to take leave of the Durkheimian sociological formulation of nostalgia for the patriarchal group.[162]

The return to Freud via Lévi-Strauss

During the period 1938–1950, Lacan was therefore not Freudian with regard to a series of theoretical points already discussed, among them the universality of the Œdipus complex, especially. Zafiropoulos holds that Lacan's return to Freud involved a "transference of knowledge from anthropology to psychoanalysis" accomplished "by means of Lévi-Strauss". According to him, this return to Freud was primarily a "subjective rectification of Lacan's relation to knowledge, and especially to Freud's knowledge".[163] Moreover, for Assoun, Lacan's thought would also develop in reaction both to ego psychology and to the ideology of communication, but also in reaction to the ideology of the object relation. Lacan would also take a look at the writings of his contemporary post-Freudian colleagues, whose work he would evaluate in light of Freud's theories.

His rereading of Freud's writings was carried out within the framework of his Seminar, which began in 1951 and whose sessions of the year 1953–1954 were collected in 1975 under the title of *Freud's Papers on Technique* as Book I of the Seminar. But, his return to Freud was publicly inaugurated with his "Intervention on Transference" given at the Congress of Psychoanalysts of Romance Languages held in 1951, initiating, with the Dora case, his rereading of the main clinical cases. According to Zafiropoulos,

> In discussing this case, Lacan immediately stresses the epistemological axis that orients his return to Freud. He does so in order to account for the way in which the subject is divided between the imaginary register, which founds her first identifications – those of the mirror stage – and the symbolic. In the latter register, Lacan locates the Œdipus complex and, more generally, the symbolic function, which he borrows from French anthropology and which includes this complex.[164]

I propose to use Zafiropoulos' work to show how, via both its notions and concepts and its structural method, Lévi-Strauss' work penetrated Lacan's mind, both as concerns his rereading of the "main clinical cases" and its conceptual elaboration during the 1950s, something which had an impact on the international and French psychoanalytic field. For Zafiropoulos, it was a matter of lifting this "epistemological repression"[165] as the precedent dealing with the Durkheimian period from 1938 to 1950.

According to him, in "The Effectiveness of Symbols" (1949), Lacan found a theory of the treatment, transference, and resistances, therefore, a "paper on technique" guiding his reading of Freud's technical and clinical writings. This notion of the "effectiveness of symbols" would incidentally be the first reference to Lévi-Strauss in Lacan's work since, using it in his interpretation of the experience of the mirror, he had mentioned it in his talk on "The Mirror Stage as Formative of the *I* Function as Revealed in Psychoanalytic Experience"[166] at the XVIth International Congress of Psychoanalysis held in 1949.[167]

Zafiropoulos considers that the "inductive value gives power and status to symbolic effectiveness and enables psychoanalytical interpretation to be rethought; it revises the symbolic organization from which the subject and its symptoms are deduced. . ."[168]

It is to be recalled that in this paper, Lévi-Strauss introduced the notion of "the neurotic's individual myth" as based on the analogy he established between shamanistic therapy and psychoanalytic therapy, then presented his "structuralist" definition of the unconscious. According to him, as symbolic formations, the neurotic's individual myths would complement socially shared mythical productions. Lacan subscribed to this intellectual viewpoint and undertook a Lévi-Straussian, structural rereading of the obsessional neurosis of the "Rat Man" in his 1953 talk rightly entitled "The Neurotic's Individual Myth",[169] which I discuss below.

Moreover, for Lacan, the structuralist Lévi-Straussian conception of the unconscious would constitute another particularly valuable tool for interpreting Freud, leading him to elaborate a new model for exploring and interpreting the unconscious, its processes, formations and products. He would seize upon the notion of symbolic function, which he would situate at the very origin of the subjective structuration, where the body image and the symbolic register are definitely connected.

What about the Œdipus complex and the superego in 1953?

In this same Book I of the Seminar, Lacan considered that the Œdipus complex was only a particular example of a much more extended system and that it had to be less a matter of looking for the universality of this complex and its form than that of the symbolic function and of its order. According to Lacan, the Œdipus complex would be a "simple" symbolic situation present in modernity; *he was therefore promoting the universal symbolic function in the psychoanalytical field*, upon which the structuring of the "subject of the unconscious" would depend. "Nothing other than this", he said, "is at stake in analysis – recognising what function the subject takes on in the order of the symbolic relations which covers the entire field of human relations, and whose initial cell is the Œdipus complex, where the assumption of sex is decided".[170]

According to Lacan, the structuring function of the oedipal myth must be interpreted against the backdrop of the knot tying together the three dimensions of the imaginary, the symbolic and the real. In his return to Freud, he reintroduced the function of death and of the dead father into the analytical experience, cornerstone of the symbolic function. In addition, he integrated the function of speech and its laws into the symbolic function.[171] As for the superego, "he gives the super-ego a symbolic status that has its roots in the symbolic exchanges that preceded even the birth of the subject. Now, superego becomes a symbolic function that comes from the Other of culture; it is a symbolic formation and a linguistic formation that determines the child's situation in relation to the symbolic system as it had existed before his birth".[172] This symbolic organisation is the subject's Other, "from which his life comes and to which he remains indebted".[173] Incidentally, this notion of debt was borrowed from Mauss' work *The Gift*.

Lacan stressed the "weight of the symbolic function and of debt on the lineage of someone who has not honoured the – always sacred – obligations of social exchange".[174] It suffices to read his "Intervention on Transference", where he gives a new interpretation of the symptoms of Dora.

"The Neurotic's Individual Myth" and the Name-of-the-Father

Let us go back to this talk given at a conference held at Jean Wahl's Collège de Philosophie in 1953 and in which the notion of "Name-of-the-Father" appears for the first time. Before looking at this notion and its sources, let me say from the start that in his rereading of "the Rat Man case history", Lacan used rules for the interpretation of myths proposed by Lévi-Strauss. Zafiropoulos considers that the logic of a neurotic life, conscious or not, familial or discursive, would therefore function in accordance with laws governing the constructions and variations of the myths, whence the title of the lecture, "The Neurotic's Individual Myth", because what Lacan stated of this case holds, according to him, for all neurotics. From the Freudian interpretation organised around the three terms of the Œdipus complex (father, mother, child), Lacan proceeded to a structural interpretation summoning in a single movement the oedipal issue and that of narcissism as he had revised it (namely, that of the mirror). Death is the fourth term of the logic paradigmatic of neurosis. In reintroducing death into the neurotic game, it is the figure of the father who finds himself divided between the imaginary register where his power prevails and the symbolic register where his fecundity prevails.[175]

In his analytic clinic, Lacan placed the fecundity of the dead father, his Name and his speech back on the agenda, and effected an epistemological rupture with respect to the theory of the paternal function.

Where does this notion of the Name-of-the-Father come from?

According to Zafiropoulos, it was inspired by Lacan's reading of the "Introduction to the Work of Marcel Mauss" and used Lévi-Strauss' structural theory of the semantic function of the floating signifier to furnish the analytic field with a theory where the Name-of-the-Father is recognised as an exceptional signifier conditioning the neurotic's symbolic thinking. With the Name-of-the-Father, Lacan proposed a western religious interpretation of the *spirit of things* figuring on this list including, notably, the *mana* and the *hau*. For him, it was a matter of identifying, amid the diversity of names of the *spirit of things,* the unity and universality of the semantic function connecting them,[176] something which would have an impact on the field of clinical research.

It was in fact during his Seminar on psychoses and his interpretation of the "Schreber Case" in 1955–1956 that Lacan analysed the impact of the foreclosure of the Name-of-the-Father as operator, placing it henceforth at the heart of the psychotic clinic. Thus, he introduced a renewed theory of psychoses into the psychoanalytical field whose structure depended on the foreclosure of the Name-of-the-Father, meaning "the absence of the zero symbol, without which the signifier and the signified cannot be knotted together".[177]

The influence of Lévi-Strauss' "The Structural Study of Myth" (1955)

During his Seminar of 1956–1957 devoted to the object relation and especially to the analysis of "little Hans' phobia", Lacan made explicit reference to this article by Lévi-Strauss. He in fact applied Lévi-Strauss' method of analysing myths to the clinic of little Hans' phobia. The structure of Hans' phobia became that of a "mythical inciting" "that makes up for the failure of the Name-of-the-Father as a zero-value symbol",[178] "where, in psychosis, the delusion appears as an attempt at a cure".[179] This reflexion opened on to a new conception of symptoms, notes Zafiropoulos, who wrote, "In treating the series of symptoms as mythic formations that stand in for the Name-of-the-Father, he finally offers us a differential clinic of the various ways in which symbolic thought is expressed in analytic experience: neuroses, psychoses, perversions".[180] He presents the symptoms as equivalents of the "quilting of the signifier and the signified" introduced by "the superego and the dead father". As for Lévi-Strauss, "myth appears as an operator that dominates all human life". Therefore, "the function of the myth is of foremost importance for Lacan".[181]

Let us go back to 1953 in order to assess the major role Lévi-Strauss' thought played in the construction of this new theoretical system created by Lacan and expressed in an exemplary fashion in the "Rome Discourse".

Given its historical position, Zafiropoulos emphasises that this report can be thought of as providing a theoretical foundation for the new Société Française de Psychanalyse. There Lacan set forth his basic project of updating the primacy of symbolic structures and of language within the objective of the Freudian discovery, the unconscious, which must go by way of the "scientific restoration" of Freudian concepts, which he wishes to show correspond in certain ways to anthropological concepts. In this manner, integrating the contemporary findings of anthropology – in this case, structural anthropology – into its theoretical corpus, psychoanalysis could find its place again, a harmonious one, among the human sciences. But, why?

Zafiropoulos suggests that it was because, for Lacan, there are first common symbolic structures that organise all these fields – and thereby place psychoanalysis and these disciplines in a close relation with each other; and second, it is precisely this common resource that has been rejected since Freud's death, given that those who deny his discovery have ceaselessly refused to take the patient's speech into account.[182]

Thus, he wishes to indicate, for example, Lévi-Strauss' head start when it came to exploring the unconscious. He explains that, "What he owes to Lévi-Strauss is nothing less than the ability to see the effects of everything that he includes in the notion of the Other: all the structures that form the field of speech and language, of which the subject of the unconscious – whether placed in a group or not – is a simple function. . ."[183]

This relationship also shows us the metamorphosis of Lacan's theory of the father, distinguishing between the father's symbolic function, the Name-of-the-Father, as the "support" of the symbolic function, and the father's person. But he distributes the paternal function over the three registers imaginary, symbolic, and real.

We have now come to the end of our exploration of Lacanian notions and concepts permeated with Durkheimo-Maussian French socio-anthropological thought from 1938 to 1950, and especially with that of Lévi-Strauss during the 1950s, not to mention the ethnographic authority of Rivers and Malinowski during the first period.

The symbolic function lain in the foundations of psychoanalysis attests to one-way conceptual borrowing from Lévi-Strauss by Lacan – from anthropology by psychoanalysis – in France, with an impact on the international psychoanalytical field. In fact it seems that Lacan was not a source of inspiration for his friend, too immersed in his anthropology and undoubtedly being much too ambivalent with regard to psychoanalysis. This French situation was radically different from what took place in the United States where, as I have shown, fruitful mutual exchanges took place between culturalist anthropologists and the new American psychoanalysis, expressing reciprocal interests, one of the common projects of which was to eliminate Freudian biologism and its universalist teleology. With Lacan and Lévi-Strauss, instinctual universality with biological overtones was replaced by the universality of the symbolic. The instinctual psychic base was abandoned so as to put into place symbolic structures external and antecedent to the subject.

However, Lévi-Strauss' influence would fade toward the end of the 1950s and mathematics would take over beginning in the 1960s. Zafiropoulos rightly speculates about what he calls a theoretical "repression" of this French socio-anthropological influence detected in the exegesis of Lacanian texts in favour of an idealisation of his philosophical (Hegel and Heidegger) and linguistic (Saussure) references, something which would also contribute to people's not catching sight of the importance of psychoanalytical anthropology in Lacan, which in a certain way brought him closer to the Freudian venture.

We have thus come to the end of our exploration of the "historical debate" and will carry on with the "contemporary debate" in the next chapter.

Notes

1 Bertrand Pulman, "Aux origines du débat ethnologie/psychanalyse: W. H. R. Rivers", *L'Homme*, 1986, No. 100, p. 122.
2 *Ibid.*
3 William Halse Rivers Rivers, "Sociology and Psychology", in *Psychology and Ethnology*, London, Routledge, 1999 (1926), p. 18. Originally published in *The Sociological Review*, Autumn 1916, pp. 1–13.
4 Op. cit., Pulman, p. 130.
5 *Ibid.*, p. 120
6 Bertrand Pulman, "Aux origines du débat anthropologie/psychanalyse: C. G. Seligman", *Gradhiva*, 1989, No. 6, p. 36.
7 *Ibid.*, p. 47.
8 Bronislaw Malinowski, "On the Principle of the Economy of Thought", in *The Early Writings of Bronislaw Malinowski*, Robert J. Thornton and Peter Skalnik eds., Cambridge, Cambridge University Press, 1993 (1906), pp. 89–116.
9 Bronislaw Malinowski, *The Family among the Australian Aborigines: A Sociological Study*, London, University of London Press, 1913.
10 Bertrand Pulman, *Anthropologie et Psychanalyse. Malinowski contre Freud*, Paris, Presses Universitaires de France, 2002.
11 Alexander F. Shand, *The Foundations of Character, Being a Study of the Tendencies of the Emotions and Sentiments*, London, Macmillan and Co. Ltd., 1914.
12 Bronislaw Malinowski, *Sex and Repression in Savage Society*, Abingdon, UK, Routledge, 2001 (1927).
13 *Ibid.*, pp. 3–4.
14 *Ibid.*, pp. 9–10.
15 *Ibid.*, pp. 10, 20, 61, 203–204.
16 *Ibid.*, pp. 32–33.
17 *Ibid.*, p. 44.
18 *Ibid.*, pp. 10, 46, 56, 63.
19 *Ibid.*, p. 60.
20 *Ibid.*, pp. 60–61.
21 *Ibid.*, pp. 62–63.
22 *Ibid.*, p. 64.
23 *Ibid.*, pp. 64–65.
24 Maurice Godelier, *The Metamorphoses of Kinship*, London, Verso, 2011 (2004), p. 250.
25 Bertrand Pulman, *Anthropologie et psychanalyse. Malinowski contre Freud*, Paris, Presses Universitaires de France, 2002, for example, pp. 6–11.
26 Published in Ernest Jones, *On the Nightmare*, London, The Hogarth Press, 1931.
27 Both papers are published in English in Vol. II of Jones' *Essays in Applied Pyscho-Analysis*, London, The Hogarth Press, 1951.
28 Ernest Jones, "The Theory of Symbolism", a paper read before the British Psychological Society on January 29, 1916 and published in *British Journal of Psychology*, Vol. 9, No. 2, pp. 181–229, October, 1918. Quoted here as appears in his *Papers on Psycho-Analysis*, London, Baillière, Tindall and Cox, 1938, p. 158.
29 Republished in Jones' *Essays in Applied Pyscho-Analysis*, Vol. II, as cited above.
30 Ernest Jones, "Mother Right and the Sexual Ignorance of Savages", *Essays in Applied Pyscho-Analysis*, Vol. II, pp. 145–173.
31 *Ibid.*, p. 162.
32 *Ibid.*, p. 169.
33 *Ibid.*, p. 170.
34 *Ibid.*, p. 173.
35 Bertrand Pulman, "Ernest Jones et l'anthropologie", *Revue internationale d'histoire de la psychanalyse*, 1991, No. 4, p. 513.
36 *Ibid.*, pp. 514–515.

37 Published in Hungarian in *Ethnographia*, 22: 128–143, 1911, pp. 193–209.
38 Géza Róheim, *Australian Totemism; A Pyscho-analytic Study in Anthropology*, London, Allen & Unwin, 1925.
39 Roger Dadoun, *Géza Róheim et l'essor de l'anthropologie psychanalytique*, Paris, Payot, 1972, pp. 116–117.
40 *Ibid.*, pp. 136–137.
41 Géza Róheim, "Dream Analysis and Field Work in Anthropology", *Psychoanalysis and the Social Sciences, An Annual*, Vol. 1, New York, International Press, 1947, p. 130.
42 Géza Róheim, *The Riddle of the Sphinx, or Human Origins*, London, Hogarth, 1934, p. 169.
43 Géza Róheim, *The Origin and Function of Culture*, New York, Nervous and Mental Disease Monographs, 1943, p. v.
44 *Ibid.*, p. 24.
45 *Ibid.*, p. 74.
46 Donald Woods Winnicott, *Playing and Reality*, London, Routledge, 1971.
47 Géza Róheim, *The Gates of the Dream*, New York, International Universities Press, 1952.
48 Republished in Géza Róheim, *Psychoanalysis and Anthropology: Culture, Personality and the Unconscious*, New York, International Universities Press, 1950, pp. 166–167.
49 *Ibid.*, p. 424.
50 *Ibid.*, p. 425–426.
51 *Ibid.*, p. 426.
52 *Op. cit.*, Dadoun, p. 248.
53 Claude Levi-Strauss, *Structural Anthropology*, New York, Basic Books, 1963 (1958), p. 19.
54 Franz Boas, "Methods of Ethnology", *American Anthropologist*, Vol. 22, No. 4, 1920, pp. 316, 318.
55 *Ibid.*, p. 321.
56 Franz Boas, "Foreword" to Margaret Mead's *Coming of Age in Samoa*, New York, HarperCollins, 2001 (1928), p. xxii.
57 *Ibid.*
58 Alfred Kroeber, "Totem and Taboo, an Ethnologic Psychoanalysis" (1920), *American Anthropologist*, New Series, Vol. 22, No. 1, Jan.–Mar. 1920, pp. 48–55.
59 *Ibid.*, pp. 49–51, 53, 55.
60 *Ibid.*, p. 53.
61 *Ibid.*, p. 54.
62 Alfred Kroeber, "Totem and Taboo in Retrospect", *American Journal of Sociology*, Vol. 45, No. 3, Nov. 1939, pp. 446–451.
63 *Ibid.*, pp. 446–447.
64 *Ibid.*, p. 447
65 *Ibid.*, p. 446
66 *Ibid.*, p. 449.
67 *Ibid.*, p. 451.
68 *Ibid.*
69 Margaret Mead, *Coming of Age in Samoa*, New York, HarperCollins, 2001 (1928), pp. 5–6.
70 *Ibid.*, p. 10.
71 *Ibid.*, p. 138.
72 *Ibid.*, p. 109.
73 *Ibid.*, p. 137.
74 *Ibid.*, pp. 137–139.
75 *Ibid.*, pp. 142–143.
76 *Ibid.*, pp. 146–147.
77 *Ibid.*
78 *Ibid.*, pp. 161–162.
79 Abram Kardiner, *The Individual and his Society; the Psychodynamics of Primitive Social Organization*, New York, Columbia University Press, 1939, p. 7.
80 *Ibid.*, p. 10.
81 *Ibid.*, p. 127, 131.

82 *Ibid.*, p. 110, 132.
83 *Ibid.*, p. 385.
84 Erich Fromm, *The Crisis of Psychoanalysis, Essays on Freud, Marx, and Social Psychology,* New York, Holt, Rinehart, Winston, 1970, p. 21, n. 17.
85 Erich Fromm, "Psychoanalysis and Sociology", in *Critical Theory and Society. A Reader,* S.E. Bronner and D. M. Kellner (eds.), London, Routledge, 1988 (1929), pp. 37–39.
86 *Ibid.*, p. 37.
87 *Ibid.*, p. 38.
88 *Ibid.*
89 *Ibid.*, p. 39.
90 *Op. cit.*, Fromm, *The Crisis of Psychoanalysis*, p. 145.
91 *Ibid.*
92 *Ibid.*, p. 147.
93 *Ibid.*, Chapter 10.
94 *Ibid.*, p. 155.
95 Erich Fromm, *The Revision of Psychoanalysis*, Rainer Funk (ed.), Boulder, CO, Westview Press, 1992, p. 56.
96 Karen Horney, *The Neurotic Personality of our Time*, Abingdon, UK, Routledge, 1999 (1937), pp. 28–29.
97 *Ibid.*, pp. 82–83.
98 *Ibid.*, p. 84, n. 4.
99 *Ibid.*, pp. 160–161.
100 Georges Devereux, "A Sociological Theory of Schizophrenia", *Psychoanalytic Review* 26, no. 3, pp. 315–142. Republished in *Basic Problems of Ethnopsychiatry,* Chicago, IL: University of Chicago Press, 1980, pp. 185–213.
101 Georges Devereux, "Mohave Ethnopsychiatry and Suicide: the psychiatric knowledge and the psychic disturbances of an Indian tribe", Washington, D.C., *Bureau of American Ethnology Bulletin*, No. 175, 1961.
102 Georges Devereux, "Culture and the Unconscious", chapter of *A Study of Abortion in Primitive Societies a Typological, Distributional and Dynamical Analysis of the Prevention of Birth in 400 Preindustrial Societies*, New York, Julian Press, 1955, republished in *Ethnopsychoanalysis: Psychoanalysis and Anthropology as Complementary Frames of Reference,* Berkeley, University of California Press, 1978.
103 Georges Devereux, *From Anxiety to Method in the Behavioral Sciences*, The Hague, Mouton & Co., 1967, p. 212.
104 Georges Devereux, "Normal and Abnormal: The Key Problem of Psychiatric Anthropology", in *Some Uses of Anthropology: Theoretical and Applied,* Washington, D.C., The Anthropological Society of Washington, 1956. Cited here as published in "Normal and Abnormal", Chapter 13 of *Cultural Psychiatry & Medical Anthropology: an introduction and reader,* Roland Littlewood and Simon Dein (eds.), London, Athlone Press 2000, p. 217.
105 *Ibid.*, p. 218.
106 *Ibid.*, pp. 262, 268, 269.
107 *Ibid.*, pp. 238, 241.
108 *Ibid.*, p. 217.
109 *Op. cit.*, Devereux, *Ethnopsychoanalysis and Anthropology as Complementary Frames of Reference*, "Ethnopsychoanalytic Reflections on the Notion of Kinship" (1965), pp. 182–183.
110 *Ibid.*, pp.136–137.
111 Émile Durkheim, *The Division of Labour in Society*, Basingstoke, UK, Palgrave Macmillan, 2013 (1893), p. 63.
112 Émile Durkheim, *The Rules of Sociological Method: And Selected Texts on Sociology and Its Method*, New York, Free Press, 2013 (1895), p. 86.
113 Émile Durkheim, *The Elementary Forms of Religious Life*, Oxford, Oxford University Press, 2001 (1912), p. 41.
114 *Ibid.*, p. 46.

115 Communicated to me personally by Camille Tarot, sociologist of religions, specialist of Durkheim and Mauss, at the seminar on "Psychoanalysis and Social Sciences" organised by me at the Société psychanalytique de Paris in 2007.
116 *Op. cit.*, Durkheim, *The Elementary Forms of Religious Life*, p. 164.
117 Camille Tarot, *De Durkheim á Mauss, l'invention du symbolique*, Paris, La Découverte, 1999.
118 *Op. cit.*, Durkheim, pp. 176–177.
119 *Ibid.*, p, 165.
120 *Op. cit.*, Tarot.
121 *Ibid.*
122 Bruno Karsenti is a philosopher who has specialised in the thought of Comte, Durkheim, and Mauss. In particular, he is the author of a work devoted to Mauss' thought, *L'Homme total*, Paris, Presses Universitaires de France, 1997.
123 Marcel Mauss, *The Gift: The Form and Reason for Exchange in Archaic Societies,* London, Routledge, 1990 (1925).
124 Marcel Mauss, *A General Theory of Magic*, London, Routledge, 1972 (1902).
125 Camille Tarot personal communication regarding Mauss' religious sociology during the seminar on "Psychoanalysis and Sciences Social" held in 2007.
126 Marcel Mauss, "Real and Practical Relationships between Psychology and Sociology", *Sociology and Psychology: Essays by Marcel Mauss*, London, Routledge and Kegan Paul, 1979 (1924), pp. 1–33.
127 Camille Tarot, *De Durkheim à Mauss, l'invention du symbolique*, Paris, La Découverte, 1999, p. 271.
128 *Op. cit.*, Mauss, "Real and Practical Relationships between Psychology and Sociology", pp. 12–13.
129 *Ibid.*
130 Information about Mauss' religious sociology communicated to me personally by Camille Tarot during the 2007 seminar on "Psychoanalysis and Social Sciences".
131 Camille Tarot, *Le Sacré et le symbolique,* Paris, Editions La Découverte, 2007.
132 Patrice Bidou, "Arguments", introduction to a special issue of *L'Homme*, "Une anthropologie psychoanalytique est-elle possible?", January 1999, 147, p. 14.
133 *Ibid.*
134 Claude Lévi-Strauss, *The Savage Mind*, London, Weidenfeld and Nicolson, 1966 (1962), p. 131.
135 Claude Lévi-Strauss, *Introduction to the Work of Marcel Mauss*, Abingdon, UK, Routledge, 1987 (1950), p. 11.
136 *Ibid.*, pp. 10, 12.
137 *Ibid.*, p. 16.
138 *Ibid.*, pp. 22–23.
139 Claude Lévi-Strauss, "The Effectiveness of Symbols", *Structural Anthropology*, New York, Basic Books, 1963, pp. 198, 199, 202.
140 *Ibid.*, pp. 202–203.
141 Claude Lévi-Strauss, "The Structural Study of Myth", *Structural Anthropology*, New York, Basic Books, 1963, p. 217.
142 Claude Lévi-Strauss, *Totemism*, London, Merlin Press, 1991 (1962), pp. 69–70.
143 *Ibid.*, p. 71.
144 Claude Lévi-Strauss, *The Jealous Potter*, Chicago, IL, Chicago University Press, 1988, p. 190.
145 *Ibid.*, p. 201.
146 *Ibid.*, pp. 204–205
147 *Ibid.*, p. 203.
148 Jacques Lacan, "The Mirror Stage as Formative of the *I* Function as Revealed in Psychoanalytic Experience", *Ecrits: a selection,* London, Tavistock/Routledge, 1977 (1949), pp. 1–9.
149 Markos Zafiropoulos, *Lacan and Lévi-Strauss, or the Return to Freud, 1951–1957*, London, Karnac, 2010 (2003).

150 Jacques Lacan, "Function and Field of Speech and Language in Psychoanalysis", *Ecrits: a selection,* London, Tavistock/Routledge, 1977 (1949), pp. 9–32.
151 Jacques Lacan, *Freud's Papers on Technique, 1953–1954,* New York, Norton, 1988.
152 Jacques Lacan, *The Four Fundamental Concepts of Psycho-analysis, 1964–1965,* New York, Norton, 1988.
153 Jacques Lacan, *Ecrits: The First Complete Edition in English,* New York, Norton, 2006 (1966).
154 Paul-Laurent Assoun, *Lacan,* Paris, Presses Universitaires de France 2003, p. 6.
155 *Ibid.*
156 *Ibid.*, p. 7.
157 Markos Zafiropoulos, *Lacan et les sciences sociales,* Paris, Presses Universitaires de France,
158 Markos Zafiropoulos, *Lacan and Lévi-Strauss, or the Return to Freud, 1951–1957,* London, Karnac, 2010 (2003). 2001.
159 Jacques Lacan, *Les complexes familiaux dans la formation de l'individu,* Paris, Navarin, 1984 (1938).
160 Jacques Lacan, "La Famille", *Encyclopédie française,* Vol. 8, *La vie mentale,* Paris, March, 1938.
161 Jacques Lacan, *Family Complexes in the Formation of the Individual.* Cited as translated by Corman Gallagher, School of Psychotherapy, St. Vincent's Hospital, Dublin 4, p. 49. Accessible online.
162 *Op. cit.*, Zafiropoulos, *Lacan et les sciences sociales,* p. 229.
163 *Op. cit.*, Zafiropoulos, *Lacan and Lévi-Strauss, or the Return to Freud 1953–1957,* pp. 9–10.
164 *Ibid.*, p. 17.
165 *Ibid.*, p. 15.
166 *Op. cit.*, Lacan, "The Mirror Stage as Formative of the *I* Function as Revealed in Psychoanalytic Experience".
167 *Op. cit.*, Zafiropoulos, *Lacan and Lévi-Strauss, or the Return to Freud 1953–1957,* pp. 45–46.
168 *Ibid.*, p. 50.
169 Jacques Lacan, "The Neurotic's Individual Myth", *Psychoanalytic Quarterly,* Vol. 48, No. 3, July 1979, pp. 405–425.
170 Jacques Lacan, *The Seminar of Jacques Lacan, Book I, Freud's Papers on Technique* 1953–1954, London, W. W. Norton & Company, Inc., 1988, p. 67.
171 See *op. cit.*, Zafiropoulos, *Lacan and Lévi-Strauss, or the Return to Freud 1953–1957,* p. 26, n. 27.
172 *Ibid.*, p. 72.
173 *Ibid.*, p. 75.
174 *Ibid.*, p. 91.
175 *Op. cit.*, Zafiropoulos, *Lacan et les sciences sociales,* p. 207.
176 *Op. cit.*, Zafiropoulos, *Lacan and Lévi-Strauss, or the Return to Freud 1953–1957,* pp. 90, 158.
177 *Ibid.*, p. 163.
178 *Ibid.*, p. 180.
179 *Ibid.*, p. 186.
180 *Op. cit.*, Zafiropoulos, *Lacan and Lévi-Strauss, or the Return to Freud 1953–1957,* p. 190.
181 *Ibid.*, p. 186, 189–90.
182 *Ibid.*, p. 137.
183 *Ibid.*, pp. 154–155.

3
THE CONTEMPORARY DEBATE

In France

With the following anthropologists

Maurice Godelier

Born in 1934 in Cambrai, France, Godelier is a major figure of French anthropology. After obtaining the *agrégation* in philosophy, then studying economics, he decided to become an anthropologist and developed an interest in a domain in the then little studied area of economic anthropology, that is to say, the study of the economic systems of peasants and tribal societies. Entering the Ecole Pratique des Hautes Etudes as "Chef de travaux" with Fernand Braudel, he later became one of Lévi-Strauss' assistants in the laboratory of social anthropology at the Collège de France. He carried out his field work among the Baruya of Papua New Guinea starting in 1967 and ending in 1988. He was the first anthropologist to work within this society of gardeners living in the mountainous areas.

In 1975, he was appointed Director of Studies at the Ecole des Hautes Etudes en Sciences Sociales. In 1981, upon the request of Jean-Pierre Chevènement, then Minister of Research, he contributed to the reform of research into the human and social sciences at the Centre National de la Recherche Scientifique. He was named scientific director of the first department of the Sciences de L'homme et de la Société of the Centre National de la Recherche Scientifique, a position he would hold until 1986. From 1997 to 2000, he was the scientific director of the Musée de L'homme. In 2000 he was awarded the Medaille d'or of the Centre National de la Recherche Scientifique for his body of work. Among his important works are: *The Making of Great Men: Male Domination and Power among the New Guinea Baruya* (1982); *The Mental and the Material* (1984); *Meurtre du père, sacrifice de la sexualité. Approches anthropologiques et psychanalytiques* (with Jacques Hassoun, 1996); *The Enigma of the Gift* (1996); *Au fondement des sociétés* (2007).

I have chosen to discuss his next-to-last work *The Metamorphoses of Kinship* (2004), in which he criticised certain of Freud's ideas as set out in *Totem and Taboo*, as well as detecting certain similarities between the way in which Freud and Lévi-Strauss conceived of the origins and foundations of the prohibition of incest. He himself presented his own hypotheses, then developed his reflexions on the socio-cultural treatment of sexuality, the way he conceived of kinship and its evolving forms. Finally, I shall look at his stand on the Œdipus complex and its universality.

Beforehand, let me point out, along with Maurice Godelier, that incest is included among all of the "misuses of sex", in the same way as necrophilia and zoophilia, for example, variously repressed and punished depending on the societies and the times, because of the threat these activities represent to the reproduction of the society and the balance of the universe. Godelier states of incest, necrophilia, and zoophilia,

> In all three cases, the criminal character of the act lies in the fact that persons or species that should be kept separate have united sexually. And the reasons advanced are the same throughout the world, based on the same logic. These species should be kept separate either because they are too different from each other (the case of humans and animals, or the living and the dead) or, on the contrary, they are too alike (the case of relatives sharing the same blood and/or sperm, or the same soul or name, or even the same food taken from the same land). In short, the proper uses of sex lie between these two extremes, between too different or too alike.[1]

Godelier points out that incest is only one particular case among others of the universal subordination of sexuality to the reproduction of society. According to him, "The social order is not only a moral and a sexual order, it is also, through and through . . . a cosmic order. And therefore the reasons invoked for forbidding and repressing these sexual practices are usually at the same time social, moral and religious (cosmic), in other words real and imaginary together and at the same time".[2] These imaginary explanations, objects of shared collective beliefs are both interpretations of social reality, therefore pertain to a "mental" (*idéel)* reality existing only in the mind and through the collective mind, but also produce social reality through their crystallisation in institutions and their staging and enactment in symbolic practices, rituals, validating and legitimising in return these collective representations. However, Godelier considers that there is something arbitrary in this collective imaginary production: "What is it then", he writes, "about human sexuality that makes societies forbid certain uses and favour others, which it nevertheless seeks to channel? Attempting to answer this question implies proposing an explanation of the origins and foundations of the incest taboo, although this can be no more than conjecture."[3]

Godelier analyses the Freudian hypothesis formulated in *Totem and Taboo* for which the murder of the father followed by the devouring of his corpse had not only been the founding act of the prohibition of incest, but had also lain the foundations of all the religions. The prohibition of incest caused exogamy and made the exchange of women among men possible and necessary. It therefore gave rise within this new form of social organisation to relations of kinship in their twofold quality of relations of descent (descendants of the same totem, of the same blood) and of relations of alliance (the groups with which men exchanged the women they had given up). Consequently, the prohibition of incest, as Freud conceived of it, had led to exogamy and to the exchange. He observes that this is the very thesis formulated by Lévi-Strauss in *The Elementary Structures of Kinship*.

What about the foundation of religion and morality?

The importance that Freud accorded to parricide and to the subsequent cannibalistic meal with the drawing in of the concepts of totem and totem animal, as well as that of sacrifice borrowed from Robertson Smith, would enable him to explain the foundations of all religions.

> Explaining all human religions by the primordial murder of a father, the memory of which lies buried and unknown in the unconscious of every individual while acting on the 'mass psyche', shows the extent to which Freud's explanation remains prisoner of Western Judeo-Christian religious representations; and it is this ethnocentrism that keeps us from adhering completely to his explanation.[4]

Thus, according to Godelier, within the evolutionist context of his time, Freud attempted to reconstruct the evolution of human institutions and to investigate their foundations, considering them to be "merely 'substitutive formations' of two events that happened a very long time ago within a 'horde' of men and women in their savage state, namely: the murder of a violent, overwhelming father by his sons and the subsequent devouring of his corpse".[5] He observed that by founding exogamy and the exchange of women on the prohibition of incest, "Freud took his place in the theoretical movement initiated by Morgan and by Tylor, who in 1888 was the first to assert that kinship was founded on the alternative 'between either marrying out [or] being killed out'. This explanation would be taken up in turn by Reo Fortune, Leslie White and finally by Claude Lévi-Strauss".[6]

Calling the myth of the primitive horde a cobbling together of an imaginary history, Godelier nonetheless credits Freud with having "advanced the scientific understanding of humankind by a big step". He especially singled out the threat sexuality represented to society and the obligation to domesticate it. All social orders, in fact, require the control of human sexuality. Moreover, he recognised that Freud had shed light on the ambivalence of human emotions, the danger to society inherent in manifesting and satisfying hostile, murderous desires and the urgent need to repress them, which did not for all that lead to their suppression. Society therefore proposes acceptable forms of expressing them. As Godelier explains,

> But instead of being content to show that humans must sacrifice something of their sexuality in order for society exist, he wanted to make his theoretical findings credible by connecting them with an imaginary event in the biological and social evolution of man. We now understand why *Totem and Taboo* was received with so little warmth by most anthropologists and notably by one of the greatest, Alfred Kroeber, who fired back a volley of criticisms. Lévi-Strauss would distance himself even further from Freud's work.[7]

Let us now look at Godelier's hypothesis.

People live in society, but also produce society in order to live, meaning they have the capacity to modify their forms of social existence by transforming their relationships with one another and with nature. Human sexuality is characterised by a disconnection between sexuality–desire and sexuality–reproduction. It is "cerebralised", functioning imaginarily and symbolically, generalised, polymorphous and polytropic. There is an effort to domesticate, socialise children's sexuality, aiming to orient it toward suitable persons. No society exists which could function without one form or another of what is called the prohibition of incest. By producing an increasingly large share of the material and social conditions of its existence, the human species is the only animal species to have become co-responsible with nature for its own evolution. Among the actions that human beings have undertaken upon themselves, the control and management of sexuality must stand in the forefront. Humanity is the only animal species that consciously and socially manages its sexuality, that explicitly, by means of oral and/or written laws, prohibits and limits certain uses that individuals are allowed to make of their sexual organs. The life of societies, like that of the people composing them, rests on two distinct but complementary and necessary obligations, that of exchanging and that of keeping and transmitting, something which distinguishes Godelier's theories from Mauss and Lévi-Strauss. These obligations are at the origin of the five forms of socially authorised union: that of marrying within one's group, with one's closest relative; that of uniting outside one's own group; a combination of the first two; exchanges without alliances; marrying outside one's group without exchange.[8]

So it is that sexuality "was forced to take on forms that were mandatory for all members of society in accordance with their respective places in the social order, and even for kings and queens when it came to the cosmic order".[9] However, he points out that "sacrificing the a-social character of sexuality is not simply an amputation. It is a kind of creation. It is acting on oneself in order not only to live in society but to produce society in order to live; this is a feature unique to humankind. . ."[10] He reminds readers that the family, unit of procreation and child raising, is this essential place of every individual's initial socialisation and of the "domestication" of the child's sexuality.

Godelier, moreover, brings up the notion of the "twin metamorphosis" at work in all societies and deriving from a twofold movement. The development of kinship relations always vested with other social relations (political, economic, religious) means that social relations foreign to kinship become an aspect of kinship, subordinating the latter to their reproduction. But, because one is a boy rather than a girl, an oldest child rather than the youngest, because of one's sex and/or to one's age, one therefore occupies a certain place in the kinship relations; one inherits means of social existence or is deprived of them. It is through this that the second movement takes place, because everything having to do with kinship is always transformed into an attribute of the sexes and is imprinted in each person's sexed body. Thus, social considerations foreign to kinship become kinship and everything that is kinship becomes sexed.[11]

It was in addressing the question of representations of the process of making human children, of ethnotheories of the person and the procreative process, that Godelier expressed his views on the Œdipus complex and countered Malinowski's thesis, still constituting a lasting reference for most anthropologists. He states several general theoretical propositions beforehand.

So it is that in many societies, the birth of a human being is not an absolute beginning and death is not the end of life. A child would everywhere be a gift from the ancestors and/or gods and the first, and only, role of human beings would be to make a fœtus out of various different substances (sperm, menstrual blood, fat, etc.). Moreover, everywhere, making "ordinary" humans normally presupposes having sexual relations, no matter what role society attributes to a given substance, male (sperm) or female (menstrual blood) in this making. In addition, the existence of sexual relations between spouses does not have any direct relationship to the descent principle that in the society determines the identity of the children who will be born out of these relations and their appropriation by a given kin category. Finally, the emphasis placed on the role of a given substance would correspond to the descent principle that is recognised in the society, but this correspondence would not always be direct, as it is among the patrilineal Baruya of New Guinea or among matrilineal Trobriands.[12]

According to Godelier, all these representations of diverse components of the person and the process of making children provide the essential social function of embedding the unborn child beforehand in the overall socio-cultural fabric of the society through three types of relationships, which from the time of its birth are "imprinted on" and "buried in" its consciousness and its sexed body. It will thus take its place in a socio-cosmic order (child of the Sun, for example), within a moral and social (kinship groups) order and in a sexual order.[13] It is first of all within kinship relations that from the time of birth each person's sexed body begins to function as a "ventriloquist's dummy for its society". Godelier comes to the conclusion that, *"In all societies, sexuality is placed at the service of a number of realities – economic, political and religious – that have nothing to do with the sexes and sexual reproduction"*.[14]

What about the Œdipus complex?

Godelier has observed that,

> It is even because the parents' reciprocal sexual access is independent of the social form of the children's appropriation that it forms the basis of the Œdipus complex. And because it is independent of any given descent rule, this basis is universal and suggests that the Œdipus complex is itself universal. If this is true, Malinowski was wrong to criticise Freud for having defined the Œdipus complex in such a way that it fitted only the structures of the 'patriarchal' conjugal family typical of Judeo-Christian societies in the West. He asked Freud to come up with a broader definition of the Œdipus complex so that it might apply equally to societies with a matrilineal descent rule, because in these societies it is often the mother's brother and not the father who exercises authority and repression on the child. But the Œdipus complex is not built around relations of authority but around the child's relations with the man who has sexual access to the mother.[15]

Some comments are called for here.

What Maurice Godelier has to say is somewhat related to the spirit of Freudian psychoanalysis. The Marxist approach to economic anthropology that he took when first engaging in research, which distanced him from structuralist thought, then his collaboration with psychoanalysts, especially that with Jacques Hassoun, within the framework of a seminar organised together during the 1990s ("Murder of the father, sacrifice of sexuality"), and the dialogue with André Green starting in 1993, greatly contributed to this.

The world of collective representations refers back to a common social imaginary shared by the members of a society. As objects of beliefs, they are symbolised in institutions and in social practices, such as rituals, for example. This link between collective representations, objects of beliefs, the social imaginary, and ritual symbolic practices is suggestive of some dialogue with the psychoanalytic notion of symbolisation. Nonetheless, it is not a matter of cultural products of the unconscious or collective unconscious phantasy, all the more so since he considers that, also finding expression in myths, the social imaginary has its share of arbitrariness.

The status and role that he confers upon sexuality, the necessary sacrifice of it, its domestication from the time of early childhood, its social and cultural fates, its creative role, participating in the production of social life for living in society, cannot fail to appeal to psychoanalysts. However, though mentioning the murder of the father and the devouring of his corpse on numerous occasions, he remains silent regarding the existence of an instinct of death and destruction. Moreover, he challenges the validity of the Freudian hypothesis establishing parricide and the cannibalistic act followed by the sons' feelings of collective guilt at the foundation of religion. Freud undoubtedly had little knowledge of polytheistic religions and was essentially referring to monotheistic religions.

Finally, with regard to the Œdipus complex, he recognised its universality and independence in relation to the descent principles, patrilineal or matrilineal, of kinship systems. Indeed, independent of the descent principle, the parents' reciprocal sexual access would constitute the universal base of the Œdipus complex, which would itself be universal. Contrary to what Malinowski thought, Godelier, considered that it was not built around relationships of authority exercised by the father or the maternal uncle, but around the child's relations with the person having sexual access to his mother. Nonetheless, he brought up the boy's Œdipus complex in its positive form, scotomising the existence of a negative form, and ignored the Œdipus complex in girls. In addition, its unconscious phantasy dimension and its role in psychic structuring also go unrecognised. But, though close to psychoanalysts, Godelier wished to remain an anthropologist, both in his manner of thinking and in his way of expressing himself. In that respect, he adopted a position different from that of his colleague, Bernard Juillerat, who chose to embrace (and to practice) a psychoanalytical anthropology inspired by Freud.

Bernard Juillerat (1937–2006) and a psychoanalytical anthropology inspired by Freud

Of Swiss origin, Bernard Juillerat was director of research for the Centre National de la Recherche Scientifique and a member of the laboratory of social anthropology of the Collège de France. As an Oceanist anthropologist, he worked among the Yafar living in the tropical forest of the West Sepik in Papua New Guinea. Without a doubt one of the major representatives of Freud-inspired psychoanalytical anthropology in France, he participated in the creation of that group and co-directed it. His principal works were: *Children of the Blood. Society, Reproduction and Cosmology in New Guinea* (1986);[16] *Oedipe chasseur. Une mythologie du sujet en Nouvelle-Guinée* (1991); *L'Avènement du père. Rite, représentation, fantasme dans un culte mélanésien* (1995); *Penser l'imaginaire* (2001).

It is through *Oedipe chasseur* and a text from *Penser l'imaginaire* that I have chosen to present his multifaceted inquiry and his rich, subtle anthropo-analytical thought.

In *Oedipe chasseur*, he points out from the start that he had never left for New Guinea with the idea of testing the Freudian theses in an extra-European community. On the contrary, it was the examination of ethnographic materials which had led him to inquire into the legitimacy of a psychoanalytical approach. It was the Yafar who had led him to Freud, and not the other way around.[17]

According to Juillerat, Freudian theory proposed to resituate the cultural products of the unconscious within the dialectic of the Œdipus complex, that is to say, within the dynamic of the ontogenetic elaboration of the subject. Maintaining a good distance from the phylogenetic thought of *Totem and Taboo*, he adopted the point of view of fellow anthropologists who considered that symbolic products such as myths, rites, or cosmologies fall within the purview of an ahistorical unconscious directly linked to the experience of individual development, but liable to ongoing translation in cultural terms, therefore to fitting into history. He was conscious that his hermeneutic approach consisting, therefore, of attributing – thanks to psychoanalytical concepts and to the influence of the thought of the philosopher Paul Ricœur – a meaning, a precise message to the mythology of a given society, even to a larger section of its culture, would generate a fair amount of criticism.

In *Oedipe chasseur*, he proceeded to analyse and interpret a great deal of mythological material in which he detected a patent oedipal symbolic and a dualistic set of problems constitutive of persons in fulfilling their destinies. Indeed, in the Tapi myth, "an underground hunt", he identified the existence of an oedipal scenario expressed in terms of hunting. He considered that the oedipal conflict that quickly comes to light there refers all of us – Melanesians and westerners – to the same imaginary core, the one which involves the subject (here male) in its twofold filiation. Reflexion of a representation born in the ontogenetic experience but metamorphosed into a sociogenesis, the action takes place in a mythic age in which the social order sought to consolidate its emancipation from the laws of nature, in which the primitive family was still torn by conflicts inherent in its twofold structure grounded in sexuality and filiation.[18]

The totemic ceremony of the Yangis ritual ensures the society's symbolic reproduction. This ritual can be perceived as the repeated symbolic production of "primitive men" *(ifegê)* from two totemic essences and, more precisely, of socialised adult men from potentially incestuous sons. It is in this sense that the Yafar designate themselves totemically as "children of the blood" (blood of the sago palm or of the coconut palm, depending on the society's moieties), that is to say, as both having come from and having been freed from the mother's blood.[19]

Let us look at the history of the Yafar heroes and the place of the Œdipus complex.

According to Juillerat, the history of Yafar heroes consists of varied reformulations of the human ontogenetic adventure. In this sense, mythology appears here as the phylogenetic recapitulation of ontogenesis. But, what these tales seek to express is more the successful *emergence of society defined as male collective*, as sons acceding to the status of father, meaning, replacing the father subsequent to a symbolic parricide. The ontogenesis elaborated as regards the Œdipus complex actually serves to put in place a sociogenesis in which the social subject evolves from a "child of the blood" still totally dependent on its mother (the *ifegê* of the Yangis) into the adult son who dominates the women and controls reproduction. An extension of individual representations to the collective plan is perceived practically on the spot there. As an organised group, the society is asking to be explained in terms of evolution, and to that end Yafar thought has used that by which humans were constituted in their personal development.[20]

What is the place of the Œdipus complex? According to Juillerat, the suitable place to be accorded to the Œdipus complex, not only in mythology, but in Yafar cosmology, eschatology, and ritual is indicated by the materials themselves.[21] He in fact considers that these materials enable one to disengage the Œdipus complex as the organising principle (or as one of the organising principles) of the way the Yafar envision the world and human beings.[22] The Œdipus complex would therefore act there as a symbolic and not as the expression of an individual or collective neurotic complex. The collective representations as they are expressed in the symbolic products that I have presented cannot be analysed as "individual psyches". Indeed, the transition from the individual dimension to the cultural dimension would in fact correspond to a simplistic, reductionist action on the complexity of the individual's mental functioning, something which enables him to maintain that the "collective psyche" as it is found in myths or rites is the result of the long sedimentation of individual psyches within the culture throughout history (and not, as Freud wanted, of the phylogenetic evolution of humankind), and the culture only takes up what is common to all.[23]

"From Originary Phantasies to Cultural Symbols, Mediations and Thresholds" (1993)[24]

Pursuing my reflexions, this is a text that deals with a limited aspect of the problem of the relationship between individual/collective, psychic/social, a place of meeting and of divergence of the two disciplines in question.

Juillerat finds that ethnologists wonder about the existence of "key symbols", fundamental primary representations detected in the cultural formations, whose recurrence in very different cultures raises questions about universals, just as Freud had identified certain originary phantasies. Being equivalent to a culture's founding representations, these "key symbols" do not correspond point by point to the originary phantasies, but are related to them by their content (sexuality, Œdipus, death). These originary phantasies can re-emerge in the form of symbols integrated into a meaning sequence, notably in mythological, ritual, cosmological, or eschatological representations.

So he asks the following questions:

- What type of relationship is there to be between phantasy and collective representation?
- What would be the transformation processes, "mediations", permitting the metamorphosis of unconscious phantasies into cultural symbols elaborated by the collective imaginary?
- Is there a theoretical "threshold" separating the substrate of the universals from the unlimited space of cultural diversity?
- How do the same universals produce different cultural results?

On the subject of the "mediations" instrumental in the transformation from phantasy into cultural representation, Juillerat appeals to the notion of *Kulturarbeit*. According to him, this involves three types of processes: the primary and secondary psychic processes, and a process of socio-cultural elaboration, a sort of historical, collective secondary process connected with external factors (natural setting, social norms, and cultural values, events. . .). He also refers to the ideas of Paul Ricœur, who envisioned the existence of multiple mediations connecting an individual phantasy to a cultural symbol presenting the same content.

The cultural products would therefore have two sources: one psychic, coming from "below"; the other socio-cultural, coming from "above", meaning from society and its established divisions. The first begins over and over again forever, while the second is transmitted and transformed in history. So, what relationship is there between the primitive psychic meaning of an established cultural representation and the "endorsement of meaning" assigned by the society? To what extent does the symbol still reflect the individual phantasy while becoming something different which is not only an element of culture defined as the "set of meanings", but also fitting itself into social relationships and into history?

Juillerat also introduces the notion of "threshold" as the border between universals and the cultural differences they underlie. To develop his argumentation he uses the example of the Œdipus complex while proposing a personal interpretation, for which the concept of threshold is supposed to define the extent to which a representation is universal and the level at which it begins to be culturally diversified. For the originary phantasies or the theoretically non-decomposable elementary symbolic forms translating them, the threshold determines the minimal structure that makes them universals, but he particularly applies it to phantasy or symbolic wholes which, like the Œdipus complex, are decomposable into smaller units. What is universal is not a given particular form of the Œdipus complex, but rather what is common to all the possible configurations of oedipal combinations, whose varied cultural expressions must be reducible to a model containing all of them. This model is not empirically proven as such. Defining the universality of the Œdipus complex consists of determining what does and does not constitute this signifying nucleus. The invariables of the Œdipus complex would be: the placing of the subject within his or her twofold filiation (with respect to a parent of the same sex and a parent of the opposite sex, or their substitutes); the fusional bond with the mother given as pre-oedipal legacy, no matter what the subject's sex; the reciprocal father/son or mother/daughter rivalry and the question of the authority (to which the submission or transgression is responding); and finally the parental sexuality phantasised by the subject. Overtly defined in this way, the Œdipus complex emerges as the setting up of a structure whose invariables can be organised in variable ways. Parricide and incest, cornerstones of the Freudian definition of the Œdipus complex as a nuclear complex of neuroses, no longer appear as anything other than extrapolations, extreme phantasies derived from the universal structures that are rivalry with the parent of the same sex and symbiosis with that of the opposite sex (or, the inverse in the case of the negative Œdipus complex having a basis in homosexuality). The male Œdipus complex is easier to define than that of the girl. In all cultures, apparently, the child–subject represented is almost always a boy.[25]

Finally, he situates his own position as being intermediary between that of "radical cultural relativism", leaving no room for universals, and that which would view cultural symbols as faithful translations of infantile phantasies.

Juillerat's psychoanalytical anthropology, grounded as it is in high quality, rigorous work in ethnography and on thoroughgoing knowledge of Freudian thought, asserts itself in the pursuit and creation of epistemologically relevant connections between anthropology and psychoanalysis. Inspired by the thought of the philosopher Paul Ricœur, he nevertheless maintains a critical distance from certain Freudian concepts, detectable in particular, in the scotomisation of the death drive, as well as in his representation of the invariable components of the oedipal structure. For example, he rejects parricide and incest, depicting them as extrapolations, extreme phantasies derived from the universal structures of rivalry with the parent of the same sex and the symbiosis with that of the opposite sex. However, he recognises the existence of an Œdipus complex in girls and the existence of the negative side of the complex. He displays great lucidity regarding the matter of the conditions of fruitful collaboration between the two disciplines on the basis of the elaboration of a psychoanalytical anthropology that necessarily presupposes the delimitation of its field, the construction of its objects, as well as the definition of a rigorous methodology. The perspicacity of his reflexions about the processes of transformation, the "mediations" permitting the metamorphosis of unconscious phantasies into established cultural representations, as well as the introduction of his notion of theoretical "threshold" as the border between universals and the cultural differences that they underlie, seems to me to have patent heuristic value.

Nonetheless, Juillerat has not forgotten, and fairly regularly voices his identity as an anthropologist based on his experience as an ethnographer, his intellectual filiation, his espousal of an intellectual tradition, and his having inherited and appropriated a historically constituted theoretical corpus.

With the following psychoanalysts

The major contribution of the group psychoanalysts with Didier Anzieu and René Kaës

Didier Anzieu (1923–1999)

Anzieu was born in Melun on July 8, 1923. After completing the *hypokhâgne* and *khâgne* preparatory classes in literature and the humanities at the Lycée Henri IV in Paris, he entered the Ecole Normale Supérieure de Paris in 1944. While preparing his Diplôme d'Etudes Supérieures in philosophy, he took psychology classes at the Sorbonne. He obtained the *agrégation* in philosophy in 1948, then prepared a *Licence* in psychology and the diplomas of the Institut de Psychologie. He thus began his first activities as a clinical psychologist at the Centre Psychopédagogique Claude-Bernard. He was initiated to psychodrama by Mireille Monod and Evelyne Kestemberg. In 1950, Daniel Lagache, who held the Chair of Psychology at the Sorbonne, gave him Freud's self-analysis as the subject for his major thesis for the *Doctorat d'Etat*, his minor thesis having been devoted to analytical psychodrama in children. Lagache also advised him to begin analysis, which he underwent with Lacan. In 1953, he began his training to be an analyst at the Société Psychanalytique de Paris under the supervision of Lagache and Favez-Boutonier. He defended his thesis in 1957. Starting in 1955, he held a professorship at the University of Strasbourg, which he retained until 1964. In 1962, he and a group of colleagues founded the CEFFRAP (a French study group for training and active research in psychology) for the coordination of social psychology and psychoanalysis. Distancing himself from Lacan, in 1964, he participated in the creation of the Association Psychanalytique de France, where he exercised various different responsibilities. He would, in addition, teach at the University of Paris X-Nanterre from 1964 to 1983. In 1972, he collaborated with René Kaës to found two book series, one for individual works ("Psychismes"), the other for collective works ("Inconscient et culture") at the Dunod publishing house. He died in Paris on November 25, 1999.

The main themes of his research were psychodrama, projective methods with Rorschach tests, groups, creativity, and the psychopathology of boundaries. Among his main concepts may be especially cited the skin-ego, formal signifiers, psychic envelopes, group illusion, and paradoxical transference.

Among his important works are: *Le Psychodrame analytique chez l'enfant et l'adolescent* (1956); *Freud's Self-Analysis* (1959); *Les Méthodes projectives* (1961); *The Group and the Unconscious* (1975); *Le Corps de l'oeuvre* (1981); *The Skin-Ego* (1985); *Le Penser, du Moi-peau au Moi-pensant* (1994).

I shall look at his approach to the debate with anthropologists in a direct manner using his text "Freud et la mythologie" (1970), and in an indirect manner with his psychoanalytical approach to groups based on his major work *The Group and the Unconscious* (1975).[26]

"Freud and mythology"

In this article, Anzieu explored and analysed the relationship of Freud and of psychoanalysis to mythology, a historical, even genetic, relationship inasmuch as a certain number of concepts central to psychoanalysis are drawn from Greek mythology: Œdipus, Narcissus, Eros and Thanatos, to cite but a few.

Anzieu analysed Freud's intellectual itinerary with regard to mythology, starting with Greek mythology and ending with the Jewish "myth" of Moses, going by way of the myth of the primitive horde and primal parricide of *Totem and Taboo*. The course he took corresponded, moreover, to an evolution in his theorisation. Seeing the Greek gods as acting upon prohibited drives and the god of monotheism as the personification of an agency with its two sides of superego and ego ideal, he situated totemism in an intermediary position between the two topics. Anzieu considered Klein's contribution particularly valuable since it played a role in reworking Freud's conception of Greek mythology – which remained based on the first topic – in light of the second topic. For him, Klein had in fact shown that the Greek gods represented the superego just as much as the id and that the "heroes" personified the different "positions" of the subject in relation to internal objects.[27]

This evolution on the part of Freud also constituted, according to Anzieu, an extension of the psychoanalytical field from the individual unconscious to the collective unconscious, which has nothing to do with Jung's archetypes.

Nonetheless, he also formulated a certain number of criticisms addressed to Freud and to psychoanalysts and especially questioned the bases and modalities of a fruitful dialogue with anthropologists and mythologists. So it is that he considered that one of the prerequisites for any possible interdisciplinary collaboration between psychoanalysts and specialists of myths was that the former would have to forego any temptation to engage in unbridled psychoanalysis with regard to the latter.[28] He especially reproached Freud for not having recognised the distinctive nature of myths or, for that matter, that of the different types of ethnographic, cultural materials. This point, he observed, is one of the ones that did the most to put a strain on subsequent relations between psychoanalysts and anthropologists. For Freud, there was, on the one hand, the clinical material, and on the other hand, the cultural data, all of which were equivalent: witchcraft, superstition, folklore, artistic creations, practical jokes were externally projected unconscious psychology, every bit as much as myths were. There Freud had really overlooked the unique nature of these cultural data while psychoanalysis' essential discovery, that of the Œdipus complex – a discovery that had opened his mind to all these rapprochements – was by its very essence linked to a myth.[29]

This is the genetic point of view in psychoanalysis, a diachronic point of view which, according to Anzieu, would sanction fruitful rapprochement between psychoanalysis and the science of myths, but one made possible on two conditions: first, the revising of Freudian stages of psychosexual development in light of Klein's contribution with the persecutory, then depressive, positions followed by the phase of reparation; and second, giving up trying to explain the development of the individual by that of the species, and reciprocally.

Anzieu then proposed to provide some guidelines for psychoanalytical participation in the study of mythology, Greek mythology in particular.

First of all, there would be the task of reciprocal exchange of information between psychoanalysts and mythologists regarding their methods, criteria, objects, and concepts. So it is that Anzieu considered that psychoanalysts must explain to mythologists that certain Freudian notions needed to be re-examined, and that Klein's contributions would constitute an indispensable extension of Freudianism and have a certain relevance to any material involving themes of bodily dismemberment, devouring, combined parents, or bad, fearsome mother, for example. He observed that both apply the same working rule, namely that the meaning of a text, an account of a patient's dream, or a Sophoclean tragedy, can only be deciphered within their context, the elements of which had to be supplied. However, he deplored the fact that psychoanalysts had too often failed to follow this rule, which led him to propose the following rule: a psychoanalytical interpretation of a myth must be based, on the one hand, on the complete text of this myth and, on the other hand, case studies displaying the specific, particular unconscious processes, analogous to those thought of as transcribed by the myth.[30]

Providing information in this way should put an end to a fundamental misunderstanding, because mythologists have often reproached psychoanalysts for always seeing the same thing everywhere. While mythologists take into consideration the particular characteristics of each myth, psychoanalysts are too often inclined to play down differences. That is why mythologists view the psychoanalytical interpretation of myths as a mechanical process always manufacturing the same product, smoothing over differences, and replacing them with platitudes.[31] Anzieu proposed two very relevant responses to these justifiable criticisms. The first consisted in recalling the polysemy of symbols. Once interpreted, that is to say, freed from their anxiety-producing affective burden, the sameness of the contents of the unconscious is an obvious fact. This explains, moreover, the difference between the poverty of unconscious thought qua thought and the richness of symbolic thought enabling the relative mastery of affects and their communication to other persons. It is in a sense true that psychoanalysis overlooks differences, but it is just that people feel that they are all similar in terms of their unconscious. This led him to his second answer, which was that the unconscious, and more particularly the Œdipus issue, was the basis of human identity and community, but the psychoanalytical clinic described inverted or early forms of the Œdipus complex. It shows how the accent is placed differently on the components of this complex depending on the neurotic organisations.[32]

According to the conception espoused by mythologists and anthropologists who conceive of myths as having the essential function of supplying members of a given society with a conceptual system giving them a way of thinking about society and nature or, in other words, with a code for thinking about reality, be it astronomical, botanical, religious, or socio-familial, Anzieu envisaged the existence of a twofold psychological coding, that of the unconscious processes, and a psychopathological coding, that is to say, a description and classification of mental syndromes. He maintained that myths are in fact also a distinguishing, a naming, a classifying, an ordering of unconscious processes and their interconnections.[33]

Finally, Anzieu took up the question of the relationships between the "individual" unconscious and the "collective" unconscious, as well as raising the question of the replacement of "debatable concepts" such as phylogenetic recapitulation. In addition, he envisioned clarifying the "too vague" notion of universality of the unconscious.

He considered that one could speak of the universality of the unconscious because of the existence of a limited number of unconscious processes that are always and everywhere the same: representations-representatives of the drive, defence mechanisms, anxiety, phantasies. However, the organisation of these processes, the ways in which they are combined, vary. They vary not only in the individual, depending on the stages of libidinal development or the neuroses, but also depending on the groups and societies. Moreover, he defended the hypothesis that the individual and collective organisation of unconscious processes are independent in terms of origin and functioning, even though the individual and collective phantasies interact, because they are made up of the same constituents. Each one functions in its own sector. Consequently, he considered that this twofold hypothesis of the universality of the unconscious and the independence of the individual and collective formations of the unconscious provides protection against the counter-transferential temptation of a narcissistic symbiosis that would lead one to misjudge the differences in the organisation of the unconscious, not only between individuals, but between groups and peoples.[34]

This most valuable conclusion "completely naturally" leads us to take a look at his ideas as presented in *The Group and the Unconscious.*

The Group and the Unconscious (1975)

Anzieu maintained that the group situation, characterised in an early phase by the anonymity of its members, awakens in individuals the anxiety-provoking image of the dismemberment of his or her ego and above all of his or her body, which would explain the resistance to living in a group, to working in a group and to the very concept of group. Thus, the ego's identity is placed in question, sensing the risk of losing itself and of breaking apart into the other people present. The image common to the yet to be unified group – because it is in the beginning stages – is therefore that of the dismembered body. That is why the first job a group has to perform on itself consists of ridding itself of this image by going beyond it. He considered that when a number of individuals brought together and riven with anxiety owing to the omnipresent image of the dismembered body have succeeded in overcoming this, in reassuring themselves, in considering themselves as human beings on the level of what is perceived and felt, in feeling pleasant, common emotion, a positive feeling out of which joint thoughts and actions can arise, then, in order to describe the changes they have just experienced and the affective tone that has become theirs, they speak of the feeling of "we", of the birth of a unit higher than each individual in which each individual participates. The group is born. It is born as a living "body". Each one recognises him- or herself as a "member" (everyday language has drawn upon this offshoot of the biological metaphor to such an extent that there is no better word designate the participants, the adepts of a group). Finally bonded together, the group differentiates, and organises. The biological metaphor remains all-powerful.[35]

This notion of group as a living "body", the notions of primitive body dismembered, then re-membered, of members designating the participants in it, correspond to the imaginary reality of social groups.

This innovative approach offered by Anzieu and group psychoanalysts is particularly valuable for our debate from the perspective of establishing fruitful links between socio-cultural and psychic realities, but also for the creation of intermediary zones between those two epistemic fields. According to Anzieu, these metaphors of group as "body" and of individuals as "members" especially aim at realising the desire of the "group's Self" to take up residence in a living organism, like the psychic functions deriving from organic functions through propping up, as Freud had postulated. So, belonging to a group will often impose upon its members physical signs or distinctive attire signifying participation in a common body. For him, this imago purported to be of a body proper to the group was in response to the nostalgic dream of symbiotic union between the members of the group in a primitive maternal womb. Along with the horde, that was one of the specifically groupal originary phantasies, meaning a phantasised representation of the origin of groups.[36]

He referred to René Kaës as one who had seen in the formation of ideology by a group an attempt to provide itself with a mental equivalent of the body proper.

Anzieu then draws us into the phantasy universe of groups, places of arousing images triggering emotions that are going to determine collective behaviour. He conceived of relations between human beings as being organised around two main poles: technology and phantasy. The technological pole enables the flow of goods and ideas, while the unconscious inter-human bond in couples, in groups, in family and social life is due to the flow of phantasy. Society would supply its members with an abundance of ways of stimulating phantasy (fomenting phantasy in the individual psychic apparatus), such as art, religion, science. Nonetheless, he pointed out that, despite the phantasy's internal groupal organisation, there are only individual phantasies, to the exclusion of phantasies common to the group. He identified the existence of an oral phantasy in a group with regression to oral sadism.

Before joining Anzieu in looking at the group's organising psychic unconscious and the principles of psychic functioning proper to the "groupal apparatus", meaning his general theory of the flow of phantasy in groups, I would like to make certain points.

Anzieu established the analogy between group and dream at a very early point (1965). Like dreams, real groups would above all be the imaginary realisation of a desire, and as in dreams, their actions would be displacements, condensations, symbolic figurations of desire. Moreover, in groups, there are no psychic processes other than those known and described in the individual psychic apparatus. Phantasy circulates among the members. The modes of thoughts and actions, their perceptions of reality are pervaded by prevalent individual phantasies emanating from certain members which become contagious or inspire resistance in the other people. According to him, the errors of judgment made by groups and their internal dissension would principally stem from that. In addition, these phantasies underlie pregenital anxieties, those of dismemberment of the body and of the psyche, persecution, depressive, and oedipal anxieties. The convergence of phantasies and their unifying elaboration can give birth to a well-defined ideology, a mythology specific to this group, but also place at its disposal the energy to perform its activities.

Anzieu considered that the fundamental dialectic resilience of the unconscious life of groups was to be constituted by the antagonistic pair groupal illusion–phantasies of breakage that would have control over their observable primary oscillations (in the psychoanalytical sense). He called groupal illusion a particular psychic state characterised by a feeling of euphoria that groups in general feel at certain times and which is verbally expressed by the members by saying: "We go well together; we make a good group; our leader is a good leader". The groupal illusion presupposes that the group has been set up as a libidinal object by its members. It replaces the individual's identity by the group's identity, with the affirmation that the individuals are identical and that it institutes group narcissism. It would represent a collective defence against the common persecution anxiety, a form of hypomanic defence. Moreover, it would illustrate the functioning of the ideal ego in groups. There would thus be a substitution of the common ideal ego for the ideal ego of each person, meaning that the group would function as ideal ego in the psychic apparatus of the participants. The counterpart of the group illusion is phantasies of breakage, in which this group-object is then invested by different forms of destruction drives.

Nevertheless, the group illusion fits into a more general process, because "the group just simply fabricates the illusion".

The groupal situation mobilises two types of identification among participants: identification with the leader, with the father, with the ego ideal; and the projective and introjective identification of the participants with one another.

Finally, the atmosphere of the group, its products, its realisations, its blockages would be linked to resonances or underlying phantasised discordances among its members or sub-groups.

Let us now take a look at the five unconscious psychic organisers of groups identified by Anzieu.[37]

The first would be the individual phantasy, combined with the phenomenon of phantasised resonance identified by André Missenard.[38] The main instigator of the phantasy is then placed in the position of groupal ego. In natural groups, businesses, social bodies, institutions, there is an institutionalisation of their founders' phantasy.

The second organiser is the imago. As Anzieu reminded us, for Freud, it was the imago of the leader that provided the groupal bond and not the prevalent phantasy of an individual.

The originary phantasies are the third organiser.

The Œdipus complex would be more than a fourth unconscious organiser of groups. To use Kaës' expression, it would prove to be a "meta-organiser" or, as Anzieu formulated this it would found the "topical structure" of groupal life, while the three preceding organisers would provide phantasy organisation.

The image of the body and the psychic envelope of the groupal apparatus would be the fifth organiser. The psychic apparatus, be it individual or groupal, would need to constitute a protective, delimiting, containing envelope for itself that allowed exchanges with the outside, what he called a skin-ego .[39] The leader of the group or the ideology would come to replace a single agency in the psychic apparatuses of the members. An envelope identity, founder of the group as such, would replace the individual diversity, and this groupal psychic envelope would present itself as leader, as ideology, as utopia. It institutes a difference between the outside and the inside.

New notions are introduced, such as those of groupal psychic apparatus and of individual or groupal psychic envelope. Their heuristic value in establishing links between psychic and socio-cultural reality would be something to examine at a later point. Independent in terms of their nature and interdependent in terms of functioning, these organisers would be present in all the groups. Generally, one of them prevails, but the complementary, antagonistic or repressed role of the others would need to be identified.

Allow me to mention, moreover, the three principles of psychic functioning proper to the groupal apparatus out of which the phantasy or imaginary life of groups flows:

- A principle of non-differentiation of the individual and the group; phantasy and imago would be of use for the imaginary accomplishments in conformity with this principle of non-differentiation of the individual and the group;
- A principle of the group's self-sufficiency in relation to physical and social reality;
- A principle of delimitation between the inside of the group and the outside.

Finally, Anzieu proposed an essential methodological point for social psychoanalysis postulating three distinct, interacting levels: the level of the individual unconscious; the level of groupal phantasy resonance; and the level of collective representations.

In my general discussion, I inquire into the impact and significance of these new, unprecedented approaches to research, which were pursued and abundantly enriched by a complexification of the issues with one of his illustrious collaborators, René Kaës.

Rene Kaës

Psychoanalyst, professor emeritus of clinical psychology and psychopathology at the Université Lumière, Lyon II, and editor of a series for the Dunod publishing house, Kaës was an eminent collaborator of Anzieu, especially at the Cercle d'Etudes Françaises pour la Formation et la Recherche Active en Psychologie (CEFFRAP), which he later directed. He was the author of numerous works, among them: *L'Appareil psychique groupal* (1976); *L'Idéologie. Etudes psychanalytiques. Mentalité de l'idéal et esprit de corps* (1980); *Le Groupe et le Sujet du groupe* (1993); *La parole et le Lien* (1994); *La Polyphonie du rêve* (2002); *Les Alliances inconscientes* (2009).

I have chosen to look at one of his works, which synthesises his experience and thought, *Un singulier pluriel* (2007), with respect to which he proposes to work out a fruitful interconnection between intrapsychic and socio-cultural realities based on his practice and psychoanalytical theorisation of groups.

The psychoanalytic approach to groups has enabled Kaës to discern three logical levels in the study of the psychic reality of groups: that of the group; that of the bonds between the subjects making it up; and that of each subject considered in terms of his or her uniqueness. This is why Kaës thinks that the group experience is essentially one of assembling or fitting together these three spaces, which creates a variable place for each of these four modalities (singular, common, shared, different). Thus, the taking into consideration of the position of the subject in the group has led him to think that the common identifications, the phantasies and shared representations, the formations of the ideal, the common dream matrix, the unconscious alliances, and the phoric functions are the points of transition and lines of rupture between intrapsychic and intersubjective space.[40]

A certain number of concepts, notions, and models have helped him to think through these multiple relationships, among them: the notion of internal groups and the concept of psychic groupality; the model of the groupal psychic apparatus; phoric functions; common, shared dream space, the unconscious alliances already mentioned; and intersubjective work. I shall present some of these.

The notion of internal groups and the concept of psychic groupality

The internal groups (primary and secondary) are groups situated within ourselves, "we are a group". The primary groups, in particular, encompass the network of identifications, the groupal structure of the ego, the group of object-relations, oedipal and sibling complexes, and the body image. Psychic groupality is that general property of the psychic matter which is that of associating, undoing, levelling psychic objects, forming assemblages out of them in keeping with laws of composition and transformation as a result of the acts of life and death instincts, as a result of repression or mechanisms without repression, by splitting, denial, or rejection.[41] By this groupality, we become "plural singular" subjects.

This concept of internal groupality gives us part of the answer to the question as to how subjects form a group. Indeed, internal groups would function as psychic organisers of the group in combination with socio-cultural organisers. Thus, each group would be characterised by a pair of predominant socio-cultural and psychic organisers from which its identity and the identifications of its members are stabilised.

Consequently, Kaës envisages the mobilisation of these two series of organisers in the process of fitting psyches together by the groupal apparatus, as well as certain necessary requirements of psychic work, several sets of processes and of modes of the fitting together.

The model of the groupal psychic apparatus

Expanding upon Didier Anzieu's thoughts, toward the end of the 1960s, Kaës proposed a model to account for the subject's relationship to the group, the arrangement of individual psyches in the group's bond, and the consistency of the group's psychic reality. Kaës thus formulated the following five basic principles of his model, which are of considerable value and significance for our debate:

1. When a shared, common psychic construction has occurred among individuals constituting a group, there is not only a collection of individuals, but a group with specific phenomena. The groupal psychic apparatus is the means of this construction and it is the result of a certain combinatory arrangement of the psyches.
2. The groupal psychic apparatus accomplishes a specific job. It connects, assembles, harmonises, and conflictualises parts of the individual psyche that have been mobilised to construct the group.

3. The groupal psychic apparatus is not an extrapolation of the individual psychic apparatus. It is a structure independent of the psyches that it assembles in keeping with its own laws. It possesses its own organisation and functioning. The processes governing shared common psychic reality derive from a logic different from that governing the individual.
4. It is this sort of fitting together that constitutes the psychic reality *of* and *within* the group, that reality organising itself in accordance with modalities, where what is "common" and "shared" prevail over what is "private" and "different".
5. The individual psychic apparatus is in part formed within this fitting together. It proceeds from it and is transformed there. It differentiates itself from it and, under certain conditions, acquires its own autonomy.[42]

How does this arrangement of the psyches by the groupal psychic apparatus come about?

Kaës envisions the existence of two series of organisers mobilised in the process of fitting together, the requirement of psychic work, several sets of processes and of modes of fitting together. The two series of organisers are the principal paradigmatic internal groups already mentioned and the socio-cultural organisers.

Concerning the modalities of fitting together, Kaës considers that the groupal psychic apparatus develops in the state of tension between two principal poles, isomorphic and homeomorphic, which structure the relationship between the subject and the whole. The isomorphic pole corresponds to the situation in which the group's organiser is identical in all the subjects who are members of the group. The formation of this pole presupposes the loss of the individual boundaries of its members. The homeomorphic pole is on the contrary characterised by the differentiation between the individual spaces and that of the group. The fitting together is then founded upon a relationship of tension between the similarity and difference of the psychic spaces.[43]

Oscillation between its two poles is therefore necessary.

Finally, Kaës points out that groups are organised around "three mental positions" corresponding to worldviews. He explains that all these positions are bearers of representations of causality and form a more or less open system for explaining the world, the origin, the end, and aims of the group.[44] It is a matter of ideological, mythopoetic, and utopian positions.

The phoric functions

Certain subjects perform intermediary, coordinating functions within the group, within the transitions between each subject's psychic spaces and the shared, common psychic spaces: in a couple, a group, a family, an institution. The persons embodying them bear these functions as much as they are borne by them. They are the message-bearers, the symptom-bearers, the dream-bearers. Kaës asks what is rightly incumbent upon the subject in the function that he or she is performing and what is assigned to him or her in this function by the groupal process. He then cites several characteristics common to these functions, among them: the functions of delegation, representation, and transmission, as well as containing, semiotisation and symbolisation.

Unconscious alliances

He calls an unconscious alliance an intersubjective psychic formation constructed by the subjects from a bond in order to strengthen in each of them, and to establish at the basis of their bond the narcissistic, objectal investments they need, the processes, the functions, and the psychic structures necessary to them that have come from repression, or denial, rejection, and disavowal. The alliance is formed in such a way that the bond takes on decisive psychic value for each of its subjects. The whole bound together in this way (the group, the family, the couple) takes its psychic reality from the alliances, contracts, and pacts that its subjects conclude and that their place in the whole obliges them to maintain.[45]

But, unconscious alliances have another dimension that concerns each subject involved in them. They require obligations and subjugations of him or her. They confer benefits on him or her. But, above all, they fashion part of each subject's unconscious and psychic reality.

Kaës discerns three categories of unconscious alliances: structuring, defensive and offensive

Structuring unconscious alliances contribute to the structuring of the psyche, such as: the oedipal pact concluded with the father (symbolic contract) and among the brothers; the contract of mutually renouncing the direct realisation of destructive instinctual aims, a condition for the advent of the community of law; the narcissistic pacts and contracts. Defensive alliances particularly include the denial pact, but also their pathological and alienating excesses, among them, the community of denial and the perverted contract. The offensive alliances seal a group's agreement to lead an attack, engage in an exploit, or exercise supremacy.

The concepts of unconscious alliances, and of phoric functions in particular, present a twofold subjective and intersubjective valence and a twofold metapsychological affiliation. We could understand them in terms of an intersubjective topography or topic, economy, and dynamic.

Kaës moreover discusses the intersubjectivity that imposes psychic work upon the psyche owing to the subject's necessarily intersubjective situation, something which leads him to propose the concept of intersubjectivity work, psychic work of the unconscious of the other person or of more than one other person in the psyche of the subject of the unconscious.[46]

Consequently, the psychic space of the bond and that of the assemblages are other places of the unconscious and, according to him, the psychoanalytic work in group situations has modified the traditional conception of the unconscious psychic conflict. Indeed, besides the intrapsychic conflict of infantile psychosexual therefore neurotic, origin, there would be an unconscious conflict between the subject and the part of his or her psyche held by another person (or more than one other person) or left in him or her (in them). Of course, the exploration of the borderline cases has also revealed the existence of another type of unconscious conflict, that between the ego and its objects.

The richness and complexity of René Kaës' thought provides material to respond to and avenues of research which are particularly precise, rigorous, and fruitful for the exploration and the psychoanalytical understanding of the relationships between the "individual and the group". That is why his contribution to the debate between psychoanalysis and anthropology seems to me to be of major importance, as is that of Didier Anzieu.

André Green

Green was born in Cairo in 1927. He lived within the principally francophone European community until the age of nineteen, then left for Paris to study medicine, followed by an internship in psychiatry in Professor Jean Delay's ward at Sainte-Anne's psychiatric hospital. That is where he met most of those who contributed to shaping his psychoanalytical and psychiatric thought. Regarding psychiatry, it was Henri Ey who would have the most significant influence on him. Green was very interested in the psychiatric clinic and in phenomenology, in Minkowski and Ey's organodynamism (as inspired by John Hughlings Jackson). Moreover, he met and participated in exchanges with a certain number of analysts who worked at Sainte-Anne's, among them Jacques Lacan, Pierre Marty, Pierre Mâle, Francis Pasche. He engaged in analysis for the first time with Maurice Bouvet in 1956. In 1957, he defended his doctoral thesis in medicine entitled "Le milieu familial des schizophrènes", which would be published in the journal *L'Encéphale* and was signed by him, Jean Delay, and Pierre Deniker.

Though the sources of his psychoanalytical thought were many and rich, Green chose the Société Psychanalytique de Paris as his place of training, affiliation, and evolution as an analyst.

It is important to mention his admiration for the thought of Lacan, whose Seminar he attended from 1961 to 1967, some concepts of which he would retain – especially that of signifier, the paternal metaphor, the Other – while rejecting certain aspects of his practice. In 1961, he discovered Winnicott, whose humanity, clinical sense, and way of talking about his counter-transference made a profound impression on him. Winnicott would play a great role in Green's interest in borderline states. In 1970, he discovered Wilfred Ruprecht Bion, then unknown in France, and was attracted to his work on thought and psychosis.

In his book on Green, François Duparc wrote that his theoretical position was situated between the body and the pure psyche, between the archaic clinic and the most Freudian metapsychology, between the mother object of primary madness and the father guarantor of oedipal triangulation, between Winnicott and Bion, on the one hand, and Lacan, on the other.[47] His thought was therefore structured by the combination of two types of analytic theorisation: on the one hand, Lacan's symbolising, paternal metaphor taking up again, and stressing, certain paternocentric tendencies of Freudian theory and, on the other hand, the emphasis on empathetic experience, relations, and the maternal environment according to Winnicott and Bion, who refined and deepened Melanie Klein's work.[48] All the while Green remained an ardent exegete of Freud's texts with a profound desire to enrich the Master's metapsychology.

He chose to become a "full-time" psychoanalyst, therefore evolving within the Société Psychanalytique de Paris, of which he would become a titular member, and even president in 1987. In particular, he contributed to an attitude of openness toward many forms of thinking, while preserving a great deal of rigour on the ethical and human levels and an unwavering fidelity to Freud.

Green's work is remarkable both in terms of the great volume of his publications, including books, articles and lectures, and of the diversity of the topics dealt with – clinic, technique, theory, but also "applied" psychoanalysis, to which I shall pay particular attention – without forgetting his passionate involvement in a certain number of ideological debates (concerning Lacan, the analysis of children, science, cognitivism, the social sciences) in order to make known, but also to defend, the deep and mysterious uniqueness of psychoanalytical thought.

Green's participation in our debate being of major significance, I shall first look at his model of the Œdipus complex and the ways in which it diverges from the Freudian and Lévi-Straussian models. Second, via certain selected themes, I shall look at his way of conceiving the relationship between psychoanalysis and anthropology.

His model of the Œdipus complex

It is in his article "Oedipe, Freud et nous" (1981) figuring in *La Déliaison* (1992), but also in his paper entitled "Inceste et parricide en anthropologie et en psychanalyse" (1999), given at the colloquium devoted to the work of Godelier held at Cerisy-la-Salle, that Green presented his model of the Œdipus complex, proposing to provide an account of its cultural, geographical, and historical variations. To begin with, he explained that, distancing himself from the Freudian conception, his reflections were the product of practice combined with a theory of major conceptual value owing to its independence from historico-cultural variables. Then, he recalled his indebtedness to Lacan and his structural conception of the Œdipus complex, thus enabling one to go beyond the ontogenetic "historical" definition of that complex in order to lend it a more general formulation, according to which, from the time of its birth, a child is caught within the symbolic oedipal framework because of the enduring nature of its parents' Œdipus complex. So, the Œdipus complex was structural there to the very extent that it was transgenerational.[49] Nonetheless, while the Œdipus complex was a human structure governing relationships among human beings, it was no less a historical phenomenon with a life, an apparent death, and an unconscious survival.

Green postulated the existence of an initial triangulation, thus rejecting the empiricist perspective only taking into consideration the mother–child relation at the beginning, and he justified that by appealing to the fact that from the time of its birth the child is recognised as being the product of the father–mother union. That is why he started with an open triangle joining the father, the mother and the child, within which the mother, positioned at the peak, is transversally connected to the father (difference of the sexes) and obliquely to the child (difference of generations). He said that his version of this model emphasises the open triangular structure where the mother has the position of the central link, because she is the only one in this tri-polarisation who maintains a twofold physical relationship with the father and with the child. He did not of course consider them to be equivalent, but the mother's body is involved there in both cases. This is why what the model shows is the lack of physical bond between the child and the father, which creates a considerable difference in the type of relationship involved with regard to the two parents. This has several consequences, in particular, the father's intervention to separate the mother and the child. Likewise, one could postulate the existence of a symmetrical desire for separation, retaliation on the part of the child regarding the parents joined in the primal scene from which it is excluded.[50]

He then insisted that, contrary to what is frequently maintained in psychoanalysis, there is not strictly speaking a dual relationship because, while the relationships between the child and the mother at birth do not actually seem also to be able to include the person of father *in praesentia*, one must, however, insist upon the fact that this primitive relationship indirectly includes the father in the mother's phantasies and thoughts. There is therefore not any transition from a dual situation to a triangular situation, but rather a transformation from the father's imaginary, phantasy status in the actual intervention from the real person of the father laden with symbolic and imaginary dimensions. This is what Green proposed to call the object's other, meaning the existence for the mother of another object that is not the child.[51]

In addition, he added that the father, inasmuch as he is the possessor of the mother and has full and complete enjoyment of her body, of which procreation is the proof, can only directly or indirectly enter into conflict with the child's desires. The elimination of the obstacle by violent death becomes, as it were, inevitable. However, one need not think, as Freud did, that it must in fact take place in reality. It suffices to invoke the generally shared nature of the phantasy of this death: parricide.[52] Green also invited us to picture the complex from three angles, depending on the vertex chosen: seen from the side of the son, it is the Freudian position; from the side of the mother, it is the *Mutterkomplex* as shown by the work of Juillerat; finally, there is the father's side.

Green made some remarks about the implications of his model, the points of divergence from the Freudian version and from that of Lévi-Strauss, with his "atom of kinship".

Divergences from the Freudian and Lévi-Straussian version

Green ruled out the idea of a prehistorical event that had really taken place and since been transmitted by phylogenesis. He derived parricide "logically" from incest, the father being the immediate obstacle to its realisation, then the inevitable incest, or incestuous phantasy, from the close physical relationship between the mother and child, made obligatory by the child's prematurity, which cannot be isolated from the physical relationship between the parents.[53] Dismissing, therefore, the Freudian phylogenetic hypothesis, he advanced the idea that the transmission of the phantasy of parricide and its non-occurrence, either in reality, or in consciousness, takes place through the repressing cultural mediation. Cultures "embroider" on the Œdipus complex by elaborating variants, displacements, condensations, extensions of the unembellished principal nucleus composed of the prohibition of incest (and by extension of incestuous desires) and the prohibition (more veiled, since it may be absorbed into the general, non-specific prohibition of homicide) of parricide. More than incest, parricide would be expressed through forms of symbolic disguise. "Social" parricide would be the object of a repression still more powerful than that involving incestuous desires.[54]

Green considered that since the analysis of the anthropological Œdipus, or Lévi-Straussian atom of kinship places the system of designations and that of attitudes into perspective and only brings together coded social roles and behaviours, it teaches us nothing about unconscious psychic reality. Its project is not in fact psychoanalytical, but anthropological in nature, the two perspectives being complementary.

To conclude, he conceived of his model as a symbolic matrix gathering together temporally ordered founding factors of subjectivity. The differences encountered from one culture to another can split the agents of certain functions (maternal or paternal) into two, complicate the network of their relationships, and bring the superego into play at an earlier or later point, but he believed that one would essentially find the same basic structure if one was willing to look behind the apparent facts. The question remained of deciphering the enigma that is the Œdipus complex. This is where the question comes up about unconscious thought as a set of formal mechanisms without which the Œdipus complex could not appear after its repression.[55]

The relationship between psychoanalysis and anthropology

I shall not go into Green's well-known summary of anthropologists' criticisms of Freudian thought and psychoanalysis, but instead look at those criticisms that he himself made of Freud's socio-anthropological thought and his reflexions on its fate and its impact on the thought and practice of contemporary psychoanalysis. Then I shall present his questions about the obstacles to the exercise of psychoanalytical thought in that socio-cultural field, as well as the conditions and modalities of psychoanalytical participation in the understanding of socio-cultural facts, not to forget the domains explorable. I shall then discuss his contribution to the investigation of some themes or sectors such as our contemporary society and its destructive manifestations, myth and mythic thought, especially. I shall finish with his criticism of Lévi-Strauss' thought and his collaboration with Godelier.

Green's criticisms of Freud's socio-anthropological thought and reflexions on its fate

Green considered that certain Freudian concepts, born at those places where socio-anthropology and psychoanalysis meet, are only really understandable when placed back into in his theoretical context. Though debatable and questionable, they should not be proscribed, but need investigation into their openness to reinterpretation, because the theoretical role they play is not eliminable. It is the conceptual function they convey that should be taken into more consideration. The passage of time has made their literal content unacceptable, which one cannot persist in defending without resigning oneself to sacrificing the reasons behind their postulation.[56]

As an example of Freud's negligence, he cited the conflict established between psychic (internal) reality and material (external) reality, which, encompassing the whole non-ego, therefore implies the lack of any distinction between lifeless and living physical reality and socio-cultural reality. Green moreover found this same negligence with regard to the object, prevalence being accorded to the status and role of drives. He pondered the fact that everything therefore inclines one to believe that Freud opted for a questionable solution by not wanting to distinguish between the external reality of the physical world and social (human) external reality, because the latter's relations with the psychic reality of the inner world were not easy to define. However, he considered such a distinction necessary nowadays, all the more so since the findings made since Freud's time – for the most part – fall under the heading of object relations that stand in opposition to many of Freud's ideas.[57] Green in fact thought that, were one to want to establish the idea of a "social reality" as the basis of a causality bearing the same name, and distinct from biological causality, one should look for its foundations in the relationship to the root of what the social relationships will be.[58] For him, it was once again a matter of the oedipal triangulation fitting into the family space as social symbolic matrix.

He analysed the impact of Freudian socio-anthropological discourse on contemporary psychoanalysis, all the more so because, given the great heterogeneity of theories and practices, there is concern about the unity of psychoanalysis.

Green observed that a significant portion of Freudian theory was based on work in "applied psychoanalysis", something which is quite different nowadays. Indeed, the combination of shortcomings and hasty interpretations of socio-cultural facts formulated by psychoanalysts met with and reinforced reluctance, even hostility, on the part of the disciplines "colonised". This resulted in a gradual refocusing on just practising therapy, which had a reductive effect on the theory leading, according to Green, to a psychoanalysis almost entirely reasoned in terms of an ontogenetic orientation, the principles of which are debatable. What is certain, he added, is that it has given up dealing with the problems that interested Freud: the reflexion on the links between the biological and the psychic; the place of human beings in the animal world; the openness to what he called the "life of the mind"; the role of culture all remained confined within the limits of an individual life, inspired by a psychologism confused with knowledge of the psyche.[59]

Questions about the presence of obstacles to exercising psychoanalytical thought in the socio-cultural field

Green also detected both the absence of definite objects and the difficulty of circumscribing the boundaries of this field. Unlike the extensive, but relatively well delimited, artistic domain, the social space is vast, complex, and hard to grasp as a whole. Hence, how is one to conceive psychoanalysis' contribution to the understanding of socio-cultural facts and what fields are to be explored? Green stated some propositions and questions that might contribute to circumscribing a field and defining a method.

So it is that he envisaged reassessing the domain attributed to drives, which are not very well harnessed and by nature conservative. He maintained that our "mythology", the theory of drives, is radically expressed through religious fanaticism, the quest for unconstrained enjoyment or the exercise of power and domination over others. In addition, creations of the imagination, works of fiction, products derived from drives and directly aimed at the unconscious of those for whom they are destined through the recurring themes of sex and crime bear witness in a different way to the omnipresence of instincts in the psyche, something which also led him to think about the need to explore the function of the social imaginary. Moreover, he invited us to examine what the work of the negative does in this socio-cultural field and to detect there the defence mechanisms used by the whole society to hide and be hidden, something which must remain in the dark. He thus recognised that psychoanalysis was far from saying everything there would be to say about the object to which it applies, in this case, but that it was important to remember that what it does have to say, no one can say, or not say, in its stead.[60]

Psychoanalytical thought should essentially focus upon the study of the so-called primitive societies and upon prehistorical society, these two complementary approaches aiming, according to Green, at the socio-historical foundations of psychic causality.

However, I have chosen to look at his reflexions on contemporary society, the collective expressions of human destructivity, and also his study of myths and mythic thought, as well as his observation of the points of divergence and convergence between those two causalities: psychic and socio-anthropological.

Taking a critical, lucid look at our contemporary western society, Green deemed that while Freud wrote of civilisation and its discontents in 1930, that discontent has evolved into an illness. He viewed war, Jewish genocide, and drugs as collective manifestations of the human destructivity, which in spite of everything is so little recognised. The socio-cultural field of the death drive being very vast, it seemed to him impossible to understand those phenomena without bringing together, in particular, causalities of a socio-historical and psychic nature. Whence the valuable recourse to psychoanalytical knowledge. He considered the Jewish genocide to be one of those collective phenomena that most puts the concept of the death drive to the test. Nonetheless, since that Freudian concept was very criticised, Green proposed considering the action of destruction drives as the expression of a de-objectalising function, realising a de-qualification of the psyche's objects, which thus lose their distinctive qualities and their originality, are reduced to an anonymous status, and at worst, reified. However, the action of the life drives would be the manifestation of an objectalising function, investing objects as love objects, or transforming certain functions or certain activities into objects enjoying the same status.

Myths and mythic thought

Let us now look at his contribution to understanding myths and mythic thought, as well as certain similarities that the latter shares with unconscious thought. To this end, I turn to his article "Le mythe: un objet transitionnel collectif" (1980).

Green asked why psychoanalysts are interested in myths. He reminded us that, starting in 1900, Freud opened up a new field to psychoanalysis: the psychoanalytical interpretation of myths, the twin sister of the interpretation of dreams. He considered it to be clear that Freud's interest in myths was based on an assumption that is very controversial nowadays, that of an encounter in the depths of the *archè*. Like the unconscious, myths would be witness to a prehistory, an imaginary construction after the fact, about what the origins of a people might have been.[61] Green put myths into a "synchronic category", where other cultural products figure, but also formations of the individual unconscious (dreams, phantasies, symptoms). As Anzieu had, he in turn noticed a major tendency on the part of psychoanalysts to underscore similarities and gather together, while mythologists were inclined to differentiate, to distinguish, and to singularise. But especially, he noted, in the cultural discourse that is myths, psychoanalysts meet up again with the discursive style of the formations of the individual unconscious gathered in listening to their patients session after session, from one patient to another.[62] That is why he formulated the hypothesis of the existence of a homology that is both structural and "historical" that justifies the relevance and heuristic value of the psychoanalytical interpretation of myths.

He emphasised that Freud's contribution to the analysis of myths was to be sought within the broader theoretical context of the mechanisms of unconscious thought described in *The Interpretation of Dreams*. If for mythologists, myths form a system – a mythology reflecting mythic thought – for psychoanalysts, phantasies forming a system reflect unconscious thought. Thus, Green reasoned, the mythic system was to the system of the thought of the myth what the preconscious-conscious system was to the unconscious system. The encounter between mythology and psychoanalysis would depend on the definition of the levels of comparison.[63]

Green raised another important question, that of knowing what the need to mythify – meaning to rewrite its history along nostalgic legendary lines – responds to in a given group.

To think through the "transitional" status of myths – between individual reality and collective reality, and both at once – he turned to the Winnicottian concepts of transitional field and object, but also to the notion of tertiary processes serving as links between the primary and secondary processes. He furthermore emphasised the ambiguity of social reality, which is both one of the spaces of external reality – encompassing in addition the physical non-human world – and one of the spaces of projection of subjective reality. Thus, like games for a child, myths partly belong to psychic reality through the relations they entertain with dreams, phantasy, and the other formations of the individual unconscious. They are obviously connected with external reality through their integration into social reality and the consensus of which they are an object. He considered that the important thing to understand well was the function and value of that collective transitional space, which creates a particular type of object in conformity with a paradoxical thought, where effects of the suspensive judgement "a myth is and is not real" are materialised.[64]

Let us take a look at the determinants of myths, of which there would be three orders: ahistorical, cultural, and individual, and their interactions.

1. The ahistorical order, where the affective, representative and cognitive unconscious universals of mythic thought find expression. They constitute a sort of empty whole to be filled by more specific kinds of determinants.
2. The cultural order, where the diachronic and synchronic data that can be associated with a culture of a given group come into play.
3. The individual order, itself constituted of ahistorical and historical, natural and cultural factors, whose symbolic matrices are unconscious in the psychoanalytical sense.

The interactions between these three orders would link the flow of messages between the individual's (unconscious) thought and the group's (unconscious) thought, their respective codes going by way of the mediation of the cultural order.[65]

What about the universals of mythic thought?

These would include the syntax of formal properties given prominence to by Lévi-Strauss and a "semantics"– discovered by Freud and developed by his successors – relative to the most general contents, unconscious affects and representations in relation to the drives that make up the common fund of humanity, a fund superficially modified by the cultural context. While myths can be conceived of as a set of propositions expressed in the language of secondary processes, their unconscious logic would be that of the primary processes, of the transitional phenomena and formal structures of Lévi-Strauss and the structuralists, formed from the perspective of the creation of a collective transitional object in a specific cultural field. It would thus be a matter of interpretation on several levels. A first level of interpretation would aim at their intrinsic relations, within themselves and in their relations with other myths. A second level would aim at the relations of myths with the cultural context, connecting the mythemes to data relative to this context. A final level would bring the mythic structures closer to structures present in the formations of the individual unconscious.[66]

Finally, how are the relations between mythic and unconscious thought to be viewed?

Green considered that they turn around the question of symbolisation, which contemporary thought has made a major issue. For him, the question of mythic thought and of unconscious thought came together in renewed reflexion on the effects of metaphor. Metaphor, interpretation. Myths interpret. Mythologists interpret myths. The metaphor that is the myth calls for its interpretation: metaphor of the metaphor. This splitting of metaphors is perhaps one of the fundamental properties of the human mind. Not symbolisation, therefore, but the symbolisation of symbolisation.[67]

Points of divergence and convergence between psychoanalysis and anthropology

Let me say to start with that Green identified three points of divergence: the relationships between structure and history; the problem of universality; and the parricide aspect of the Œdipus complex.

According to him, if one considers that history and structure find that the historical and socio-anthropological disciplines fields are particularly suited for development as axes around which to organise the human condition, one immediately grasps the differences with the manner in which psychoanalysis conceives of their interrelations. While history refers to memory, psychoanalysis deals with a faulty memory.[68] Indeed, this memory dominated by the atemporality of the unconscious, therefore, not in line with linear temporality, is subjected to a certain number of unconscious psychic processes, among them repression, the return of the repressed, compulsive repetition, and afterwardness in particular. According to Green, the structures of psychoanalysis are built upon the heterogeneity of the constituents of the psyche, a heterogeneity that develops their diverse energetic, topical, dynamic dispositions.[69] They function discontinuously and tend "toward a form" rather than being formal.

The problem of universality would also bring the two disciplines into conflict. While for psychoanalysis, the sense of universality is founded on the unconscious psyche and its instinctual base, Green thought that for Lévi-Strauss and structuralism, the universal was only conceived of directly in relation with the facts of a natural order. However, I might object to this by saying that Lévi-Strauss does not represent all of anthropology and consequently that other anthropological conceptions of universality do exist.

But, for Green, since the end of Lévi-Straussian structuralism, and with Godelier as a new interlocutor, the crux of the debate lies in the relationship between incest and parricide, the latter setting the two disciplines in opposition.

Indeed, according to him, the discussion about parricide was a real issue. First of all, he recognised that nothing in the experience of anthropologists could lead them to take into consideration the thesis of the murder of the primal Father. According to Green, we know that that was one of Freud's most daring speculations which, contrary to the forbidden desire for the mother, which is fairly easy to connect with the prohibition of incest, cannot be substantiated by any observable fact. He imagined that Freud would reply that the power of religion could be considered as a trace of the same order for parricide as the prohibition of incest is in matrimonial rules. Green saw contemporary anthropologists as having found themselves facing two possible options: either demolish the Freudian thesis, retaining practically nothing of it – that was Lévi-Strauss' choice; or accept it partially by proposing an interpretation more in line with their own conceptions, as Godelier did. Indeed, the issues at stake extend beyond the mere debate about the question of the reality or nonexistence of the murder of the primal Father. Pierre Kaufmann (1975) had seen well that it was a question of the theory of culture according to Freud.[70]

Unprovable by any observable fact, the hypothesis of parricide reflects fundamental differences between psychoanalysis and anthropology, that bearing upon the method and that bearing upon the object of observation. Only the psychoanalytical technique can bring unconscious contents like phantasies to light, while the ethnographic method can only objectify empirical facts accessible to "realistic" observation. Thus, the parricide phantasy will never be able to be a fact – ethnographic data – which does not mean that it does not exist. Green raised the question of the retaining of this speculative, but also heuristic, hypothesis of parricide and answered that it is because we remain sensitive to certain of Freud's arguments. There is no society in which spirits do not play an important role and in which the dead ancestors do not fulfil a function inspiring fear and respect. It is therefore essentially relative to this universal fear of death, not only as the end of pleasure, but also as the time of judgement, of appearance before the tribunal of the ancestors, that parricide can be surmised further down the road, so to speak. Since anthropologists only actually study societies in which the prohibition of incest is in force, this itself is a solution that kills two birds with one stone. It explicitly prevents incest and implicitly prevents parricide, if one agrees that the primitive cause making parricide irresistible is that which underlies incestuous desire: enjoyment of the mother.[71] Green cited Godelier's irrefutable arguments, which we shall look at later on.

Among the convergences between the two disciplines, Green emphasised the dominant role they accord to interpretation and their sharing of the same point of reference, that of the concept of meaning. Nonetheless, they differ about the question of the scope of the data and of the object of interpretative process more than about qualification by interpretation. Moreover, he observed the predominance of the symbolic, a concept common to the human sciences, but raised questions about the diversity of meaning attributable to it and about its relationship to other aspects of thought or psychic life.

How did he define the relationship between cultural causality and psychic causality?

In keeping with Freud's thought, Green looked at the psyche's twofold determinism, biological and cultural, between nature and culture, socio-anthropological causality therefore representing one of the polarities of psychic causality. However, cultural causality is also dependent upon common psychic organisation, finding support in it and proceeding to operations of transformation, socialisation, and "culturalisation". That is one of the aspects of *Kulturarbeit* mentioned by Freud. He also considered that certain aspects of psychoanalytical theory, especially the fates of drives, among them sublimation, would be best shown by the study of culture, through its major products as represented by religion, mythology, art, law, the economy, and other institutions.

The fact that the form of the relations that set themselves up between these two causalities have a common reference in the concept of meaning suggested to him the idea of a back and forth movement between action and reflexion, between collective participation and solitary retreat. Withdrawing back to the subject does not lead to the retrenchment of the collectivity, but rather to the internalisation of the foundations of collective life. It is the individual internalisation of these symbolic values that confers stability and permanency on each culture under consideration. This internalisation plays its role in intrapsychic conflictuality and can be found at the origin of turmoil having an impact on the outer world during changes of cultural paradigms. It is this going back, or return which is become interiority, that in the eyes of psychoanalysts is revelatory of psychic causality, arising out of its biological determinants on the one hand, and out of its cultural determinants on the other.[72]

Criticism of Lévi-Strauss' thought

Green considered that, hoping to re-establish the dialogue with anthropology interrupted up until then, psychoanalysis thought it might find a privileged interlocutor in Lévi-Strauss' work. However, he thought that "dialogue" was an inappropriate word, because for a very long time it had actually been a question of monologue.[73] And he added that it was only after Lacan's death that he had taken up his dispute with psychoanalysis – with Freud rather – in *The Jealous Potter*.[74]

First of all, Green observed that, although his field was not that of Greek culture, the Œdipus complex was a repetitive, nagging, practically obsessive theme in Lévi-Strauss' work. He found that the prohibition of incest as the "rule of rules" had been interpreted in diverse ways in the course of his work.

Noting the criticisms that Lévi-Strauss had made of psychoanalytical theory, in both the "finale" of *The Naked Man* and in *The Jealous Potter*, he mentioned, in particular, the revival of the notion of subject, which Lacanian theory cannot do without, but also the major conceptual role of affects, the theory of symbolism, the exclusive recourse to the "psycho-organic" code in the interpretation of myths. He detected in Lévi-Strauss an imperious, objectivist, formalising need, sometimes pushed to the point of caricature, which went hand in hand with a naturalism.

The structuring symbolic function, social in nature, is rooted in the brain and expels the individual unconscious, thus proceeding to a desubjectivation. The individual is caught in a twofold determinism, biological and social, the much too bothersome psychic then being cast out.

Green noted another major area of conflict between psychoanalysis and Lévi-Strauss' anthropology. It is a matter of the concept of psychic work elaborated by psychoanalysis. He in fact considered that Lévi-Strauss' analyses, both in the area of kinship and in that of myths, could in a certain way be connected with this. But, it is a matter of the work of the symbolic function, not of the individual unconscious. In addition, Green reproached Lévi-Strauss for having remained silent about the comparisons that were to be drawn from the work of elaboration of kinship systems and that which is at work in myths or other cultural products.

Moreover, Green detected, in both Lévi-Strauss and Lacan, the desire to rid themselves of the burden of excessive historicism, a suspicious attitude toward the signified and the content, the setting aside of any reference to affects. It was a matter of emptying the unconscious of any idea of force, substance, meaning.[75]

Finally, he placed Lévi-Strauss' thought within its post-war historical context and within an ideological setting in conflict with Marxism and Freudianism, explaining that, from a very impersonal perspective, he considered Lévi-Strauss' thought to be symptomatic of the culture of the second half of the twentieth century in France and that, completely apart from Lévi-Strauss' personal responsibility, he himself evaluated this work by adopting an ideological stance taking into consideration the structured body of theoretical positions defended in the human sciences. Upon that occasion, he situated the "structural conviction" within the dominant ideas of the time and saw it as a reaction against history and dialectical materialism, and also against psychoanalysis, therefore, Marx and Freud.[76] Nonetheless, in his article "Le Mythe: un objet transitionnel collectif" (1980), Green all the same identified certain connections between psychoanalytical thought and structuralist thought, especially when Lévi-Strauss detected a thought at work in myths, as Freud had for dreams. In addition, Lévi-Strauss implicitly had accepted the idea that mythic thought was a projective system, but this would only be a system of forms, the contents being ignored.

What about his collaboration with Maurice Godelier?

His exchange with Maurice Godelier began during a lecture given by the anthropologist to the Société Psychanalytique de Paris on November 21, 1993, where Green had been asked to act as his discussant.

In his talk entitled "Incest and parricide in anthropology and in psychoanalysis" given at the colloquium about Godelier's work held in Cerisy-la-Salle in 1996, Green clearly debated the anthropologist's ideas, identifying three points of agreement and some points of disagreement.

There was an attempt to interconnect natural causality and cultural causality, taking into consideration both the evolution of primates – therefore, human phylogenesis and sexuality, the prematurity of the little human being determining his long period of dependency – and the role of epigenesis, all of these factors influencing psychic causality.

Godelier accorded a central place to human sexuality become generalised, which takes on two forms, sexuality–desire and sexuality–reproduction. He therefore recognised the sexual drives and the affects connected with them. For him, this sexuality was a factor in social disorder, encouraging organisation of society and that of the individual. The prohibition of incest was to be based on a necessary sacrifice of a part of one's sexuality, protecting from social disorder and participating in this organisation.

By drawing up rules society constructs a social order, but also produces social relationships, and therefore the social, just as it ensures its reproduction. According to Green, the principal fact was the construction of the social out of and against the sexual. There would be a "ventriloquy" of the sexual. The social body constitutes a network of relationships in which the sexual is implicitly represented.[77] For him, these points of agreement constituted a very solid platform permitting the opening up of the discussion in a very fruitful manner.

What were the important points of disagreement?

According to Green, Godelier maintained that it was not sexuality that phantasises society. It was society that phantasises sexuality. He said that he himself would be tempted to reply, neither one nor the other. Sexuality phantasises the body, the difference between the sexes, the difference between generations, reproduction, power, death, etc. He called all that primordial. As for society, he considered that its goal was to establish an order of human beings that it wanted to have pass as being an order of the world. Nature and culture meet in this elaboration.[78]

The disagreement about the interdependence of incest and parricide is a major one. I have already discussed this at length above, but here Green argued on the basis of the writings of the Hellenist Walter Burkert and those of James Frazer concerning the murder of the divine king. Researching the historical and prehistorical sources of Greek religion, Burkert had in fact considered that hunting, sacrifices, and funerary practices seemed connected at a time when the gods were not yet believed to be individualised powers. He defended the idea, which had already been that of Freud, that murder was at the foundation of the cultural order and that it was at the origin of the evolution of social and spiritual structures. He wrote that the presentation of the theses of a Hellenist concerned to go as far back as possible into Greece's past shows that Godelier's objection that the ideas defended by psychoanalysis are too dependent on Judeo-Christian ideology could not be valid.[79] In Frazer's case, he described the varied, more or less indirect forms of this killing of the divine king as being in decline.

I shall take up this considerable contribution made by André Green in my general discussion in Chapter 4.

In the United States

Addressing the contemporary debate in the United States is no easy task! Indeed, an initial question necessarily arises as to the fates of the movements and ideas of some of the figures already studied, such as those of Kardiner and his "culture and personality" school, Róheim's psychoanalytical anthropology, as well as Devereux's ethnopsychiatry and complementary ethnopsychoanalysis, or Fromm's analytical social psychology. Providing an answer would seem rather difficult. In addition, one might also inquire into the sources of inspiration of certain contemporary figures, among those we are going to look at, namely Melford Spiro and Gananath Obeyesekere.

In the face of so much uncertainty, I have chosen to stay on the safe side and look at some major figures.

Weston La Barre (*The Human Animal*, 1954; *The Ghost Dance. Origins of Religion*, 1972); and Werner Muensterberger (*Man and his Culture: Psychoanalytical Anthropology after 'Totem and Taboo'*, 1969) were definitely influenced by Róheim.

Irving Hallowell was also inspired by the American Psychological School. He would be one of Melford Spiro's mentors. One of his important works was *Culture and Experience* (1967).

Robert Paul, psychoanalyst and anthropologist, especially worked on Tibetan society from a Freudian perspective. He published his study in a work entitled *The Tibetan Symbolic World: Psychoanalytic Explorations* (1982).

Finally, during the 1980s, Gilbert Herdt tried to analyse ritual homosexuality in a New Guinean society (the Sambia people). In addition, he collaborated with the psychoanalyst Robert Stoller, a recognised specialist in studies on sexual identity and its psychogenesis. Among his publications are: *The Guardians of the Flutes, Idioms of Masculinity* (1981); *Ritualized Homosexuality in Melanesia* (1984); *Intimate Communications, Erotics and the Study of Culture* (1990, in collaboration with Stoller).

Melford E. Spiro

Spiro was one of the main representatives of contemporary American anthropology. He founded the Anthropology Department at the University of California, San Diego and was a member of the American National Academy of Sciences. Juillerat considered him to be the pivotal figure of the school of psychological anthropology and Freudian-inspired anthropology.

He combined an old interest in the philosophical problems of human existence with important ethnographic research. In his words,

> In an important sense, my intellectual interests have always been more philosophical than scientific, and just as in the Middle Ages philosophy was the handmaiden of theology, so for me anthropology has been the handmaiden of philosophy, a tool for the empirical investigation of some central questions concerning the nature of man. Although I have worked in four different

> societies – the Ojibwa, Ifaluk, an Israeli kibbutz and Burma – I have never been interested in ethnographic description, per se; and although I have published on a variety of institutions – family, kinship, politics, socialization, and religion – I have had little interest in institutional analysis, as such. Ultimately – so at least I have believed – these enterprises are useful to the degree that they can illuminate some aspect of the nature of man. Since, however, anthropology is primarily interested in society and culture, and since until recently it has been much more concerned with socio-cultural differences than with universals, my choice of anthropology – rather than, for example, psychology – might seem rather strange. In the light, however, of the intellectual and political zeitgeist of the intellectually formative years of my life, this choice was not so strange after all.[80]

Spiro was greatly inspired by Hallowell, his mentor at Northwestern University, and through him by psychoanalytical theory and the theory of learning. As he explained, "From Hallowell's writings and teachings I came to realise that culture does not directly impinge on behavior, but is mediated through personality processes relating to individuals. The contours of these processes, I came to believe, were best delineated by Freud".[81] Kardiner also played a major role.

> From Kardiner, too, I became convinced of the importance of "projective systems" for the understanding of those aspects of culture that are not "reality" based. There remained, however, a missing ingredient. If social actors monitor their own behavior in accordance with cultural norms and rules, it was necessary to explain the acquisition of culture in each generation of social actors. Here the social learning theorists – and especially Miller and Dollard – provided the key.[82]

Spiro principally addressed the need to take into consideration both the psychological and cultural forces and structures as integral parts of the explanation of human behaviour, which set him radically apart from anthropologists and sociologists. He in fact considered that psychological factors are a necessary and explicit part of any acceptable theory of culture and of human action. He found it hard to imagine a genuine, heuristic theory of culture that could endure without an attempt to integrate a theory of the human mind. He regularly used aspects of psychoanalytical theory in his explanations and theoretical constructions. Although he essentially subscribed to the ethnographic method, he also argued for the existence of deep "motivational structures" at the basis of all human behaviour, both rational and irrational. Thus, his systematic use of psychoanalytical theory – traditionally criticised and often rejected by anthropologists owing to its culturally determined nature conferring upon it the status of ethnoscience, consequently unusable ethnographically speaking – led him to elaborate a theory of "panhuman" nature, which is one of the hallmarks of the originality of his thought. He maintained, moreover, that psychoanalysis provides the best coherent theoretical scheme available connecting the "panhuman" structure of the family to the concepts of individual motivation, on the one hand, and to the concepts of socio-cultural organisation, on the other.

Among his works may be cited *Kibbutz: Venture in Utopia* (1956–1971) and *Children of the Kibbutz* (1958–1975), an analysis of the psychological dimensions of socialisation and the acquisition of values and utopian aspirations. *Buddhism and Society* (1971) develops the themes of religious needs and social organisation, of personality and of culture. It particularly examines the meaning of divergences between their real beliefs and the normative doctrines of Buddhism for its devotees. *Œdipus in the Trobriands* (1982) proposes a new analysis of Malinowski's data which shows the existence of an oedipal constellation among the Trobriands. The Œdipus complex is structurally invariant, but variable from functional and cultural points of view.

Based on his work, *Culture and Human Nature* (1995), which is a collection of essays covering the years from 1961 to 1984, I propose to present some themes of his theoretical elaboration that led him to construct a coherent, rigorous scheme. I have chosen to look at his criticism of cultural relativism, the relations between culture and personality and the position he took with regard to the problem of the universality of the Œdipus complex.

Criticism of cultural relativism

Spiro proposed to explore the errors of traditional anthropological reflexion that had led to the adoption of cultural determinism and, from there, to the relativist cultural view of human nature. As he wrote, "this conceptual structure falters, I believe, on two related, but separable, theses, both of which are (I believe) untenable. These are: (1) culture is the exclusive determinant of personality; and (2) personality consists exclusively of the internalization of culture".[83]

He in fact thought that the determinist cultural theories of behaviour and personality were developed in the first place as alternatives to and refutations of biological determinism. He considered that the invalid conclusion about the lack of any invariant pancultural psychological characteristics was based on three errors: that of believing that the intercultural variability of social behaviour and personality implies that the organism is a black or empty box; that of confusing "culture" and "a culture" in the expression "cultural determinism"; that of the non-distinction between the "phenotypical" and the "genotypical", or between an "obvious, evident structure" and a "latent, deep structure".

As opposed to "particularist" cultural determinism, he therefore defended a "generic" cultural determinism and argued for the existence of transcultural characteristics of the human mind. Thus, human feelings and the manner in which they function are determined, not so much by the characteristics of the particularist cultural patterns as by the transcultural characteristics of a generic human mind. However, the fact that these characteristics are in turn to a large extent determined by the transcultural characteristics of a set of universal patterns was "axiomatic" for him. This generic cultural determinism, which is based on certain hypotheses about the universality of human social and biological characteristics, their symbolic expressions, and their cultural transformations, is very different from the particularist cultural determinism of Benedict's relativist school, for example. He in fact considered the process of enculturation to be a process by which a new-born child learns to be an Iflaluk, an American, a Burmese, thus learning to be radically different from the others. However, generic cultural determinism considers enculturation first of all as a process of humanisation, meaning a process by which, by being an Iflaluk, the new-born child is also transformed from a mammal into a human being. To the extent that it is culture that makes us human and that an "enculturated" American or Burmese is also human, the deep structural similarities of their cultures, and of all the other cultures, comprise a set of universal cultural patterns which, in interaction with a common biological heritage and common traits of social interaction, create a generic human mind. To sum up, despite the differences of structures apparent in their cultures, the minds of all human beings function in accordance with the same principles. This is the psychic unity of mankind.

Of course, but what about the specific participation of the psyche because this discourse assumes that, though universal, the human mind is exclusively the product of biological inheritance and culture, therefore denying any existence prior to the human psyche.

Culture constructs reality and all science would be ethnoscience (like psychoanalysis, western ethnoscience) according to the relativist school. Viewing anthropology as "the study of human beings" would have been replaced by that of contemporary anthropology to become "the study of humans" – the two characteristics of diversity and relativity of the cultures having become its hallmark – something which hinders any attempt to uncover intercultural patterns and to formulate explanatory theories. This would therefore be tantamount to challenging anthropology's status as a "science".

The Œdipus complex

In earlier writings, Spiro had endeavoured to attain two separate, but related, objectives: the first was to show the great weakness of the empirical foundation of Malinowski's empirical theory enabling him to argue for the existence of a matrilineal complex in the Trobriand people; the second consisted in showing the existence of proofs indicating, on the contrary, the presence of a particularly marked Œdipus complex among the Trobriands. What then is the impact of these discoveries for human societies in general?

Almost all anthropologists, representing the full range of anthropological thought, accept the conclusion of the existence of a "panhuman motivational disposition" to incest as a highly probable hypothesis,[84] despite its opponents in agreement with Westermarck, for whom sexual indifference or aversion, rather than attraction, develops between any persons (including family members) living in proximity to each other from an early age. Since this aversion develops naturally, it would account for the relative rarity of incestuous behaviour. Moreover, the incestuous dimension of the Œdipus complex renders its aggressive dimension, that directed against the paternal rival for love of the mother, all but "axiomatic", Spiro considers. For him, "the only appropriate response to the question, 'is the Œdipus complex universal?' is 'How could it possibly not be?'"[85] He considered that if "there were a human society in which mothers did not have male consorts – so that the son had no adult rival for the love of the mother – in such a society, the Œdipus complex (by definition) would not exist. So far as we know, however, no human society of that type exists, or has ever existed".[86] He mentioned even the findings of Kathleen Gough (1953)[87] among the Nayar, an Indian caste of the Malabar Coast, who argued for the existence of an Œdipus complex despite the fact that these women typically take a series of lovers rather than living with a permanent consort. What would he say about the Na of China?

Nonetheless, according to him, asserting the universality of the Œdipus complex does not imply that it is interculturally uniform but assumes variability between societies, therefore, intercultural variability on the basis of ethnographic data. He then envisaged demonstrating this thesis on the basis of his detection of the existence of three important dimensions of the complex: its structure, its intensity, and its consequences.

By structure, he means members forming an oedipal triangle, objects of the boy's aggressive and sexual desires. These are not necessarily his biological parents. The variability of kinship systems would consequently imply corresponding, expectable variability in the structure of the oedipal triangle:

> If, then, there is no theoretical reason why the adult members of the Oedipal triangle must consist of the boy's biological mother and father, it might well be the case that in some society this triangle consists of the boy, his sister, and his mother's brother. Malinowski's claim that this is the case in the Trobriands was rejected not on theoretical, but on empirical grounds: neither the composition of the Trobriand household nor the social relationships that obtain within the nuclear family display the characteristics that might expectably produce that particular structural variant of the classical Oedipal triangle. For exactly the same reason, neither this nor any structural variant of the classical Œdipus triangle has been reported at a total societal level for any other society, which does not mean that such a variant or variants may not occur in individual cases or in certain subgroups in some societies, or that some variant may not be reported in the future for some (as yet unknown) total society.[88]

However, its intensity and consequences exhibit intercultural variability that is not simply a matter of theoretical expectation, but is an ethnographic reality. With Spiro, let us look at the variability of the "fates" of the complex, which has important socio-cultural consequences, they too variable. They can variously take the form of extinction, repression, or incomplete repression.

Spiro considered that the differences in socio-cultural consequences are particularly marked when we compare societies in which extinction and repression are dominant outcomes with those in which incomplete repression prevails. He writes,

> Hence, those societies in which incomplete repression is the dominant outcome of the Œdipus complex are societies in which the implementation of the taboos on mother–son incest and father–son aggression by the enculturation and socialization techniques... is not entirely successful in achieving their internalization. This being the case, rather than relying on the boy's own psychological resources – extinction, repression and reaction formation – to ensure compliance with those taboos, many of those societies achieve compliance by means of socio-cultural resources, as well.[89]

Which ones are they? It is principally a matter of the practice of child extrusion and painful initiation rites. "These customs", Spiro writes, "ensure compliance with the twin Oedipal prohibitions by reducing the opportunities for incestuous and aggressive temptation or by strengthening the incomplete repression of the boy's sexual and aggressive Oedipal wishes".[90]

The extrusion of children from the parental home leads them to be moved into an age-graded dormitory, a men's house or a children's village, for example.

Achieving the same goal, the initiation rites consist of different practices, varying from culture to culture, such as hazing, isolation, physical torture, ordeals, or sexual mutilations (circumcision, subincision, for example). As Spiro explains,

> these rites arouse in the boys intense fear and anxiety – often, in my view, castration anxiety – regarding the father and or the father-figure initiators..., thereby serving to break the boys' incestuous attachment to their mothers... and inhibit their aggression to their fathers... That these painful and often brutal rites also provide a culturally sanctioned (and ritually limited) opportunity for men to express their complementary Oedipal hostility to boys – rationalized, of course, by the ideology of helping them achieve socio-cultural maturity – seems equally obvious, as Reik suggested some years ago... Indeed, from these descriptions I would argue that societies which practice initiation rites of the ferocity found in – and perhaps confined to – New Guinea and Australia are societies in which the incomplete repression of the childhood Œdipus complex is most pronounced.[91]

Among the other sociocultural consequences accompanying the variability of the outcome of the Œdipus complex, Spiro mentioned the societies within which the oedipal conflicts require repression and permanent counter-investment, the complex possibly then undergoing structural transformations as a result of defensive displacements and projections significantly affecting other relationships and social institutions. He refers to Jones' contention that the boy's hostility towards his maternal uncle in Trobriand society would be a defensive displacement of his oedipal hostility for his father. The same would be the case among the Nayar. But, he also observed displacements, projective movements – associated with a symbolic expression of repressed oedipal conflicts – regarding the political, economic, and religious institutions. So, he considered that "the continuing debates over the Œdipus complex are debates not merely about a passing episode in the psychological development of the child. Rather, they are debates about a psychological constellation which, as this discussion has attempted to show, has pervasive cultural, social, and psychological consequences".[92]

Let us now look at what Spiro called "the making of a scientific myth"[93] out of certain claims made by Malinowski to which anthropologists as a whole have uncritically subscribed.

Indeed, the very heart of Malinowski's claim that the structure of the nuclear complex (as he preferred to call it) is culturally variable, not only in principle, but also in fact, consists in claiming that, although the biological mother is the principal mothering figure in the Trobriands, it is the sister who is the main object of the boy's libidinal desires. Yet, this paradoxical affirmation was refuted by Malinowski's own proofs. He had argued that "just as the strong incestuous desire for the sister in the Trobriands is reflected in the 'strong' brother–sister taboo, the weak desire for the mother is reflected in the 'weak' mother–son taboo".[94] Unfortunately, he did not have any ethnographic evidence for the "putative" weakness of the mother–son taboo. For Spiro, this anomaly regarding the reported absence of an incestuous attachment to the mother remaining unresolved was reason enough for scepticism:

> That this report, then, has not received the skeptical reception that normally greets an anomalous scientific report is not only... a remarkable fact, but one which itself constitutes an intriguing intellectual problem: Since its solution could shed important light on the influence of scientific paradigms on the acceptance and persistence of scientific ideas, it is to be hoped that an investigation of the problem might some day be undertaken by an intellectual historian or a historian of science. Although the causes for the unskeptical reaction to this anomalous report are still to be discovered, its consequence – with some notable exceptions – has been an uncritical acceptance of the putative Trobriand matrilineal complex. I would suggest, then, that if this report had been subjected to the probing scrutiny to which anomalous scientific findings are usually subject, the matrilineal complex would have been rejected as empirically unsupported rather than achieving the status of an incontrovertible finding of anthropological science. Nevertheless, it is not its weak empirical foundation that led me to characterise the Trobriand matrilineal complex a "scientific myth". This characterization stems, rather, from the uncritical acceptance of the reported finding – the absence of an incestuous attachment to the mother – on which its plausibility hangs, despite the fact that this finding is not only once, but twice, anomalous. A myth, Malinowski taught us, enjoys uncritical acceptance because it serves important functions for those who believe it to be true. It would be well, therefore,

> if our hoped-for historian were to address yet another question in the course of his investigations: what functions might have been served by the acceptance of this myth? Indeed, since the role of the "will to believe" in the acceptance of scientific ideas is as prominent as the role that William James attributed to it in the acceptance of religious doctrines, it is entirely possible that the answer to this second question might simultaneously provide the answer to the first.[95]

Spiro's inquiry into the determinants of this scientific myth is particularly pertinent, especially as regards certain characteristics of the history of knowledge and the numerous issues at stake in it. Moreover, despite the interesting analysis of the Œdipus complex, it is curious to note that, though inspired by Freud, he does not envisage the existence of the negative side of the Œdipus complex, therefore its complete form, just as he omits the girl's Œdipus complex. Unfortunately, this observation cannot be expanded upon here.

I have now arrived at the end of my presentation of some themes of reflexion and research developed by this American anthropologist at the meeting point of Kardiner's school and Freud-inspired anthropology. Having chosen certain topics enabling one to discover his thought and modes of expression, as well as his broad, fruitful contribution to the psychoanalysis/anthropology debate, I have had to give up examining other areas of his research, such as his reflexion on the problem of conforming to cultural norms and the notion of "moral anxiety", or his criticism of symbolic and structuralist anthropology eliminating any sexual and aggressive themes (cf. Lévi-Strauss and Mary Douglas).

Gananath Obeyesekere

An anthropologist of American and Sri Lankan descent, one of the major representatives of psychoanalytical anthropology in the United States, Gananath Obeyesekere studied anthropology at the University of Washington. In 1956, he studied "culture and personality" under Melville Jacobs, who encouraged him to read and discover more of Freud's work. During those years, he decided also to take a course in psychiatry given by Professor Gert Heilbrunn at the Medical School. A little later, he met Melford Spiro who had joined the faculty at the same University. This anthropologist taught him much about psychoanalytical anthropology and, moreover, became a faithful friend. In 1964, he obtained his Ph.D. in anthropology. From 1968 to 1972, he was a professor and chairman of the Sociology Department of the University of Sri Lanka. From 1972 to 1980, he taught anthropology at the University of California, San Diego. Then from 1980 to 2000, he taught at Princeton University, while also serving as the chairman of its Anthropology Department from 1983 to 1988. He has been Professor Emeritus since the year 2000. During his rich scholarly and academic life, he has received many awards for his abundant research work in Sri Lanka and South Asia, on Buddhism and Hinduism.

Among his important works may be cited *Land Tenure in Village Ceylon: A Sociological and Historical Study* (1967), which is indirectly a return to his roots in Sri Lanka, since it is the study of a village similar to the one in which he was born and which he left when he was about four years old to live in Colombo. This "monograph" is to a great extent influenced by British social anthropology, and particularly by the work of Edmund Leach, one of its illustrious figures, whom, moreover, he would meet at Cambridge University in 1964. Other works include: *Medusa's Hair: An Essay on Personal Symbols and Religious Experience* (1981); *The Cult of the Goddess Pattini* (1984); *The Work of Culture* (1990); *Imagining Karma: Ethical Transformation in Amerindian, Buddhist and Greek Rebirth* (2002); *The Awakened Ones: An Essay on the Phenomenology of the Visionary Experience* (2008).

Among those who had inspired, stimulated, and nourished his thought in a major way, Obeyesekere mentioned the anthropologists Spiro and Leach, Freud, obviously, and the philosophers Paul Ricœur and Ludwig Wittgenstein. He does not share the "naturalist" conception of psychoanalysis adhered to by Spiro and defends instead a hermeneutic "Diltheyan" conception of the nature of the human sciences, including psychoanalysis. In spite of his admiration for Leach, he rejects his structuralism in favour of a subject-centred anthropological orientation giving priority to content over form. Ricœur's work helped him to realise a hermeneutic "reorientation" of Freudian psychoanalysis and Wittgenstein's work encouraged a certain relativism in his anthropological thought. I shall return to this at a later point.

He has especially reproached Kardiner for having established a "positivist tradition" in psychoanalytical anthropology, for having transformed psychoanalysis into "positive" sociology, and for having analysed symbolic forms in accordance with the psychopathological model, turning his colleagues among the culturalist anthropologists against him.

Let us look at one of his major works, *The Work of Culture, Symbolic Transformation in Psychoanalysis and Anthropology*.

In his preface, Obeyesekere describes the book as "a product of considerable rethinking" of the Lewis Henry Morgan lectures that he had delivered at the University of Rochester in March 1982[96] about the study of the relation between culture and deep motivation through symbolic forms and their processes of symbolisation. The notion of the "work of culture" found in Freud's work unifies the book, which tackles diverse themes, among them, rituals, myths, history, and the Œdipus complex, but also a critical reflexion on Freudian metapsychology and the divergences and convergences between anthropology and psychoanalysis.

Among the notions studied in this presentation of his thought are: "deep motivation"; "the work of culture"; "family resemblance"; "forms of life"; the metaphor of the "muddy bottom"; the idea of "symbolic remove and levels of symbolisation".

Freudian thought and anthropology

It was psychoanalysis that permitted Obeyesekere to understand the interrelationship between deep motivation and culture. Unlike most anthropologists who label

Freudian theory dogmatic, he considers that Freud constantly revised his metapsychology. Moreover, he reproaches Freud for his inability to consider human beings within their historical and socio-cultural context and encompassed by social institutions.[97] Among the points of Freud's metapsychology that Obeyesekere criticises figure the second topography of the psychic apparatus, his theory of drives, and the problem of the clinical, pathological model. He also deals with the interest of psychoanalysis and its two models – represented for him by the interpretation of dreams and the major clinical cases – for the practice of psycho-ethnography, or even just ethnography.

Ricœur's hermeneutic interpretation of Freud suggested to Obeyesekere "a way of breaking out" of the clinical pathological model for the study of culture, art, literature, and religion, for example. As dialectic movements, the notions of regression and of progression (the latter implicit in the theory of sublimation) can find expression in phenomena such as dreams and phantasies, and also help to understand the cultural products arising out of complex symbolic transformations of infantile unconscious motivations.[98]

According to him, the evolution of Freudian metapsychology had taken place through a misalliance between his theory of instincts and a theory of motivation based on ideas and emotions belonging to human relationships. He considers that the "trouble with Freud is that he felt obliged to develop the traditional *assumption* about drives into a theory, and later into an ontology, without the proper biological foundation on which to erect such a metapsychological edifice". However, he finds it "hard to reject the existence of drives" because the "theoretical edifice of psychoanalysis will collapse if it can be shown that human beings do not possess drives such as sexuality, elimination, dependency, aggression, and so forth, however they may be derived". It therefore seems to him that psychoanalysis "must assume the existence of drives (primary and secondary), but one must bracket them for the time being, till we know more about them from biology, academic psychology, and other sciences that might want to study them". He questions Freud's having inferred the existence of an aggression drive as being something as innate as sexuality from his observations of the human condition, rather than from experimental work in biology.[99]

This is why Obeyesekere considers Freudian metapsychology to be shaky, because it is based on this theory of drives. Moreover, he considers the theory of motivation to be more useful, but that it cannot exist without the theory of drives. He concludes these reflexions by rejecting propositions and speculations on the theory of drives presented both in *Instincts and Their Vicissitudes* and in *Beyond the Pleasure Principle*.[100] For him, this theory of drives is, therefore, the object of particular ambivalence, something which helps us understand his project of a hermeneutic "reorientation" of Freudian theory. It seems that he cannot accept the idea of the existence of an instinctual life as the foundation of unconscious psychic life.

What about the second topography?

Obeyesekere favours and accords major, primordial value to the first topography which, he sees as containing "concepts and ideas that are not too tied to European thought and hence could be employed to study cultures that place a premium on unconscious processes", while "the second topography of ego-id-superego is at best of limited value in the study of other cultures, since it locks us into a compartmentalist view of the mind" and into real Cartesianism characterised by the centrality of the ego and that of the consciousness in Descartes that Freud had initially broken away from by giving priority to the unconscious over consciousness.[101] He believes that the "second topography was a transformation of the first, but now articulated to a Judaeo-Protestant conscience", that both the superego and the id had been structured in terms of "a Judaeo-Protestant conscience". Obeyesekere refers to his fieldwork in South Asia where he had been able to observe that where there is "a greater back-and-forth movement among the three structural components of the mind, the contents of the id can be transformed, through the work of culture, into personal symbols or collective representations". In the case of personal symbols, he proposes an Asian reformulation of Freud's celebrated formula from "where id was, there shall ego be" to "where ego is, there shall id be." [102]

After these various criticisms, Obeyesekere questions the usefulness of Freudian "metatheory" in psychoethnography, asking whether this metatheory can "be reconciled with a key objective of any ethnography, which is to describe and render intelligible an alien life world".[103]

On the one hand, he hypothesises that Freudian case history can be used for groups because it "belongs to the same genre as the ethnography: it combines description and analysis; it is historical; it shuns operationalism for contextualization; . . .it expresses reality but can never replicate it".[104] On the other hand, the method of interpretation of dreams can be applied to ethnography. He writes that in fact the "dream text is the descriptive account of the dream . . . the description is followed by an interpretation that renders the text intelligible in terms of the dreamer's deep motivation . . . this model can easily be applied to ethnography (and not just to psychoethnography). One could have a thick description . . . followed by an interpretation based on a set of metatheorical rules, if one recognises that the description itself is influenced by these rules".[105]

The Œdipus complex

In rethinking the Œdipus complex among the Trobriands, Obeyesekere does not adhere to Malinowski's thesis, but calls the matrilineal Œdipus' or matrilineal complex's "objectified" "nuclear family complex" a different form of the Œdipus complex. This Trobriand complex would not, however, be a variant of the nuclear Œdipus complex.

Using mythological and clinical data, he presents the Hindu Indian Œdipus complex and the Buddhist Sri Lankan Œdipus complex in boys.

According to him, the family relationships underlying the Indian Œdipus complex are characterised by a powerful, symbiotic, mother–son bond combined with an erotic component, while the father–son relationship is marked by the father's jealousy and authority and the son's loyalty. The oedipal crisis is resolved by the son's identification with his mother, which mobilises the female component of his bisexuality, and by submission to the father.

The paradigmatic myth of this Hindu Œdipus seems to him to be that of Ganesa. The myths recount both the mother's erotic feelings and the incestuous relationship with her son and her domination over him. Moreover, these myths and popular tales emphasise filicide, the sons being killed, mutilated, castrated (symbolically or really) by the father. There is therefore no parricide. The son's attempts to possess his mother and take the place of his father are totally abnormal and reprehensible. Any thought of that kind would lead to reprisals by the father, as in the myth of the emasculation of Indra or Siva's decapitation by Ganesa.

For Obeyesekere, this oedipal configuration different from that of the western model raises questions regarding the existence of a universal Œdipus complex. Would this Indian complex be a transformation of the western Œdipus complex? He in fact considers that the Indian son has been born into a family system in which the relationships are culturally predetermined, and within this context, the Œdipus complex will be structured in terms of these family relationships, rather than in accordance with the western model, which does not exist there. Consequently, the development of the Indian Œdipus complex as a psychic structure and mythic model must necessarily take a different form from that of the western model.

The typical form of the complex in Sri Lanka is characterised by the brother's incestuous desires for the sister and by parricidal wishes. The myth of Sinhabáhu is the paradigmatic myth of the Sri Lankan Œdipus complex. The son kills his father and marries his sister, desired mythologically as a sexual object.

Concerning the father–son relationship, Obeyesekere therefore detects a fundamental difference between Hinduism and Buddhism. The Sri Lankan Buddhist glorifies the son who kills his father, while the Indian Hindu glorifies the son who submits to his father, the predominant model, among other rarer ones. Moreover, he reminds us of the impact and importance of Buddhist and Brahman values on the formation of the Œdipus complex and its mythical representations.

On the basis of these data, he invites readers to engage in a completely personal reflexion contesting any universality of oedipal myths and complexes in the sense of the existence of an invariant structure or model, contrary to the ideas of his colleague Spiro. They should, however, show us "family resemblances", a term inspired by Wittgenstein's relativism enabling him to escape from the constraining universalist perspective of the Freudian conception.

Indeed, adding homosexuality and the sibling complex to the complete form of the Œdipus complex, he says,

> what we have is id, in my phrase, "an erotically desirable circle of familial kin." Within this circle each culture (or some cultures) isolate in their fantasy lives a group of kin that are significant for the neuroses. These are the "Oedipal" kin; and the complex that emerges in the psychosexual development of the child is the "Œdipus complex." This complex can be represented at different degrees of remove in culturally significant Oedipal *myths*.[106]

Obeyesekere moreover considers that "the Œdipus complex is a 'fictitious term' constructed on the basis of circular reasoning".[107] Finally, he sees the western Œdipus complex as representing a "form of life", one "scenario" among many others exhibiting "family resemblances" within or through cultures, all "derived as forms of life from the identical universal muddy bottom".[108] This is a metaphor symbolising our common human nature, with its basic human behaviours and its "existential" universals and, according to Obeyesekere, the ground of our human nature is psychobiological.[109] We shall learn more about this from the work of the different specialists involved which anthropologists will then be able to reflect upon and use. He believes that this perspective "liberates us from a straightjacket of a single, universalist Œdipus complex into a more humane and richer view of other life worlds", but he confesses that he does not know whether the "fiction" he has created is any truer than Freud's.[110] Finally, he considers that "it is impossible to infer a universal (and uniform) Œdipus complex on the basis of a universal form of a human family life, as it is to infer a universal family model from a common human nature".[111] There are at best "family resemblances".

This conception of the Œdipus complex displays obvious relativist aspects. In certain respects, it gives us the impression of finding the "nuclear family complex" specific to a given society, as maintained by Malinowski. Obeyesekere seems to favour the cultural structuration of family relations constituting the bases of multiple oedipal scenarios exhibiting "family resemblances" among themselves, the whole resting upon the "muddy bottom" or psychobiological human ground.

The notion of "work of culture"

In order to think through, and make intelligible, certain aspects of the relations between culture and unconscious deep motivation, Obeyesekere resorts to the notion of "work of culture" inspired by Freud and the notion of "work of art" proposed by Ricœur.[112] He is also influenced by Ricœur's theory of symbols, in that it provides rules for interpretation, psychoanalysis is a hermeneutical system.[113] As the point of departure of his discussion of relations between symbols and deep motivations, he posits the existence of the "two movements of meaning in relation to the sources of motivation – that of progression and of regression, which in turn may appear separately in different symbolic forms or dialectically within the same form".[114] So, he considers it necessary to develop Ricœur's idea in terms of a psychoanalytical anthropology, whose basic problem would be the manner in which unconscious motivations are transformed into symbolic forms, be they personal symbols, myths or collective representations. Thus, a pre-established cultural system of symbols would enable individuals to express and control their psychic unconscious conflicts of infantile origin. The symbols employed would be intelligible to members of the society within that specific cultural context. The term "work of culture" designates this set of processes of symbolic transformations of unconscious motivations into cultural symbols that are bearers of meaning for the individual, involving both the person and the culture. In other words, if the ideational representations are "primary objectifications" of unconscious processes, we have to describe or identify the mechanisms at work in the more complex "objectifications", at a higher level, which are carried into relations between the unconscious processes and the culturally constituted symbolic forms. Obeyesekere introduced the parallel notions of "*levels of symbolic remove* from deep motivations" producing "different *levels of symbolization*", some closer to, some more distant from the motivations that initially (psychogenetically) triggered the symbolic formation". He said that he uses levels of symbolic remove "because *all* cultural symbols are *removed* from their motivational springs", unlike a neurotic symptom which would be, "more or less, a direct precipitate of the motive".[115]

Obeyeskere realises that there are situations in which it is impossible to "draw a fine line" between symptom and symbol, but considers that

> the idea of symbolic remove and levels of symbolization resolves this difficulty by recognizing that some symbolic forms are closer to, or isomorphic with, symptoms while others are far removed from them; whereas for Freud, as well as for those anthropologists who deal with cultural defenses and projective systems, there was indeed an isomorphism, if not a simple replication, of symbol and symptom.[116]

Since these symbolic forms are essentially constituted of images, they display an "ontological" affinity with unconscious formations such as dreams. Nonetheless, Obeyesekere wants to make it clear that, these forms "are not themselves unconscious phenomena, they exist in the consciousness, yet they connect with the unconscious processes . . . Both personal symbols and collective representations are, however, cultural products, and consequently they are embodied in language, in which one talks about them, and in myth, which contains stories about them".[117]

The model of this "work of culture" would be dream work, with its processes of the transformation of the unconscious motivations of childhood into images and dream symbols. The dream is then conceived of as "a symbolic set". "But", Obeyesekere explains,

> dreams are not culture, though they may be the stuff from which some types of cultural forms are psychogenetically derived. Culture is a symbolic order far removed cognitively, ontologically, and ontically from dreams. A psychoanalytic study of cultural forms must move from the dream work to more complex processes that can help us comprehend these more complex forms. One must move from the work of dreams into what, following Freud himself, I call "*the work of culture*".[118]

As an example, he gives South Asia, where he was able to observe greater tolerance of phantasy and of the primary process, as well as greater "fluidity of the barrier separating the three structural components of the mind". He considers that this much greater tolerance permits "the transformation of fantasy into culture, the constant invention, creation and re-creation of personal and collective symbols that permeate the life of the individual and the society".[119]

This question of the processes of symbolic transformations from deep motivations is reminiscent of Juillerat's concern about the mediations between originary phantasies and cultural representations. He too used the expression "work of culture". Recent research has led me to see his conception of "work of culture" as representing one aspect of what is covered by the notion of *Kulturarbeit* in Freud's work.

Unlike his many colleagues, Obeyesekere displays profound knowledge of Freudian thought and the critical attitude he takes is stimulating and constructive. In addition, the remarkable depth of his reflexion – nourished by philosophers, notably – combines with a rich experience of the Asian and eastern worlds. The avenues of research that he endeavours to explore – that of symbolic transformations from deep motivations, the notion of "work of culture" to account for this, its connection with dream work as a model – are particularly attractive and subtle and raise questions having definite heuristic value. Nonetheless, it is interesting to note that by using the term "work", on the model of "dream work", he reduces it to rules and processes without inquiring into its correlative energising, economic, dynamic dimension. Meaning must certainly take precedence over energisation, but the processes and symbolic transformations cannot take place without expending energy. This is something that "witch metapsychology" has also taught us.

Notes

1 Maurice Godelier, *The Metamorphoses of Kinship*, London, Verso, 2011 (2004), p. 319.
2 *Ibid.*, p. 323.
3 *Ibid.*, p. 391.
4 *Ibid.*, p. 397.
5 *Ibid.*, p. 399.
6 *Ibid.* The square brackets appear in the original (Translator's note).
7 *Ibid.*, p. 400.
8 *Ibid.*, pp. 450–451, 468–473.
9 *Ibid.*, p. 474.
10 *Ibid.*, p. 475.
11 *Ibid.*, p. 496.
12 *Ibid.*, pp. 305–307.
13 *Ibid.*, p. 306.
14 *Ibid.*, p. 314. The italics appear in the original. (Translator's note).
15 *Ibid.*, p. 305.
16 Bernard Juillerat, *Children of the Blood. Society, Reproduction and Cosmology in New Guinea*, London, Bloomsbury Publishing, 1997 (1986).
17 Bernard Juillerat, *Oedipe chasseur. Une mythologie du sujet en Nouvelle-Guinée*, Paris, Presses Universitaires de France, 1991, p. 40.
18 *Ibid.*, p. 55.
19 *Ibid.*, p. 220.
20 *Ibid.*, p. 242
21 *Ibid.*, p. 245.
22 *Ibid.*, p. 245.
23 *Ibid.*, p. 229.

24 Bernard Juillerat, "Des fantasmes originaires aux symboles culturels: médiations et seuils" (1993), in *Penser l'imaginaire*, Paris, Payot, 2001.
25 *Ibid.*, pp. 69–70.
26 Didier Anzieu, *The Group and the Unconscious*. London, Routledge, 1984. Originally published as *Le groupe et l'inconscient*, Paris, Dunod, 1975. The page references are to the original French edition.
27 *Op. cit.*, Anzieu, "Freud et la mythologie", p. 144.
28 *Ibid.*, p. 119.
29 *Ibid.*, p. 124.
30 *Ibid.*, p. 137.
31 *Ibid.*, p. 136.
32 *Ibid.*, pp. 136–137.
33 *Ibid.*, p. 140.
34 *Ibid.*, p. 144.
35 *Op. cit.*, Anzieu, *Le groupe et l'inconscient*, pp. 40–41.
36 *Ibid.*, p. 200.
37 *Ibid.*
38 André Missenard, "Identification et processus groupal", in D. Anzieu, A. Béjarano, A. Missenard, and J.-B. Pontalis, *Le travail psychanalytique dans les groupes*, Tome 1, Paris, Dunod, 1972.
39 Didier Anzieu, "Le moi-peau", *Nouvelle Revue de Psychanalyse*, No 9, pp. 195–208, 1974.
40 René Kaës, *Un singulier pluriel*, Paris, Dunod, 2007, p. 38.
41 *Ibid.*
42 *Ibid.*, pp. 105–106.
43 *Ibid.*, pp. 120–121.
44 *Ibid.*, p. 123.
45 *Ibid.*, p. 192.
46 *Ibid.*, p. 219.
47 François Duparc, *André Green*, Paris, Presses Universitaires de France, 1996, p. 18.
48 *Ibid.*, p. 19.
49 André Green, "Inceste et parricide en anthropologie and en psychanalyse", in P. Descola, J. Hamel & P. Lemonnier (eds.), *La Production du social. Autour de Maurice Godelier, Colloque de Cérisy*, Paris, Fayard, 1999, p. 215.
50 *Ibid.*, p. 217.
51 *Ibid.*
52 *Ibid.*, p. 218.
53 *Ibid.*, p. 219.
54 *Ibid.*
55 André Green, "Oedipe, Freud et nous", *La Déliaison*, Paris, Belles Lettres, 1992, pp. 145–46.
56 André Green, *La Causalité psychique*, Paris, Odile Jacob, 1995, p. 115.
57 *Ibid.*, p. 117.
58 *Ibid.*, p. 119.
59 *Ibid.*, p. 262.
60 *Ibid.*, p. 134.
61 André Green, "Le mythe: un objet transitionnel collectif", *La Déliaison*, Paris, Belles lettres, 1992, p. 148.
62 *Ibid.*
63 *Ibid.*, p. 155.
64 *Ibid.*, pp. 168–169.
65 *Ibid.*, pp. 174–175.
66 *Ibid.*, p. 177.
67 *Ibid.*, p. 179.
68 *Op cit.*, Green, *La Causalité psychique*, p. 126.

69 *Ibid.*, p. 127.
70 *Ibid.*, pp. 182–183.
71 *Ibid.*, pp. 189–190.
72 *Ibid.*, p. 240.
73 *Ibid.*, p. 153.
74 *Ibid.*, p. 153.
75 *Ibid.*, pp. 168–169.
76 *Ibid.*, p. 206.
77 *Op. cit.*, Green, "Inceste et parricide en anthropologie et en psychanalyse", p. 222.
78 *Ibid.*, p. 223.
79 *Ibid.*, p. 226.
80 Melford Spiro, *Culture and Human Nature*, New Brunswick, NJ, Transaction Publishers, 1994, pp. 3–4.
81 *Ibid.*, p. 8.
82 *Ibid.*
83 *Ibid.*, pp. 22–23.
84 *Ibid.*, p. 75.
85 *Ibid.*, pp. 87–88.
86 *Ibid.*, p. 88.
87 Kathleen Gough, *The Traditional Kinship System of the Nayars of Malabar*, Cambridge, MA, Harvard University, 1954.
88 *Ibid.*, p. 89.
89 *Ibid.*, p. 92.
90 *Ibid.*
91 *Ibid.*, pp. 93–94
92 *Ibid.*, pp. 97–98.
93 *Ibid.*, p. 98.
94 *Ibid.*, p. 102.
95 *Ibid.*, pp. 102–103.
96 Gananath Obeyesekere, *The Work of Culture, Symbolic Transformation in Psychoanalysis and Anthropology*, Chicago, IL, University of Chicago Press, 1990, p. xvii.
97 *Ibid.*, p. 249.
98 *Ibid.*, p. xviii.
99 *Ibid.*, p. 249.
100 *Ibid.*
101 *Ibid.*, p. xx.
102 *Ibid.*, p. 252.
103 *Ibid.*, p. 256.
104 *Ibid.*, p. 271.
105 *Ibid.*, p. 266.
106 *Ibid.*, p. 88.
107 *Ibid.*, p. 94.
108 *Ibid.*
109 *Ibid.*, p. 101.
110 *Ibid.*, p. xxi.
111 *Ibid.*, p. 95.
112 *Ibid.*, p. 16.
113 *Ibid.*, p. 52.
114 *Ibid.*, p. 53.
115 *Ibid.*, p. 57.
116 *Ibid.*
117 *Ibid.*, p. 282.
118 *Ibid.*, p. 55.
119 *Ibid.*, p. 64.

4

GENERAL DISCUSSION

Remarks and commentary

What, and how, is one to think about this conflictual history?

This history especially poses the problem of the relations between two disciplines, one of which feels attacked, intruded upon in its own territory, and so reacts defensively in a variety of ways. The Œdipus complex – and through it the methodological and theoretical corpus of psychoanalysis – would be the agent of contamination and aggression.

The historical debate

Let us recall, on the one hand, that Rivers and Seligman themselves discovered psychoanalysis by reading *Studies on Hysteria* and *The Interpretation of Dreams* during the years 1916–1917, and, on the other hand, that Seligman was the first anthropologist to question the universality of the Œdipus complex, then asking his student Malinowski to go and test the validity of Freud's thesis among the Trobriands, in a matrilineal society.

Nonetheless, it was Malinowski who laid claim to being the one who elaborated the form and content conferred on this debate, which have since become paradigmatic for anthropology and the community of anthropologists in general.

He in fact took an ethnographical approach to the Œdipus complex based on phenomenological observation, and went about "reducing" the complex by only taking into account that of the boy in its positive, exclusively direct form, therefore scotomising that of the girl and its negative, inversed form. Moreover, he considered that the relationship of rivalry between the son and the father was based on the latter's authority and not on the fact that he was the possessor of the mother's body and the only one enjoying access to it. It is to be stressed that, in contrast to the more nuanced position adopted by contemporary anthropologists, this mode of understanding and exemplary distortion of the issues were adopted by the international anthropological community during that historical period of the debate.

Then, Malinowski transformed this "reduced" form into a "bio-behavioural" complex inspired by the work of the psychologist Alexander Shand, subject then to the influence of social factors. Consequently, he "biologised" the Œdipus complex, interpreted as being an attribute of "human nature", then "relativized" it and established it as a "nuclear family complex" subject to and determined by the family organisation characteristic of a given society. So, according to him, Freud was to have had the great merit of discovering the nuclear family complex of patriarchal societies, while he himself had discovered that of matrilineal societies! Furthermore, he discovered the fundamental correlation between the nuclear complex and the type of family structure linked to a specific social organisation – that is, its socio-cultural relativity.

His ethnographic authority enabled him to impose his relativist thesis, which anthropologists would appropriate for multiple reasons, transforming along the way the Œdipus complex, a "bio-behavioural" complex, attribute of human nature, into a normal "social formation" (in Kroeber, Kardiner, and even Lacan) or a pathological one (in Mead, Horney).

Thus Malinowski answered the question of his mentor Seligman and in so doing invalidated the Freudian thesis of the universality of the Œdipus complex. He also discovered and instituted cultural relativism. From that point on, the identity of each of the two disciplines was established and would be characterised by certain lasting traits over the course of this debate.

Through the Œdipus complex, psychoanalysis presented a biological dimension, with its exploration of the diverse aspects of "human nature", whose universality it claimed. In addition, representing all of psychoanalysis in the eyes of the anthropologists, the biologism of the Freudian theory did not take into account sociocultural factors – that is, it ignored the discoveries, writings, interests, and contributions of anthropologists and sociologists to the enrichment of human knowledge. Psychoanalysis therefore imposed its central thesis of the universality of "human nature" upon anthropologists, and in so doing asserted its epistemological identity.

As for anthropology, then in a critical period of its development, it built a new identity for itself, on the one hand, by the establishment of the model of "ethnographical authority", and, on the other hand, by discovering and demonstrating the determining importance of the socio-cultural factors influencing and shaping "human nature". As a consequence, it imposed a new idea of societies and human cultures, that of cultural diversity, singularity, and relativity, which did not become simply a dogma, but also the new and lasting distinctive feature of this discipline. This new reading and translation–interpretation of cultures would be shared and developed by both European and American anthropology and also adopted by the psychoanalysts Fromm and Horney.

A historical explanation is necessary in order to understand this change and the nascent socio-anthropological relativism's need to make claims and assert itself. It was a matter of distancing itself from the initial theoretical approach in the history of this discipline – namely, evolutionism, defender of the thesis of the unity of the human mind on the basis of the readings and speculations of "armchair" researchers. Certain aspects of psychoanalysis seemed too reminiscent of this way of thinking, which had become a totalitarian ideology, that is, the view that the unity of the human mind and human history is inexorably uniform. Thus, the pioneering institution of controlled field-work, that is, of direct observation by trained and specialised research workers would from then on underpin the new sovereign ideology of cultural relativism. It would be especially predominant in Great Britain and the United States.

In contrast, in France, in spite of Durkheim's, Mauss', and Lévi-Strauss' rejection of evolutionist ideology, the original position of French socio-anthropology was characterised by the combination of the unity of the human mind and the diversity of cultures and histories – that is, it demonstrated great complexity, while rejecting psychology or putting it at the service of anthropology.

To be noted is the position of Lacan and his two periods, in the course of which he successively adhered to the ideas of Durkheim, Malinowski, then to those of Lévi-Strauss, as well as those of the American psychoanalysts, Fromm, Horney or Kardiner, who had integrated cultural relativism.

The contemporary debate

Unlike the historical debate, the contemporary debate has some nuances.

Indeed, one finds more self-criticism and circumspection on the part of the psychoanalysts, as well as seeing, in France, the creation of "intermediary" disciplines, group psychoanalysis, offering theoretical tools for the understanding of socio-cultural facts having undeniable heuristic value, thus enabling us to open up and enrich our debate. To be noted in particular are the notions of phantasy and of phantasy-resonance among the organisers of groups, the flow of phantasy in groups, the notion of group imaginary body and of group envelope, of group psychic apparatus, unconscious alliances, group formations of compromise, such as ideologies, mythologies, and utopias, while anthropologists are demonstrating better knowledge of psychoanalysis and its diverse branches.

Thus, they would re-examine the Œdipus complex, no longer by rejecting its universality outright, but, for example, by splitting it, breaking it apart, and selecting from it what is a matter of universality. Even if many of them are acknowledging its universality, some continue to ignore its complete form, meaning they scotomise its negative form, and neglect that of the girl. They are acknowledging that the boy's rivalry is not established with the family figure vested with authority, but with the one who possesses and enjoys access to the mother's body, something which does not change in accordance with the principle of patrilineal or matrilineal (Godelier, in particular) descent. Moreover, taking into consideration the "logical" cohesion of the parricidal and incestuous components, some, like Juillerat, have viewed the latter as extreme forms of a "less violent" nucleus combining maternal symbiosis and paternal rivalry. However, he himself has also brought up the existence of a main oedipal symbolic at work in the multiple cultural products of the unconscious.

Others, like Godelier, placed great emphasis on the disorder engendered by free human sexuality if it is not regulated, whence the making of a necessary sacrifice. The prohibition of incest was the original model for these social rules making possible the domestication and socialisation of sexuality. While he acknowledged the incestuous component of the Œdipus complex, in contrast, he rejected the parricidal component. What is predominant, as Green remarked, is therefore the rejection of parricide and its multiple metonymic extensions, its rich and diversified symbolisations. Spiro distinguished three dimensions in the Œdipus complex: its structure, its intensity, and its socio-cultural consequences. He defended the universality of the oedipal structure and the existence of the intercultural variability of its intensity and its socio-cultural consequences. Finally, Obeyesekere defends the idea of an identical "muddy bottom" to talk about the universal psychobiological sources of the Œdipus complex, "form of life", "scenario", which presents "family resemblances" through its multiple historical, socio-cultural forms, combinations, and configurations. He differentiates then the historical Œdipus complex from that of the myths and the diverse family configurations largely influenced by religious values, multiple symbolic forms. It needs to be pointed out that he has essentially worked in Buddhist and Hindu South Asia. Although defending the idea of a "deep motivation" and its relationship to culture, through the mediation of diverse symbolic transformations ("work of culture") producing personal symbols and collective representations, he seems to reject Freud's theory of drives, only retaining the hermeneutic dimension of psychoanalysis.

However, something remains conspicuously missing in this debate: the castration complex, object of an even more radical denial! Only Juillerat and Spiro emphasised the existence of castration anxiety.

On the basis of these many observations, I propose to depict the way in which anthropologists have interpreted the Œdipus complex – as compared to the way psychoanalysts have seen it, then the way anthropologists have viewed psychoanalysis, as well as how psychoanalysts have seen anthropologists, all the while keeping in mind that there are some variations in these views and that their forms have evolved.

Ways of viewing the Œdipus complex

As I already mentioned, for psychoanalysts, the Œdipus complex was first discovered in boys in its positive, then negative, form, attaining a complete form elaborated in 1923. It was presented as being the apogee of infantile sexuality with the castration complex as its crowning moment and the way to its resolution in boys. The girl's Œdipus complex was addressed late, along with feminine sexuality. But, the Œdipus complex was also understood by Freud as a primal phantasy containing the three other ones (seduction, castration, primal scene). The Œdipus complex appeared as a structure, in Lacan, then as a model, in Green.

For the latter, the twofold difference between the sexes and the generations at work within any family space constituted the foundation of the Œdipus complex in its anthropological dimension.[1] The meaning of the Œdipus complex was therefore to be neither a phase, nor even only a complex, but a psychic structure constitutive of the subject, giving rise to cultural reformulations, meaning to collective symbolisations. Consequently, the Œdipus complex grounds human identity and community.

Unfortunately, anthropologists have most often confined themselves to the Œdipus complex in boys, in its positive component, ordinarily fastening on to the incestuous side of the desire and obscuring the parricidal wish. They therefore remained ignorant of the evolution of the Freudian and post-Freudian conceptualisation, the very complexification, of this central concept, which is so rich both in its structuring conflictual dimension and in its phantasy dimension, freezing it and reducing it to the first stage of its elaboration, "clinging" to an exclusively phenomenological approach, an object therefore of socio-cultural variations, something which could only seriously fetter any possible discussion. So it is that I find a surprising contrast between these two ways of viewing the Œdipus complex, that of the anthropologists and that of the psychoanalysts.

The way of viewing psychoanalysis

Anthropologists, particularly those active in the historical debate, seemed to have reduced psychoanalysis to a purely speculative theory – aspiring to make universalist claims – and fundamentally ethnocentric. Some separated the methodology from the theoretical corpus in order to use the former and reject the latter. Others selected certain concepts. This "reduction" and breaking up of psychoanalysis into parts would be the result of repeated scotomising and splitting underlain by defensive needs and identity issues, notably.

The contemporary relativist perspective of anthropologists contrasts with the universalist perspective of psychoanalysis. Even though the search for universals is characteristic of structuralism, it is in conflict, in another way, with that of psychoanalysis, which is suggestive of that of evolutionism. Indeed, anthropology may have possibly found in psychoanalysis three fundamental aspects of its own "evolutionist childhood":

- purely speculative, ivory tower, armchair thinkers without experience in the field;
- the assumption of the universality of the human mind and of the uniformity of human history, in the manner of ontogenesis;
- an ethnocentric prejudice transformed into an "ethnocentrist scientific norm".

However, modern, "mature" anthropology demands full recognition of cultural diversity, a relativist approach to beliefs, customs, and institutions, fieldwork as a major reference, and the rejecting of any ethnocentrism. That is why espousing the psychoanalytical thesis of the universality of the Œdipus complex (as the anthropologists interpret it) would represent a regression back to an evolutionist position from which one had to keep one's distance.

By reproaching psychoanalysts for engaging in speculative thought and for their lack of experience in the ethnographic field, anthropologists obscure the very source of the psychoanalyst's investigation, which is clinical work, the field specific to psychoanalysts and the meeting place of their patients' many unconscious phantasies and drives and the diversity of peoples' beliefs, customs, and institutions, according to Devereux. This is something I shall return to later on.

Finally, anthropologists consider that psychoanalysts tend to reduce the diversity of ethnographic materials to some universals and fail to differentiate between the multiple interactive aspects of historical and socio-cultural reality, the sources of its so very great complexity.

View of anthropologists developed by psychoanalysts

Psychoanalysts readily identify anthropologists with patients expressing resistance to truths revealed by them, such as the universality of the Œdipus complex, and through it to all the phantasised, instinctual, and unconscious profundity of psychic life (cf. Jones with Malinowski, or Róheim with the culturalists).

Moreover, psychoanalysts underscore anthropologists' regular ignorance of the very existence of that complex unconscious psychic reality that psychoanalytical theory endeavours to make accessible and intelligible, as well as their lack of any genuine interest, something leading to incomprehension, evasiveness, and serious distortions of the notions and concepts. This would be the case with the unconscious and drives, with repression and return of the repressed, infantile sexuality, and phantasy, for example.

Elements for understanding this conflictual history

A certain number of concepts and notions can help us discover some avenues for understanding the issues involved: the major anthropological concept of acculturation and its aspects of diffusion and assimilation, the processes of cultural trends and of historical accident among the historical circumstances of cultural change, as well as the notions of reinterpretation and syncretism, trauma, and identity. Recourse to two analogies will, moreover, help us to conceptualise this history: the first identifies psychoanalysis and anthropology with two cultures; the second, according to Didier Anzieu's theories (1975), with two "imaginary" bodies placed in contact with one another.

In the anthropology of cultural change, Rivers' and Seligman's sudden discovery of Freud's writings corresponds to a "historical accident", which had an impact on the evolution of this science-culture and on its relations with psychoanalysis. In psychoanalytic terms, the historical accident finds expression in the collective "traumatic event". The psychoanalytic theoretical "corpus" and methodology are innovations, "cultural items" and "foreign bodies" to be welcomed, assimilated, transformed and/or totally or partially rejected. It is the same with the concepts of the unconscious, repression, transference and resistance, phantasy, infantile sexuality, the Œdipus complex, as well as the notions of latent and manifest, for example.

But it was *Totem and Taboo*, which – owing to its intrusion, and the inoculation of the universality of the Œdipus complex into the "socio-anthropological body" – through afterwardness – was to give full "traumatic" value and meaning to this discovery of psychoanalysis. Starting there, and with the writings of Malinowski, then of others, we can interpret or "translate" a certain number of facts related in terms of phenomena of acculturation, finding expression in diverse ways and producing different results.

However, let us point out with Devereux that new contacts between two culturally different groups represent a critical situation for them, which gives rise to the phenomena of resistance, to acculturation in particular, that form the very foundation of the process of "antagonistic acculturation" introduced by him in 1972 in *Ethnopsychoanalysis and Anthropology as Complementary Frames of Reference.*

I, in fact, think that, following Malinowski, anthropology's resistance to accepting the cultural item "the universality of the Œdipus complex" might have been translated by anthropologists as follows: "Yes, we accept this Œdipus complex as a family complex in patriarchal societies exclusively, but not in matrilineal societies, where another type of nuclear family complex exists".

Malinowski was in fact the exemplary creator of this acculturative phenomenon. He created the nuclear family complex, a "syncretic" product, by reinterpreting the Œdipus complex as being the family complex of patriarchal societies. That manipulation of the Œdipus complex, underlain most probably by an unconscious phantasy, "resonated" with the expectations, phantasies and ideas of the "collective body" of the anthropologists. This family complex quite quickly became a social formation – with Kardiner (1939), in particular – attesting to its well-established "assimilation". The new identity of the anthropologists was built and crystallised around this acculturative phenomenon. From then on, it would be based on fieldwork, on the rejection of evolutionism and on phenomena of acculturation to certain concepts, notions, and elements of the psychoanalytical method – that is, on the anthropological translation and manipulation of them.

As I have already mentioned, it was with *Totem and Taboo* that the traumatic dimension of the discovery of and encounter with psychoanalysis acquired its full value and meaning, thus justifying the manifestations of resistance and antagonistic acculturation on the part of the "anthropological body". From that point on, this would also shape the history of their conflictual relations. However, the impact of this intrusion of psychoanalysis into the socio-cultural "body" was all the more traumatic for anthropology because it occurred at a critical moment in its history, therefore during one of great vulnerability – namely, at a time when evolutionism and its postulate of the unity of the human mind was in decline and soon to be overtaken by the new paradigm of cultural relativism combined with the model of "ethnographical authority".

However, this situation of acculturation also resulted in the creation of new "acculturative" disciplines, among them: Roheim's and Kardiner's psychoanalytic anthropology, Fromm's analytical psycho-sociology, and Devereux's complementary ethno-psychoanalysis and ethnopsychiatry, in particular, but also that of Spiro and Obeyesekere.

I am tempted to add that the issues at stake in this debate would also, and especially, be of an identity and ideological order, rather than of a scientific order. Moreover, to be noted is the prevalence of discourse and attitudes conveying requirements of differentiation, singularity, and autonomy, which are manifestations of a need for protection from the danger of intrusion, for example.

Epistemological and methodological characteristics of anthropology and of psychoanalysis

Anthropology

What, Mondher Kilani asked, was the work of the anthropologist if not that continuous mediation work on identity and difference?[2]

The principal and fundamental object of anthropology is the culture conveyed by human society, notably through the study of its institutions, its customs, its beliefs, its representations, its social organisation. There is the idea of a construction of the object of study and ethnographic data on the basis of a theoretical frame of reference, an anthropological one in this case.

From the field to the anthropologist's discourse

Ethnologists choose their field, the group or tribe they plan to study, and the factors determining this choice are multiple, among them unconscious psychic factors connected with certain characteristics of their personalities, with possibilities of identifying with certain groups, in particular. This process of identification with the group frequented and observed enables them to "appropriate" it afterward. It will become "his/her" group, "his/her" tribe.

The ethnographic field is a quite singular situation within which, immersed in a particularly anxiety-generating, stimulating, alienating historical, socio-cultural reality for a specific length of time, the researcher is going to establish different types of relationships: with the people native to the village; with his or her special informants; with the natural environment; with his or her varied and multiple affective and emotional states (excitation, anxiety, hypomanic and depressive episodes, and feelings of loneliness, relative disorientation, joy and uneasiness, etc.) produced by his or her experience in the field; with writing, notetaking having psychically defensive and scientific practical functions. The ethnologist is therefore immediately exposed to socio-cultural alterity, to a feeling of strangeness – mixed with what is familiar, nevertheless. That is why his or her interest is immediately directed toward what is singular about the society or societies observed and studied, toward a comparative study establishing differences and similarities, but also toward transformations. He or she therefore displays an attachment to a certain cultural relativism.

In this field, direct observation, foundation of a "realist" epistemology, is based on seeing, on a rhetoric of looking, itself strongly oriented by our own expectations and our own preconceived cultural ideas,[3] as the anthropologist Francis Affergan has explained. But what the observer sees is also accompanied by talking and listening in a relationship with one or several privileged "informants", a place of negotiation of their respective points of view, but also, a place of tension and compromise between two subjects involved in two different types of historicity. As Kilani has explained, anthropologists are historically and culturally situated by the questions they ask their field and by the manner in which they seek to understand the world, just as the responses given by the informants are themselves the result of interpretations mediated by their culture and history.[4] They endeavour to construct knowledge together. Yet, this relationship remains asymmetrical, and the informant or informants will establish a "cultural" transference, to borrow Obeyesekere's expression, onto the ethnologist who will feel the counter-transferential affects, something which I shall discuss later on in relation to Devereux.

The procedures involved in establishing documentation and "stabilising" "facts" out of notes, recordings, and filmed and photographic materials give field "data" an initial form, according to Kilani.[5] This work of reorganising, therefore, of imposing a proper order on what is supposed to correspond to the elements of indigenous knowledge implies later work to schematise, classify, rank. Consequently, the ethnographic facts prove to be artefacts taking on, for example, the appearances of description, and immediately raise questions about the reference and the modes of reference to experience in the field,[6] as the epistemologist Marie-Jeanne Borel has aptly expressed it.

But the ethnographic field is inconceivable without its complementary phase, the time of writing, meaning the "textualising", the transcription of the knowledge and of the experience of this field in the form of a monograph, with its rules and principles, mainly addressed to colleagues, which Malinowski instituted and made canonical. This unique field experience, in many senses a high point in an anthropologist's life, must necessarily be communicated in a standard form and a common language to the professional community, the researcher then feeling borne and judged by it.

What is this discourse of the anthropologist?

Another epistemologist, Silvana Borutti, has characterised the discourse of the anthropologist in terms of its fictional nature. According to her, through the fictional effects of a series of procedures of a literary kind, the knowledge of an indigenous people is transposed into the terms and schemas of a fiction which, moreover, has a great deal of practical power with regard to information and comprehension. This discursive fiction is a privileged means of creating (understood as "poiesis") and producing knowledge in human sciences in general.[7]

Among the notions and concepts used, it is to be pointed out that some remain stable and lasting, despite different interpretations according to schools of thought, while others prove to be more specific to domains and theoretical currents, therefore varying with the history and the different fields of the discipline.

The following are some key notions and concepts: culture, society, ethnicity, belief, tradition, institution, value, norm, ideology, representation, symbolism and symbolic, exchange, cultural relativism, structure, acculturation.

Among the principal domains are: kinship, social organisation, material culture, art, languages, technology, ecology, economy, politics, law, religion, and the universe of representations of the world, of the society, of the individual and of the person, with which I shall associate the corresponding notions.

The theoretical models of reference vary from one school of thought to another, and researchers use them as schema to interpret the data they have collected and constructed. The functionalist, structuralist, Marxist, "culture and personality", cognitivist, psychoanalytical, deconstructionist, and constructivist approaches may serve as examples.

For some contemporary anthropologists psychoanalysis has, as I have been able to show, become the new theoretical model, the heuristic value of which can no longer be denied for the interpretation of a certain category of data, that of the "cultural products of the unconscious", an expression suffering from some ambiguities.

What about the present situation in anthropology?

Today, many anthropologists observe that the end of the twentieth century was marked by a series of second thoughts regarding their own discipline, regarding its objects, history, discourse, concepts, epistemological foundations. For example, in the United States there was postmodernist deconstructionism. US anthropologists in fact noted both the breaking apart of the objects henceforth to be reconstructed and the shakiness, if not the unsoundness, of concepts not having a universal foundation, whence the need to rework the discipline.

Psychoanalysis

The principal, specific object of psychoanalysis is the unconscious, its processes, its individual and collective products. A science of the unconscious, it is a method of investigation as well as a psychotherapy. Freud always defined it as a "natural science", therefore, an explanatory science based, nevertheless, on interpretation, the exemplary model of which is *The Interpretation of Dreams*. As a psychological science of the unconscious, it represents and constitutes a bridge, a link between the medical sciences and the cultural sciences, precisely owing to the characteristic nature of the unconscious, neither individual, nor collective, but both at once. That is why the outer/inner contrast becomes obsolete with psychoanalysis, the unconscious being both inner and outer within humanity.

The field of psychoanalysis

Psychoanalysis' field is the clinic and its original, standard arrangement, the couch/armchair of the patient/analyst relationship. The parameters governing the analytical setting aim to create a situation analogous to dreams. The heart of analytical activity, whatever the modalities of the situation may be in which the analyst is brought to work, is made up of the patient's free association, coupled with the floating listening and benevolent neutrality of the analyst, who is receptive both to his patient's transferential movements and to his or her own counter-transferential processes pervaded with reveries and thoughts, they too floating. André Green (2002) expressed this quite well by saying that it is definitely in listening, by positioning oneself at the head of the couch that one opens up to resonating to the patient's unconscious by letting one's own resound.[8] Analysts therefore listen to their patients' "living" discourse, ready to interpret, meaning to translate, their products, multiple expressions of their unconsciousness, into the language of secondary processes. Psychoanalysis transforms the psychic apparatus into an apparatus of language and Green proposed talking of going back into oneself by making a detour through one's fellow human being to describe this psychoanalytical activity.

Within this arrangement there is a disjointedness between this stable "setting" of the therapy and the moving, necessarily dynamic, therefore living, analytical process upon which it develops. The analyst's self-analysis is an essential instrument to this clinical situation so specific to psychoanalysis. Moreover, this clinical field is also the site of the emergence and production of a type of thought, "clinical thought", as Green put it so nicely, a source of later conceptualisation and theorisation, for the psychoanalyst and psychoanalysts in general.

Clinical thought and psychoanalytical work

André Green maintained that in psychoanalysis there is not only a theory of the clinical, but a clinical thought, meaning a specific, original mode of rationality derived from practical experience.[9] It is recognised when theoretical elaboration gives rise to associations referring to one or another aspect of psychoanalytical experience in the reader, as psychoanalyst or psychotherapist.[10]

What does clinical thought consist of, how is one to grasp it?

For Green, clinical thought forges concepts that recount the unconsciousness' reasons, the diversity of responses that its advances call for, as well as their transformations into hallucinatory "realisations", into actions, into psychosomatic reactions, into rationalisations. It would be fitting to relate the clinical, no longer only to the one who is suffering, but also to the one charged with hearing this suffering owing to a particular sensibility, namely the analyst.[11] Nonetheless, Green points to the inevitable and lasting existence of an unbridgeable gap between theory and practice, appealing to Jean-Luc Donnet's conviction that theory will never be able to adhere completely to the clinical, nor cover the full expanse of its field. The clinical will never be an application without any remnant of theory, entirely elucidated by it. Clinical thought must always keep this gap and ineradicable residue in mind, and accept that they may never be completely eliminated. Nowhere does uncertainty weigh as heavily as it does in psychoanalysis.[12]

Green considered that clinical thought truly began with the account of the analysis of Dora and was pursued with the four other cases making up the corpus of the five psychoanalyses.

If psychoanalytical theory builds itself up on the basis of experience, clinical thought is therefore a way station, the stage prior to any theory seeking the assent of those claiming that psychoanalysis deserves the status of being a fundamental discipline. The theory is only elucidated, fits in, deepens, and multiplies its connexions by extracting its potentialities, its interpretation of the psyche from experience in order to gain access to what remains hidden. Any psychoanalysis that does not concern itself with clinical thought would be the exercising of a sterile, ornamental, frivolous discipline.[13]

Green adds that to constitute a discipline, a thought, the presence of a third party, who listens to what the two others say to each other and hear, is indispensable, something which explains why analysts resort to writing. It is interesting to observe and discover this necessary presence of a third party, both in ethnology, through the writing of monographs, and in psychoanalysis, as well as the asymmetric, dialogical nature of the analysing/analysed relationship and that between researchers and their informants.

Finally, what precisely is the goal of the psychoanalyst's work?

With Green, I answer that it consists of a broadening of patients' awareness (through transference – whether interpreted or not – and resistance) of their modes of functioning, the nature of their conflicts, and the relationship of the latter to their lives, and finally their relationship to what they are saying and to the other person's listening. All this combined constitutes the aim of the psychoanalyst's work. It should lead to significant changes translating into greater freedom and, for this reason, be accompanied by a more profound, more extensive activity of representation. Healing is a side benefit, as Freud himself admitted.[14]

The fundamental notions and concepts of Freudian thought

To begin with, it seems to me useful to recall the "principal subject-matter of psycho-analysis and the foundations of its theory" stated by Freud in 1923 as being the "assumption that there are unconscious mental processes, the recognition of the theory of resistance and repression, the appreciation of the importance of sexuality and of the Œdipus complex".[15] For my part, I propose: the unconscious, repression and the return of the repressed, the Œdipus complex and the castration complex, the theory of drives, the theory of the libido and its stages – fixation and regression, compulsive repetition, afterwardness – infantile sexuality, unconscious phantasy, narcissism, the Eros and destruction drive dualism, sublimation, identifications, the two theories of the psychic apparatus, defence mechanisms, symptoms, neurosis, dreams and dream work, affect, representation, symbolism, symbolic and symbolisation, transference and resistance, meaning and interpretation, in particular.

Green reminded us that psychoanalytical concepts are metaphorical and considered the category of meaning to be the category proper to psychoanalysis. He believed that the psychic level of meaning was reached when the category of "the similar other" comes into play. According to him, the psychic is born out of the encounter between an event taking place within the subject (feeling, knowledge, representation, etc.) who finds his or her reflexion or complementarity in the similar other.[16] The guiding line of the psyche oscillates between two orientations, intrapsychic and intersubjective, both producing meanings and creating objects. Moreover, Green notes that, while drawing sustenance from both nature and culture, the psychic goes about creating itself and that for him nature and culture are the parents of the human species.[17] Indeed, in Freudian theory, the situation of the psyche arises as emerging from the twofold influence of its cultural and biological components, as is clearly attested to by the second topography of the psychic apparatus.

Some reflexions on the models of Freudian psychoanalysis

In his remarkable work *Introduction à l'épistémologie freudienne*, Paul-Laurent Assoun reminds readers that Freud developed his analytical knowledge using terminological and conceptual material borrowed from nineteenth-century epistemological references and models, those of his mentors, to which he remained attached all throughout his life.

Beforehand, let us state Assoun's view, the nexus of the Freudian epistemological problem: for him it was true that at the heart of Freudianism there was the energy problem and a theory of meaning and Freud never separated the fate of the energy problem and that of his theory of meaning.[18]

The epistemological foundations of Freud's creation would be threefold in nature: monist, physicalist, and agnostic.

Its monistic foundation assumes that as a "natural science" psychoanalysis refuses to engage in any "battle of methods", and for it, *interpretation is an explanation.* Psychoanalytical procedure is therefore not to be split into an explanatory part and an interpretative part. Freudian epistemology is based on a radical monism, rejecting therefore all dualism.

Its physicalist foundation refers to the founding physicochemical model. The very appellation "psychoanalysis" is in fact in direct analogy with this model. Analysis signifies "decomposition", "taking apart", and the atomistic image is the basis for the analogy with chemistry: the drives, as components of psychic life, being comparable to the ultimate constituents of matter, reducible to force. So, unfolding in accordance with the physics-physiology-psychology sequence, this natural science was based on a great determinist need to assign a cause, reconstitute the process.

As for its agnostic foundation, the object of psychoanalysis is the unconscious, which would be nothing other than the "thing-in-itself", to borrow Kant's terminology, meaning the unknowable. Freud in fact argued for the scientificity of psychoanalytical knowledge and at the same time proclaimed that there was an absolute limit to knowledge

What, then, is the structure of this Freudian epistemological identity and what are its models?

In his essay on "The Unconscious" in his "Papers on Metapsychology", Freud wrote, "I propose that when we have succeeded in describing a psychical process in its dynamic, topographical and economic aspects, we should speak of it as *metapsychological* presentation".[19]

Supported and inspired by one of his mentors, the physiologist Ernst Brücke, Freud pursued a whole anatomo-physiological line of thought to reach the topic. He would later transfer his positivistic orientation and his technique of observation onto the clinic. The physiological was first readable on the anatomical structure.

The dynamic dimension was inspired by the "Herbartian" model elaborated within a tradition of German psychology going back to the early nineteenth-century philosopher Johann Friedrich Herbart, who considered that the psyche was investigable because it had an atom, a basic motion called *representation. There was no psychic fact that was not representational.* Freud would therefore borrow a language and categories from him and when he based psychic activity on representation, he modernised this Herbartian schema with all its dynamic connotations. As for the affect quantum, it was an integral element of the psychic process remaining essentially representational. Herbart therefore introduced the properly psychological dimension into the metapsychological object. Owing to its mediation, the central theory of the conflict – designating the opposition of psychic places in the topographical order – becomes dynamic. Thus, the dynamic is correlated with the topographical schema beforehand and afterwards with the economic dimension by the interplay of forces that develops into a relationship of quantified forces. By this means, the concept of force will return to its physical origin.

Finally, Assoun notes that the *economic* is rooted in the "Fechnero-Helmholtzian" model. By attributing a quantitative dimension to psychic phenomena, as well as making quantification imperative, Freud modernised the issues involved in nineteenth-century scientific psychology. That is what made the theory of the libido the basis of the metapsychological edifice. Remember that Gustav Fechner was the founder of psychophysics and Hermann von Helmholtz an eminent physiologist. The connection between physiology and psychology went by way of quantification. The fundamental principles of the Freudian energy problem directly derived from Fechner's energy theory. In this way, Freud specified the principle of stability as a principle of constancy-inertia. I would also like to draw attention to the Freudian terminology having energy connotations: investment, discharge, abreaction, libido, affect quantum, for example.

To be mentioned as well is Freud's attraction to the monism of the German Darwinist Ernst Haeckel as cultural and scientific reference.

What about the evolution of the theories and practices of psychoanalysis?

Today, psychoanalysis is essentially present in Europe and the Americas, and the time when Freud's work was the common and sole reference point of psychoanalytical thought has come to an end. Indeed, the interpretations of the psyche and the practices differ according to the persons engaging in them, according to the diverse analytic movements (Kleinian, Bionian, Winnicottian, Lacanian, that of Ego psychology, of the proponents of the theory of the object relation with Fairbairn, of Kohut and the theory of self, of the developmental perspective and observation of the infant, of the intersubjective approaches, for example), in the different regions of the globe. There is a non-homogenous European psychoanalysis distinct from those of the Americas, themselves very different and all influenced by their history, their culture, and their national identity.

What can then be said about the unity of psychoanalysis today? Is there unity in the face of the heterogeneity of the theories and practices?

According to Green, extreme uncertainty reigns nowadays about contemporary psychoanalytical thought, and in most psychoanalytical milieux, engaging in any substantive debate about the main issues at stake in the theory inspires fear. Moreover, as he observed, in the wake of the hostility manifested by the social sciences, notably towards work in "applied" psychoanalysis, this singular evolution of psychoanalysis has been characterised by a refocusing on psychoanalytical practice alone. As I have already explained, this refocusing has had a reductive effect on the theory, leading to a psychoanalysis almost entirely thought out in terms of ontogenetic direction, therefore remaining confined within the limits of an individual life. In addition, it had the effect of transforming the theory of the psyche to which Freud aspired into a theory of relations, object relation, intersubjective, interpersonal.

I therefore find that a serious crisis exists, affecting both contemporary psychoanalysis and contemporary anthropology, which therefore draws them closer together in certain respects.

Divergences

Anthropology's object is therefore culture and society, meaning the varied, multiple, historically and geographically determined collective modalities of organisation and life. Through this quite rich diversity of historical and socio-cultural forms, we could inquire into the essence of this order of collective reality, its principles and rules of functioning, then extract the fundamental categories of the culture in itself. Its twofold status of collective exteriority and individual interiority is a major characteristic. An exploration of the intercultural patterns would therefore be necessary, as well as that of the different models of culture created by human beings. From this perspective, a specific methodology was developed and instituted, also mobilising, following the irreplaceable, exceptional experience in the field, procedures of abstraction, schematisation and modelisation that I have already mentioned.

Among the concepts, notions and domains specific to anthropology, apart from those of culture and society, some emerge and function as "identity markers". This is so, for example, for those of institution, custom, tradition, norm, ideology, and acculturation, as well as of domains of myths, rituals, cosmologies and religions, social organisation, kinship systems, economic and political factors, power, law, technologies, linguistic facts, and the artistic field. They are immanent to the collective life of human beings, to their organisation, their social relationships, their products, and their history. While they involve and commit the life of every individual, this would be inasmuch as he or she is an "active" member of a society, participating in its production and its reproduction. Human beings acquire the status of being human by becoming "social, moral beings", cultural beings, through the twofold process of enculturation and socialisation, cultural introjection and social incorporation. However, we shall see that other concepts and notions, as well as other domains, are shared with psychoanalysis, but their meanings and their approaches differ. Such is the case with the symbolic and symbolisation, representations, the prohibition of incest, with belief, value, structure, especially.

As for psychoanalysis, as I have stated, its original object was the unconscious, its processes, its collective and individual products. The arrangement and characteristics of the psychoanalytic treatment model, as well as the dream–object, represent the paradigmatic conditions and the "royal road" for the exploration of this object specific to psychoanalysis, with which it is identified. These technical conditions therefore favour the construction of "psychoanalytical data", the "observation" of a singular type of reality – unknown up until then in the history of knowledge – the unconscious psychic reality, with its heterogeneity, fundamental conflictuality, splittings, processes, and contents, dreams, phantasies, symptoms, representations and affects, in particular. As a result, the ethnographic method cannot construct psychoanalytical data, any more than the psychoanalytical method can elaborate ethnological data. Consequently, this approach makes a contribution to answering the question about "the socio-cultural existence" of the Œdipus complex: it is a psychoanalytical fact about unconscious psychic reality, and not an ethnological fact observable in the field. It is a matter of a process of interpretation, of translation within the psychoanalytical theoretical frame of reference, of ethnographic materials conceived of, notably, as symbolic products, meaning as cultural products of the unconscious.

Certain concepts and notions presented above belong exclusively to the psychoanalytical theoretical corpus and lexicon, and very early in the history of this debate, some anthropologists found some of them particularly enticing – namely, the unconscious, latent and manifest content at the service of a hermeneutic approach, repression, identification – while rejecting the others, such as those of unconscious phantasy, infantile sexuality, drive, and libido, notably. Indeed, psychoanalytical methodology, as well as certain concepts and notions, found favour with some anthropologists, while their clinical foundations were ignored, even denied.

Inversely, I have observed that psychoanalysts have above all been interested in ethnographic materials to the detriment of anthropology's concepts and theoretical dimension.

The phenomena of acculturation therefore appear to be just as selective among cultures as among scientific disciplines!

Convergences

According to Devereux in *From Anxiety to Method in the Behavioral Sciences* (1967), the fundamental characteristic of the behavioural sciences, to which both anthropology and psychoanalysis belong, is the actual and potential reciprocity of the observation between observer and observed, which constitutes a relationship that is theoretically symmetrical, but is in reality asymmetrical in these two disciplines. Moreover, he noted the data of behavioural sciences are threefold:

1. The behaviour of the subject of observation.
2. The "disturbances" produced by the existence of the observer and his or her observational activities in the observation framework.
3. The behaviour of the observer: his or her anxieties, defensive manoeuvres, research strategies, "decisions" (with respect to attributing a meaning to his or her observations).[20]

Devereux noted that the most characteristic data are phenomena triggered by the observation itself. Indeed, in most of these sciences, the basic data are the "statements" (the behaviour) of the subjects. They also include the perceptions of the observer. In the "triggering" situations, as much as in the study of the perturbations caused by the observer and the observation, the royal road to objectivity is the imaginative exploitation of the distortions to which the methods of triggering subject the data. Let us recall, moreover, that he emphasised that anthropology studies what is specifically human in culture, and psychoanalysis studies what is also specifically human in the psyche. It is in fact a matter of two human sciences exploring the diverse modalities of the "making" of mankind, as well as its multiple manifestations and "faces".

I shall therefore first look at their common object, mankind, and their necessarily different, because specific, modes of approaching this object.

A group of anthropologists have introduced the notion of "anthropopoïesis", which they have defined in this way: conceived both as "rebirth" of humans as social beings (anthropogenesis) and as a process of creating humanity's fictions and models, anthropopoïesis is precisely a notion encompassing phenomena which, constitutive of human civilisation, cross cultures to inform anthropology's very procedures. While socio-cultural practices make human beings through the intermediary of different institutional and ritual constraints in accordance with normative models often elaborated, depicted, and transformed into traditions in genealogical accounts, the attempts at synthesis by the anthropologists themselves are marked by the models of human beings and their construction.[21] Thus, anthropology can concede that beyond the base of the biological capabilities distinguishing human beings from animals, human beings' existence in general precedes their essence, an essence which is to be made, to be created, a malleable essence which can only be constituted collectively in interaction with other human beings through a historical process which is never definitive. These anthropologists emphasise two characteristics associated with human beings as social beings with a culture: their innate incompleteness and their potential overabundance.

So it is that, in inventing culture and society, human beings above all give birth to human reality. In addition, these human beings are born several times: the first birth is a matter of a physiological process, and culture intervenes to interpret and organise it; the second is social and is a matter of "fictional" constructed, "invented" processes. The second birth would be connected with a conception of human biological incompleteness, and culture would fulfil a function of completion, according to the anthropologist Clifford Geertz.[22]

Let us now look at some other socio-cultural sectors, apart from rites of initiation, in which the construction of mankind is apparent, namely, ethnicity, cannibalism and masks, especially.

According to the anthropologist Ugo Fabietti,[23] ethnicity involves two kinds of processes: the production of the social individual and the making of an identity for the group, a "collective Self". This group affiliation is the result of a symbolic, practical activity leading to placing individuals into specific categories reflecting distinctions of a collective type – "limits". The differentiation and identification are complementary and opposite aspects of the continual process of "constructing limits" that seems to accompany the whole of human history, in particular, by producing discourse whose goal is to isolate specific features, and therefore meaning spaces in which to relate their own existence. To be underscored is the need to root the identity of groups in biology, biological kinship, and therefore in nature, which is apt to foster a portrayal of the cultural difference linked to natural differences.

The anthropologist Mondher Kilani has observed that cannibalism also contributes to the making of mankind. It would in fact have this capacity to configure models or anti-models of mankind with which societies identify or, on the contrary, of which they are wary. According to him, this capacity to configure mankind persists through a metaphorical power of cannibalism. The cannibalistic metaphor enables the creation of fields of similarity with other social phenomena which it helps to decipher better.[24] He especially distinguishes savage cannibalism, metaphorisation of all the disorders, essentially through imaginary figures, such those of the ogre, from ritual cannibalism. Moreover, the prohibitions of cannibalism and incest define the boundaries of culture.

The ethnological category of masks is also interesting to consider. Indeed, according to Francis Affergan, masks permit the very redefinition of culture, which becomes the place where humanity produces itself, where it fashions its own image. Human beings make different versions of humanity through the mediation of the animal or divinised world, therefore, of mankind in roundabout, symbolic ways. In order to make what is the same, what is the same goes by way of what is other.

This notion of making a detour through what is other particularly resonates with the characteristics of the human psyche and psychoanalytical thought.

Finally, with Françoise Héritier,[25] let us look at some dreams or phantasies of the imaginary world that humanity has inherited in relation to procreation and their cultural attempts at realisation: the dream of immortality, the imagery surrounding the pregnant man, the desire for self-reproduction (eliminating both the obligation to have sexual relations in order to procreate and the recognition of alterity), the construction of an ideal society governed by the idea of being among one's own (by virtue of consanguinity and inherent territoriality, of gender, of being among members of one's own sex).

Nonetheless, these universal phantasies pertaining to the ever alive omnipotence of primary narcissism run up against the rock-bottom observations: we are born and we will die, and we only procreate during the finite time of our lives; sexual relations between a man and a woman are necessary to procreate; only women bear children and children of both sexes; the generational order of births is not reversible.

Héritier then notes that, like certain traditional institutions, the modern techniques of procreation endeavour to realise certain of these abiding human phantasies.

The so very rich and elaborate reflexions of these anthropologists lead us to consider the manner in which psychoanalysis, for its part, observes, analyses, interprets this human object that it shares with anthropology.

In 1992, Green judged the task of psychoanalysis to be paradoxical in that in psychoanalytical practice it strives to grasp the distinctive features of a given patient as well as is possible and yet the result of its research and the theory stemming from it aims to define the most general traits determining human subjectivity.[26] Sharing Anzieu's point of view, he considered that people differ a great deal in terms of the products of their conscious activity, but resemble one another more in the products of their unconscious psychic life. Anzieu in fact talked about the monotony of the contents of the unconscious as being a self-evident fact explaining the difference between the poverty of unconscious thought qua thought and the richness of symbolic thought, something which anthropologists have observed, since it constitutes their principal object through its multiple cultural expressions. This poverty of unconscious thought is characterised by the existence of a limited number of processes at work which are the same always and everywhere; whence the affirmation of the universality of the unconscious with, especially, its representations-representatives of drives, its defence mechanisms, its phantasies, its anxiety. However, the organisation of these processes, their manner of combining is variable, not only in individuals, but also relative to groups and societies. Anzieu also posited independence of the individual organisation and the collective organisation of these processes, both in their origin and in their functioning. Green considered that we have to think about the connection between "primary" reason and "secondary" reason. According to him, this primary reason, which works hand in hand with secondary reason, implies that we use other categories to think about being, having, space, time, causality, etc. The closer one comes to this other reason, the more relative the influence of cultural, social, geographical, historical data becomes.[27] In this regard he agreed with Anzieu.

Historically and traditionally, anthropologists have reproached psychoanalysts for ignoring cultural differences, for having reduced the richness of symbolic products to a paucity of unconscious psychic processes or contents. Anzieu answered them by arguing that by virtue of their unconscious all people feel that they are all alike. The unconscious, and more particularly the issues surrounding the Œdipus complex, found human community and identity.[28]

Consequently, the non-recognition of the universality of the unconscious and of the Œdipus complex would lead to the denial of the existence of a human community and identity, meaning what it is that founds the essence of mankind and its subjectivity.

I consider that the universality/relativity distinction so important in this conflictual history has lost its heuristic value and power. It is in fact very probable that it was at the service of identity, but non-scientific, concerns. In reference to biology, the distinction would be immediately obsolete because universality and diversity coexist and are immanent to the very essence of living things. By virtue of this common object which is mankind and its multiple historical, cultural, and psychic expressions, both psychoanalysis and anthropology will very obviously see the universal and the particular in all data. Everything will depend on the level and mode of observation, therefore, on the type of construction of the object observed, as well as on the analytic perspective and the theoretical model orienting the interpretation. We shall be able to extract the universal from the particular, as well as to try to understand the processes of differentiation and particularisation. All that is a reflexion of the richness of living beings, in which psychic reality participates just as much as the historical and socio-cultural reality does.

As Devereux reminds us, the psychic unity of humanity is an undeniable fact, since the differential moulding of the same drives and the same defences adequately accounts for the differences of both ethnic and individual characteristics. Moreover, "the most characteristic trait that all men have *in common* is their capacity to be *more different* from their fellows than a lion can be from other lions".[29]

Here, the biological analogy therefore acquires all its meaning and effectiveness.

I believe that, although the psychoanalysis/anthropology debate has enriched us regarding the inextricable, reciprocal relations between scientific and ideological interests, and also between identity and scientific issues, through the multiple operations of scotomisation, splitting, distortion, evasion, and repression, it has, however, considerably impoverished the unified knowledge of mankind that is the object of anthropology in the full, primary sense of the word. Knowledge of the human sciences has therefore definitely suffered from this.

I hypothesise that Freud's discovery of the unconscious, which constituted a major epistemological revolution in the history of the sciences, possesses a potential to "catch fire", which is still continuing to manifest its effects in the different fields of human knowledge. We have yet to assess the full impact of it, even if Green noted an ignorance of the unconscious[30] in the sciences still in our time. And, it is definitely the unconscious that constitutes that principal, fundamental factor of unification of knowledge of the human sciences, as Freud had discovered very early on, then Devereux clearly stated. Lévi-Strauss had probably already understood this and, preoccupied with the functioning of the human mind, as well as feeling particularly ambivalent about psychoanalysis, he replaced the Freudian unconscious with his own creation, the structuralist unconscious amounting to the symbolic function, to be differentiated from the subconscious, a product of the transformation of the Freudian individual unconscious, another of his creations. Apart from the discovery of the unconscious and its universality, it was at the same time discovered – with Freud and his writings on "applied psychoanalysis", among them the "traumatic" *Totem and Taboo* – that it was individual and collective, being both inner and outer, belonging to socio-cultural and psychic reality. Yet, there would be an independence of the collective and individual formations and organisation. Thus, through the symbolic function, Lévi-Strauss studied the organisation and collective manifestations of the unconscious processes to the point of defining culture as a set of symbolic systems.

So I consider that the conflict crystallised in the problem of the universality of the Œdipus complex is the product of a displacement. It in fact indirectly expressed that engendered by the discovery of the universality of the unconscious and its two poles, individual and collective, intrapsychic and socio-cultural. As long as it remained intrapsychic, its discovery was bearable, under certain conditions, but unpalatable nonetheless. But, by venturing beyond its bounds, Totem and Taboo *triggered the reactional hostility on the part of anthropologists inherent to this very intrusion into their own field. However, through afterwardness, this hostility above all also expressed and signified the violence of the rejection of this discovery of the unconscious, which, moreover, up until our time, remains so little understood and quite mysterious.*

Common confrontation with alterity

While anthropologists and psychoanalysts share the human object, a familiar object with which it is easy to identify, they are also confronted with a face of alterity, although of a different nature. Indeed, the indigenous person that the ethnologist encounters represents the stranger, an external face of alterity, strange and disturbing in certain respects, but also strangely familiar. Listening to the unconscious processes of their patients and their reverberations within their own psyches, psychoanalysts encounter another, intrapsychic, face of alterity, that of multiple instinctual representatives, of disturbing and strangely familiar offspring of the unconscious. This dialectic of the same and the other, of the familiar and the strange, at work in the ethnologists' and psychoanalysts' field is particularly anxiety-provoking, and in later sections, with Devereux, we shall take a look at what protective measures researchers mobilise.

What about the concepts and the nature of them?

Psychoanalysis shares with the socio-anthropological disciplines the metaphorical nature of their own concepts. Green reminded us of this for psychoanalysis, and Kilani has explained that the most fundamental concepts of sociology and anthropology are metaphors, living metaphors which have not been subjected to the purification and abstraction that would make them into concepts. Next, since the symbolic imposes itself upon anthropologists as the essential component of culture, their investigation of rituals, myths, belief systems, and models of kinship necessarily brings them to encounter metaphor on the way. However, far from being a handicap – in the sense of weak heuristic productivity – to the extent to which it creates meaning, the presence of metaphor in the work of anthropologists instead possesses cognitive value.[31]

The common concepts seem to me to be those of meaning and significance, but also representation, the symbolic and symbolisation. However, while anthropologists explore their collective dimension, psychoanalysts are interested in their intrapsychic-individual dimension. Their respective definition would be determined by reference to theoretical models, therefore endeavouring to account for an empirical reality and specific processes. Nonetheless, Héritier has emphasised the anchoring of symbolic thought in the body, thus connecting up with the psychoanalytical conception. Yet, the very nature of the unconscious, of its formations and its processes, makes it possible to establish links, build bridges, between these two orders of socio-cultural and psychic reality. This is in fact one of the epistemic characteristics of psychoanalysis, as it had already been defined by Freud, and quite rapidly scotomised, both by the psychoanalysts and by the anthropologists. In that respect, psychoanalysis is fully identified with its object, the unconscious, something which it does not seem anthropologists have done with culture, but rather with the symbolic for a certain anthropological current.

In addition, another area of rapprochement between our two specific objects, the unconscious and culture is to be mentioned. Both enjoy a twofold status, inner and outer, intrapsychic and socio-cultural. As is the case with the unconscious, culture is also an intrapsychic reality present in each individual, therefore, in each of the members of a given society, through the psychic agencies of the ego, the superego and the ego ideal. Let us recall in passing that Freud wrote of the "institution of Superego". This bodily and intrapsychic experience, product of the process of enculturation, or of "cultural introjection", as per my own formulation, is a condition of the humanisation and socialisation of every human child.

This reflexion can, moreover, develop within the framework of a notion that would seem to be common to and utilisable by our two disciplines. It is a matter of *Kulturarbeit,* originally a German term introduced by Freud, but never defined, which has been variously translated into 'cultural work', 'work of civilization', 'cultural activity'. I myself recently undertook to define and construct this new notion from an exclusively Freudian perspective. It now seems to me to be opportune to discuss it here, especially since it has the invaluable heuristic merit of connecting socio-cultural and psychic realities, of being able to account for interrelationships between psyche and culture and to foster collaboration between psychoanalysts and anthropologists. This notion seems to be close, in certain respects, to that of anthropopoïesis mentioned above, but also to that of "work of culture" developed by Obeyesekere.

The Freudian notion of *Kulturarbeit*

Introducing the notion

We discover the first occurrence of the notion of *Kulturarbeit* in *The Interpretation of Dreams*, precisely where Freud deals with the "dream of embarrassment due to nakedness" in the section devoted to typical dreams. Indeed, he writes there of "paradise", "a group phantasy of the childhood of the individual", when human beings were naked and without shame in one another's presence until shame and anguish awoke, expulsion followed, and "sexual life and the tasks of cultural activity began".[32] This cultural activity is to be understood as the realisation, accomplishment, of human "cultural development" in its individual and social dimension, as well as in the life of society.

Then, in "'Civilized' Sexual Morality and Modern Nervous Illness", Freud used the term five times – undoubtedly as synonymous with cultural activities – associating it from the start with the process of sublimation supplying necessary energy. He wrote that, "civilized sexual morality is a sexual morality obedience to which. . . spurs men on to intense and productive cultural activity".[33] Later on, in "Thoughts for the Times on War and Death", we discover its appearance as work accomplished collectively, therefore producing a common endeavour.[34]

In 1927, in *The Future of an Illusion*, *Kulturarbeit* is mentioned four times in different acceptations. Indeed, on two occasions, Freud writes there of "coercion in the work of civilization" to which people are subjected,[35] then of the "work of civilization", which protects us from feelings of helplessness in face of the superior force and dangers of Nature,[36] for example.

The term is found two times in 1930 in *Civilization and its Discontents*, where Freud wrote that, "The work of civilization has become increasingly the business of men, it confronts them with ever more difficult tasks and compels them to carry out instinctual sublimations of which women are little capable",[37] but also produces the cultural superego expressing its demands via an ethic regulating social relations. Finally, in "Dissection of the Psychical Personality", Lecture XXXI of the *New Introductory Lectures on Psycho-Analysis*, the "work of culture" would seem analogous to psychoanalytic work and its therapeutic endeavours. For the ego, it is a matter of a work agenda for gradually conquering other pieces of the id, "Where id was, there ego shall be. It is a work of culture, not unlike the draining of the Zuider Zee".[38]

In addition, throughout Freud's work, we find numerous allusions, references, implicit, but also explicit, to *Kulturarbeit*, both in his socio-anthropological writings and in other texts. I am thinking, for example, of the notion of "individual culture" acquired during the period of latency in *Three Essays on the Theory of Sexuality*;[39] the "susceptibility to culture resting on the transformation of instincts[40] and "the process by which an individual rises to a comparatively high plane of morality"[41] in "Thoughts for the Times on War and Death" and other expressions.

I hypothesise that there is a latent, quasi-continual, presence of *Kulturarbeit* just below the surface, both in Freud's writings and in his mind. So, this notion would be something to discover through its multiple contents, processes, functions and meanings scattered throughout his writings. Let us explore them.

My construction of the notion of Kulturarbeit

Phylogenetic aspects of Kulturarbeit

From a phylogenetic point of view, according to Freud, the first stage and manifestation of *Kulturarbeit* was that accomplished by human beings in order to create culture with its institutions, its basic rules, its customs and ritual practices, its beliefs, and its systems of representations, the first product of a hypothetical "collective mind", as he termed it.

According to him, the collective murder of the father of the primal horde, followed by his being devoured by the company of sons, set this in motion. Feeling profound emotional ambivalence towards their father, at once loved, admired, feared and hated, the latter satisfied their hostility by the criminal deed and their desire to identify themselves with him by the cannibalistic act. Then their tenderness expressed itself in the form of collective repentance and a sense of guilt on each one's part, which then incited them to reinstate the father figure through the creation of a substitute, of a symbol, Durkheim would say, the totem, but also to establish basic prohibitions, those of totemism, consistent then with the two repressed desires of the Œdipus complex and also determined by the need to preserve the cohesiveness of the clan of the brothers based in particular on sublimated homosexual bonds. For Freud, these prohibitions therefore reflected the most ancient prohibitions created by human society: the prohibition of incest, the prohibition of murder and the prohibition of cannibalism.

Among these first primal institutions, Freud cited religion, morality, law, and the beginnings of a social order or an initial form of social organisation, which are interdependent.

In his "Short account of psycho-analysis", he explained that they have as their "fundamental aim the enabling of the individual to master his Œdipus complex and to divert his libido from its infantile attachments into the social ones that are ultimately desired".[42]

According to Freud, this human culture "rests on two pillars, one of which is the control of natural forces and the other the restriction of our instincts",[43] that is to say of the "primal animal status" of human beings; whence the collective and individual aspects of *Kulturarbeit*.

Kulturarbeit was in fact to become work involving two poles or fields of activities, social and individual; the latter combining the two spaces, physical and psychical.

Collective Kulturarbeit

Let us first of all look at the social pole. It is a matter of social work in Durkheim's sense of the word (Durkheim 1893), presupposing, therefore, social division.

On many occasions, mainly in *The Future of an Illusion* (1927) and *Civilization and its Discontents* (1930), Freud discussed the needs and functions of culture, its duties and obligations towards its participants, as well as its expectations, demands, and rights with regard to them. Structured in terms of the twofold difference of sexes and generations, every society maintains a social division of the activities necessary to its good functioning and establishes systems of prohibitions, dictates, norms, and values, as well as creating numerous institutions and systems of collective representation. All that contributes to its own production, its organisation, its cohesiveness, its self-preservation, and its reproduction. It is also supposed to respond to the basic material and psychical needs of its members. From the perspective of its self-preservation and of its members' need for safety, it also sets up measures for protecting against multiple dangers, in particular, those coming from its natural milieu, but above all those inherent to human hostility among its members or strangers to the community. Culture therefore works to neutralise this aggressive human instinct, on the one hand, by continually seeking modes of social relations ensuring its cohesion. According to Freud, these would mainly consist of inhibiting the aim of sexual instincts, favouring enduring social bonds, sublimating the homosexual libido, and kindling strong feelings of identification. On the other hand, another means would be the creation of a store of cultural ideals, collective representations – religious ones in particular – but also works of art, qualified as "psychical assets", something I shall come back to. These in fact participate in the development of a common inheritance constituting a cultural identity and generating feelings of social belonging.

The establishment of a cultural superego, agency belonging to the collective mind, according to Freud, comparable to the individual superego and corresponding to the latter, under the influence of which cultural development would be carried out, would produce these cultural ideals and impose its demands, the non-observance of which is punished by "fear of conscience" or "social fear". Among the latter, ethics brings together those concerning social relations. It would participate with the superego in the neutralisation of the aggressive instinct. Freud conceived of it as "a therapeutic attempt – as an endeavour to achieve, by means of a command of the super-ego, something which has so far not been achieved by means of any other cultural activities".[44]

Through the aggressive, narcissistic, libidinal renunciation required, culture imposes sacrifices on those participating in it. So, it is duty-bound to compensate them by offering them compromise solutions, a source of surrogate satisfactions. These are, Freud thought, the cultural ideals and works of art which procure a society's members new forms of satisfactions of a narcissistic kind. In addition, religion would be another gift of culture to those participating in it. Its "grandeur" rests on the accomplishment of three functions corresponding to the satisfaction of people's basic needs: the desire to know; relief of their anxiety in the face of life's dangers and vicissitudes, and comfort in unhappiness; and finally, precepts, prohibitions and restrictions, by way of rules for conducting their lives. It is an attempt to control the world of the senses by means of the world of infantile wishes ever alive in every adult.

Religion would also offer a social solution to the ambivalent conflict with the father owing to its being a universal neurosis protecting all subjects from individual neurosis. In addition, it forces prohibition of thought in the service of its self-preservation.

According to Freud, these religious representations are born out of the need to make human helplessness bearable, meaning that situation of human anxiety and weakness inherent in the ultra-powerful world of the forces of nature. They have an infantile model, therefore, are built out of memories of the helplessness of the individual's own childhood and that of the human species.

Moreover, all culture works towards the constitution and transmission of a heritage which would include a hereditary portion, "the archaic heritage". For Freud, this notion of archaic heritage therefore seems to establish a link between phylogenesis and ontogenesis, the latter constituting an abbreviated recapitulation of the development of mankind. This goes back to Ernst Haeckel's biogenetic law that "ontogenesis recapitulates phylogenesis", or rather psychogenesis recapitulates sociogenesis, according to Elias.[45] Archaic heritage would involve innate contents and specific instinctual and thought dispositions. Certain contents in its inventory become mixed up with acquired innate dispositions, as with primal phantasies and the developments of the ego and the libido. Let us cite, among others: the symbolic or "symbolic language" or "symbolic relation" consisting in thought relations between diverse objects, representations that are constituted during the historical development of language and must be repeated during the individual development of the language; "extensive" instinctual ambivalence referring to the historical development of the coexistence between impulses with an active aim, the oldest ones, and later impulses with a passive aim, whence the notion of extensiveness of ambivalence; primal phantasies as "disposition to re-acquisition" during individual development; and affects, residues of recollections of prehistoric times.

Culture therefore has a duty to transmit this heritage to its participants, securing then intergenerational bonds, those with the history of humanity, but also those with the members of society sharing this "common cultural property".

But *Kulturarbeit* also consists of cultural development work, which operates using the same means as those of the individual, presenting analogies with the organic process and involving inevitable changes. Freud showed us that it is hindered by some forms of resistance – notably by the superego and past ideal formations – with regard to new situations.

In addition, Freud draws us a picture of male/female sexual differentiation with regard to culture, *Kulturarbeit*, and sublimation. While in the beginning, women "laid the foundations of civilization by the claims of their love", they later came into opposition with its development, exercising then "a retarding and restraining influence" because they represent "the interests of family and of sexual life". And, "the work of civilization has become increasingly the business of men, it confronts them with ever more difficult tasks and compels them to carry out instinctual sublimations of which women are little capable",[46] something which can only be accomplished to the detriment of their interest in women and sexual life, consequently estranging them from their roles as husbands and fathers.

Finally, every society has expectations and rights with regard to its members, as well as possessing and imposing multiple requirements upon them. Among these, Freud differentiated those that are "useful", of vital importance, from those deemed "useless", but nevertheless important, such as beauty, cleanliness and order. The claims of justice, on the other hand, help regulate social relations, something which now brings us to the individual field of *Kulturarbeit*.

Individual Kulturarbeit

One of the aims of *Kulturarbeit*, Freud thought, is to make all subjects moral and social. So, following his thought through his numerous writings, I shall distinguish the work accomplished by every society on the body and bodily functions of its members from the psychical work realised by the ego and imposed by culture upon each one of its participants from childhood on.

The work on the body and bodily functions

The major stages of the life cycle of every individual (birth, puberty, initiation, marriage, death) would be marked by "rites of passage"[47] often involving procedures performed on the body (deformations, piercings, extracting or sharpening of teeth, circumcision, excision of the clitoris, and other types of ablation, scarification, tattooing), modifying the natural state of the body, and performed in accordance with rules particular to each society. This bodily marking enables a collectivity as a whole, as well as for each one of its members, to express the specific character of a collective and/or individual identity. Through it, a person manifests his or her status and social affiliation. Among the multiple modes of bodily marking, circumcision attracted Freud's interest, especially in *Totem and Taboo* and *Moses and Monotheism*.

Thus, in *Moses and Monotheism*,[48] he presented circumcision as a sign of the "sanctification" of the Jewish people by Moses, their founder, a visible sign marking this people off from others, thus becoming a sign of identity, a source of narcissistic satisfaction. Moreover, as a symbolic substitute for castration, it would symbolise this people's submission to their founding father.

This work of bodily marking asserted itself as a form of work of collective symbolisation characteristic of *Kulturarbeit*.

I would also like to mention the work undertaken with respect to certain bodily functions, in particular with respect to every human child's excretory functions, something I call "sphincter training" or toilet training.

Work on the psyche

As for the psychical work accomplished by the ego, Freud presented two dialectically opposed and complementary processes: the humanisation of the "human animal" through "introjection of socio-cultural components" and its socialisation or incorporation into society conferring upon it multiple social roles and statuses, therefore transforming the "human animal" from the state of "individual" into that of a "person", to use Mauss' term,[49] or of a "subject".

By the process of humanisation of the "human animal", I understand the pressure exercised by society and its culture, therefore, by "reality", by the "external world", in keeping with the expressions used by Freud, both upon the constitution of a differentiated psychical apparatus and the specific characteristics of its functioning and upon the obligatory instinctual transformation consecutive to renunciation. The psychogenesis of humanity, according to Freud, is characterised by an essential process of internalisation, of psychisation of phenomena and human experiences, from sensory perceptions to representations. Prohibitions, inhibitions and external constraints will also be internalised to constitute, at a later point, "historical sediments" belonging to mankind's archaic heritage and transmissible during the ontogenesis of each person.

The constitution of a differentiated psychical apparatus and the specific characteristics of its functioning as found in Freud's writings

If one places oneself within the context of the first topography, the substitution of the reality principle for the pleasure principle leads to a series of adaptations of the psychical apparatus involving, in particular: the institution of the activities of consciousness (attention, act of judgment, thought process. . .); the emergence and development of the preconscious system animated by the thought processes whose connection with word representations conditions access to the consciousness; repression (primal, and in the strict sense), and the establishment of the first, then second, censorship.

From the perspective of the second topography, according to Freud, if we must attribute the differentiation of the ego and the id not only to primitive humans, but – since it is the necessary expression of the influence of the external world – also to much simpler living beings, then, because born out of experiences that determined the establishment of totemic culture, the separation between the ego and the superego would represent the most significant traits of the development of the individual and of the species.

Sense organ of the entire apparatus, the ego dominates access to motility, but has slipped thought work in between need and action. It maintains alliances with culture and its current demands, although it is also in conflict with reality, which refers to the historical conflict between individual and society. It shares with culture the same aspiration to unity, that of Eros.

Plunging its roots into the id, and heir to the Œdipus complex, more precisely to the castration complex, through its functions of self-observation, of conscience and of ideal, the "institution of the superego" constitutes one of the major accomplishments of *Kulturarbeit* realised on each individual's psyche. This creation–establishment of the superego is a "most precious cultural asset in the psychological field".[50] The people in which it is realised go from being the adversaries of culture they once were to being vehicles of culture; whence also the idea of "participants in the culture".

Built upon the model of the parental superego, becoming "impersonal" later on, the child's superego fills up with the same content and thus becomes "the vehicle of tradition and of all the time-resisting judgements of value which have propagated themselves in this manner from generation to generation",[51] something which also ensures psychical continuity between them. However, yielding only slowly to the influences of the present, therefore to changes, the past continues to live in the "ideologies of the superego". This is why mankind never lives entirely in the present.

The obligatory instinctual transformation subsequent to renunciation

In *Three Essays on the Theory of Sexuality*, Freud considered that the organisation of human sexual development into two phases, those of childhood and of puberty, separated by the latency stage, represented "one of the conditions of the aptitude of men to developing a higher civilization, but also of their tendency to neurosis".[52]

Indeed, "in the space of a few years the little primitive creature must turn into a civilized human being",[53] meaning that he or she will have had to take a major shortcut to traverse a quite long portion of the development of human culture so as later to become "what we call a normal man, the bearer and in part the victim, of the civilization that has been so painfully acquired".[54] This is precisely the object of *Kulturarbeit* for every human child or, expressed in another way, the task of education which, according to Freud, is representative of the "cultural demands in the family" and would be sustained by the child's playing, guided especially by the desire to grow up and be an adult.

Acting upon the sexual instinct and upon the aggressive instinct, this instinctual transformation-reorganisation necessarily active all throughout each person's life is put in place during "ontogenesis", which according to Freud would be "organically determined and fixed by heredity".[55]

After the "programmed dissolution" of the Œdipus complex, because of the threat of castration (in boys), it would be characterised by:

- the repression of infantile sexuality accompanied by its major reaction-formations, which are disgust, shame, pity, morality, as well as the barring of incest, but also those connected with anal eroticism (order and cleanliness) so important for culture and contributing to the formation of character;
- aim–inhibition expressed by feelings of tenderness for family and friends;
- the establishment and development of the work of sublimation of the ego, which will be considered later on;

- the development of feelings of identification, both parental ones constituting the nucleus of the superego and ones involving the formation of character of the ego playing a role in the construction of a post-oedipal sexual identity;
- a limiting of narcissism, and the development of object-love, the transformation of selfish impulses into social instincts by adding erotic components of a homosexual nature;
- the twofold reversal of instinct, in particular of sadism into masochism, would be clearly favoured by *Kulturarbeit* – these sadistic instincts may also be subject to other socially acceptable fates, in particular, their sublimation associated with the energy of scopic pleasure would be at the origin of the instinct to know;
- finally, the "instinct of destruction, moderated and tamed, and, as it were, inhibited in its aim, must, when it is directed towards objects, provide the ego with the satisfaction of its vital needs and with control over nature".[56]

Freud nevertheless detected a difference between the sexes, especially as concerns the building up of the reaction-formations of the latency stage and the structuration of the superego.

In *Three Essays on the Theory of Sexuality*, he noted that this building up takes place earlier in a little girl, and encounters less resistance in her, than in a boy, just as engaging in the repression process seemed greater, or of greater significance. Moreover, when manifesting themselves, partial sexual instincts prefer to take a passive form. On the other hand, the auto-eroticism of the erogenous zones would be the same in both sexes; whence the absence of sexual difference in childhood.

Later, with regard to the superego, Freud points out to us that in girls, their distinct structuration leads to a different level of morality. The "switching off" of the castration anxiety would be replaced by another form of anxiety, that of loss of object-love dependent on external conditions. And, Freud reminds us, "the superego is never so inexorable, so impersonal, so independent of its emotional origins as when we require it in men".[57]

Around the age of eleven years, the advent of that flood tide of sexual need, in fact finds in these reaction-formations dykes that prescribe for it outlets called normal and make it impossible for it to revive the perverse instincts subjected to repression.

The ban on incest having been established during the latency stage, parents can perform their task, which is to guide their pubescent child in the choice of the sexual object that will exclude them as primary love-objects and will be oriented towards strangers.

At the same time that they overcome and reject their plainly incestuous phantasies, adolescents must accomplish, Freud tells us, "one of the most significant, but also one of the most painful, psychical achievements of the pubertal period. . . detachment from parental authority, a process that alone makes possible the opposition, which is so important for the progress of civilization, between the new generation and the old".[58] For every adolescent, this detachment from the family becomes a task that society often helps him or her solve by means of puberty and initiation rites, explained Freud in *Civilization and its Discontents*.[59]

On the socialisation of the individual

This work of instinctual transformation-reorganisation would determine every individual's conditions of socialisation. This process would also involve each one's "socialisation of sexuality", meaning the acquisition of a genital sexuality in the service of reproduction, having subordinated pregenital instincts and involving a convergence towards the same goal and object of flows of tenderness and sensuality during puberty. This socialised sexuality said to be normal would cause culture to progress, affirmed Freud, in "'Civilized' Sexual Morality and Modern Nervous Illness". Moreover, one would find aim–inhibition and sublimation of the homosexual libido at work contributing to the establishment of lasting social bonds, friendship, the formation of social feelings based on identifications stemming from reaction-formations against hostile and jealous impulses, a substitution of ideal cultural objects for each person's ego ideal, thus a prevailing of objectality over narcissism in the individual libidinal economy. Indeed, within society, the curtailment of narcissism – therefore, of singularities – to the benefit of similarities and object-love could but inhibit the hostile impulses arising out of narcissistic self-assertion intolerant of the slightest difference that could then find satisfaction outside the society in question, which indicated to Freud that (object) love is a factor favouring culture.

What can now be said of the role of sublimation in this process of the individual's "incorporation into society"?

This social, non-sexual, fate of pregenital instincts immediately fits in at the boundary line between two realities – intrapsychic-individual and collective, socio-cultural – realising then the transition from one to the other and the essential connection between them. Several of Freud's texts attest to this. For instance, in *Three Essays on the Theory of Sexuality* and "'Civilized' Sexual Morality and Modern Nervous Illness", he accorded "cultural value" to the capacity to change the aim of the sexual instinct.

In *Civilization and its Discontents*, Freud established particularly interesting connections among sublimation, work, libidinal economy, and social integration in every individual. He in fact presented professional work as a sublimational activity procuring psychical benefits and also determining a primordial condition of the social existence of every subject, something which, moreover, raises questions regarding the limits of the social field of sublimations.

The work of sublimation would thus consist of psychical work accomplished by the ego of every subject experiencing the double pressure of the superego and of culture. Both individual and collective, it consists of a process of derivation, after desexualisation, of perverse sexual instincts from their initial aim towards aims that are non-sexual, socio-cultural, but nevertheless "psychically related to the former". These new aims and objects concern social activities, cultural products – material as well as ideological, scientific, artistic – contributing to the life of the said culture, this symbolic universe enveloping and unifying every human community.

Inspired by Freud, who tried to define the concept of instinct, I would say that regarding its individual pole, Kulturarbeit *is the psychical work required of all individuals by culture, relayed and supported by the superego, with a view to connecting them to social realities, meaning to incorporate them into society, therefore, to their participation in culture.*

Nonetheless, if the essential goal of *Kulturarbeit*, as well as of Eros, seems to me to be the creation of multiple psychical, psychosocial, and social ties, to be noted is the frequent, even quasi-permanent, existence of situations of undoing of ties, even of excessive ties, therefore, of failures of *Kulturarbeit*, on both the individual and social level, very probably proceeding from vicissitudes in the shifting, unstable balance of forces of linking-integration (Eros) and undoing-disintegration (instincts of destruction) within individuals and society.

Thus, these failures of *Kulturarbeit* can be conceived of as, on the one hand, pathological social products, like war and other regressive collective manifestations and, on the other hand, as individual pathological products.

Finally, I shall close this examination of the similarities between psychoanalysis and anthropology by looking, with Devereux, at the anxiety engendered by the materials – mobilising then defence mechanisms – and the counter-transferential situation experienced both by ethnologists in the field, in the relationship to the group chosen and to their informants, and by analysts, with the clinico–analytical couple they form with patients. The reflexion developed by Devereux is of considerable significance for exploring and understanding the places in which these two human sciences converge.

Indeed, when engaged in observation, the researcher is inevitably exposed to materials that trigger or can trigger anxiety, which mobilise in them different sorts of defence mechanisms, sources of counter-transferential distortions of these very materials. So it is that Devereux defined counter-transference as being

> the sum total of those distortions in the psychoanalyst's perception of, and reaction to his patient which cause him to respond to his patient as though he were an early imago and to act in the analytic situation in terms of his own – usually infantile *unconscious* needs, wishes and fantasies.[60]

And he added that it "is strictly a matter of convention that the relevant reactions of the informant or of the analysand are called 'transference' and those of the field worker or of the analyst 'counter-transference'".[61]

Indeed, among the sources of the distortions that researchers impose upon observation, recording and interpretation of their materials figure, besides the researcher's personality, the models of the culture to which they belong, their social implantation involving the influence of their cultural and ethnic status, class affiliation, and the influence of ideology. In the vast field of measures shielding against anxiety,

Devereux especially brought up "professional" defences such as methodological positions and technical devices. He preferred to discuss the actual manifestations of these distortions, which he classified into three categories: the relationship to data, the relationship to informants and to the tribe as persons, the "complementary role". Concerning the relationship to data, he cited: the inexactness of facts, contradictions, and obscure written expression often caused by unconscious scotomisations, but also selectivity and the different types of it; preference for a domain of study, but also the manner of using and interpreting data, what is called "exotic" selectivity.

One of the major sources of anxiety derives from identifying with the other person and with other people, human beings like ethnologists and psychoanalysts, and resonances with certain aspects of the unconscious psychic life of these researchers. Indirect self-observation, the ability to be both in the position of subject and of object of observation are common to both disciplines. So a methodological and ideological defensive measure consists in establishing protective distance while seeking to exaggerate differences between oneself and others, by looking for what is unique and specific, something which leads, according to Devereux, to denying the psychic unity of humanity and to attributing a "special" psychology to each ethnic group. He remarks that this tendency is fairly marked among the ethnologists hostile to psychoanalysis, who tend to ignore the latent traits counterbalancing the obvious extreme cultural traits. He considered that this was the case with cultural relativism, dealing as it does with others and their practices as depersonalised objects of observation. Consequently, the "real, though unacknowledged and unconscious, aim" of these distancing and "objectifying" measures would be "the interruption of the all-important dialogue of the unconscious".[62] However, Devereux considered that an "authentic behavioral science will come into being when its practitioners will realize that a realistic science of mankind can only be created by men most aware of their own humanity precisely when they implement it most completely in their scientific work".[63]

Finally, Devereux considered that a rapprochement could be made between ethnologists and psychoanalysts, notably, by using psychoanalytical techniques in the ethnographic field, and also by sharing the key concept of culture and one of their objectives consisting of a comprehension of the essence of the culture.

Just as the unconscious becomes a "unifying object" of human sciences, therefore linking anthropology and psychoanalysis, culture becomes another common object, to be shared scientifically. As the unconscious is individual, intrapsychic, and socio-cultural, culture is extra-individual, collective, but also individual, intrapsychic and bodily. Freud had begun to detect this with *Totem and Taboo* and had amply demonstrated it in *Civilization and its Discontents*. The notion of *Kulturarbeit* that I have presented accounts for this complex dialectic reality in an exemplary fashion. Róheim, then Devereux, also expressed this in their writings. *Consequently, through their primary common object – human beings – psychoanalysis and anthropology in fact share two major attributes of its "humanity": the unconscious and culture. The Œdipus complex acting to establish the connections and the notion of* Kulturarbeit *could then acquire the status of interdisciplinary concept accounting for this new epistemological reality.*

Finally, I must not fail to point out a similar attitude adopted by anthropologists and psychoanalysts with regard to their ways of viewing empirical reality and the theoretical corpus of their interlocutors. Both in fact tend to reduce the richness and complexity of their respective fields, psychic reality and socio-cultural and historical reality. They likewise do not have a good understanding of their concepts, their theoretical models and the history of their disciplines. These characteristics enable us to understand, at least partially, certain misunderstandings as well as the multiple reciprocal distortions and manipulations that have occurred. All this raises a major question regarding conditions conducive to a scientifically fruitful collaboration between these two sciences. Before proposing some elements of a response to this question, let us inquire into the relevance of these new disciplines, which I term "products of acculturative phenomena".

Reflexions on the new "acculturative" disciplines

During the course of this debate, people have repeatedly said and written that with *Totem and Taboo* Freud created psychoanalytical anthropology. This interpretation gives a way of explaining the "true" creation of a discipline. As Freud had already defined it on multiple occasions, psychoanalysis indeed establishes a "bridge" between the medical and cultural sciences. By the very nature and characteristics of its object of exploration, the unconscious, psychoanalysis would therefore necessarily have to be in quest of its diverse expressions, individual and collective, intrapsychic, bodily and socio-cultural. So, in writing *Totem and Taboo*, Freud pursued and developed his multidimensional investigation of the unconscious in accordance with his own psychoanalytical methodology, valid and applicable for him, in an undistinguishable manner, in both the intrapsychic and the socio-cultural field, the two being considered analogous. He dealt with socio-cultural data as psychic facts extracted from their socio-cultural and historical context, which was one of his great methodological errors, and other analysts followed him in this. And what if he had known of the Maussian notion of "total social fact"?

Róheim's psychoanalytical anthropology

If Freud is considered to have created psychoanalytical anthropology with *Totem and Taboo*, Róheim was the first ethnologist and psychoanalyst in history. It was he who founded the field, conferring upon it objects, methodology, some concepts, a representation of culture and socio-cultural facts. He is the one who established and developed it as a new discipline, the product of an acculturation, of a meeting of psychoanalysis and anthropology. But what psychoanalysis was it a matter of and what were the anthropological domains concerned?

Róheim would call himself a Freudian, but his psychoanalytical anthropology was also inspired, and amply so, by Ferenczi's and Klein's ideas, which enriched it but, as I have noted, brought with it the risk of distorting Freudian concepts. The influence of the biologist Louis Bolk would also have an effect on his ontogenetic approach to culture. Having as objectives the affirmation of the unity of human beings and mankind and the exploration of the popular, traditional and cultural expressions of the unconscious, the anthropologist–psychoanalyst would necessarily be a practising psychoanalyst who would himself observe and collect the materials in the field, which he would analyse and interpret at a later point. So we understand that this anthropologist–psychoanalyst was Róheim himself, serving as an exemplary model and "ideal type" for future researchers – of which there would not be very many, given these high standards.

From this perspective, the methodology advocated would be that of the psychoanalyst working within specific socio-cultural contexts with "adjustments" imposed by the specific nature of the field. The study of dreams of indigenous peoples, the analysis of children's games, the exploration of symbolism in myths, rituals, customs, stories, but also an investigation of sexual life would therefore be necessary. While Róheim recognised the reductive nature of psychoanalysis, tending to reduce heterogeneity to homogeneity, the richness of the multifaceted to some essential figures, as he was too preoccupied with detecting collective and individual expressions of the Œdipus complex, and did not seem to be aware of another reductive aspect of his approach consisting of underestimating the complexity of the historical, cultural and social reality he was studying. Characterising a culture by its particular type of ontogenetic trauma is of that order. His selective, therefore reductive, approach can only attack the scientific value of his work, something which, moreover, his anthropologist colleagues have done.

Abram Kardiner's psychoanalytical anthropology

Things are completely different with Kardiner and his approach aiming at exploring the relationships between the individual and his or her society. His psychoanalysis was not Freudian, but American, centred rather on the ego and its mechanisms of adaptation. In addition, the epistemological context in which it evolved was dominated by behaviourist psychology and culturalist anthropology. Kardiner presented us with a rather mechanical vision of the relationships between the individual and his or her society, according to which, cut off from his or her conflictual, phantasising, instinctual and unconscious dimension, the individual is reduced to a list of fundamental biological needs and a system of adaptation to the external world, to institutions conditioning him or her, while the culture is transformed into a catalogue of primary and secondary institutions. The basic personality concept characteristic of a given culture that Kardiner endeavoured to introduce and define was located between the two types of institutions. Moreover, he conceived of society as rather a homogenous, undifferentiated, totality, without multiplicity and hierarchisation of groups or divisions, and the essential conflictuality of social relationships. Based on empirical study, his theorisation rejected the somewhat speculative Freudian concepts. Besides, Kardiner distorted those he retained and oversimplified socio-anthropological concepts. Nevertheless, he chose to collaborate with anthropologists, with Ralph Linton in particular, who provided him with ethnographic materials to interpret in accordance with his anthropo–analytical approach and tried to think through the complexity of individual/society relations.

Erich Fromm's analytical psycho-sociology

Fromm tried to establish connections between Freudian psychoanalysis and Marxist sociology by particularly stressing the action of economic factors upon the moulding of the individual's psyche through the intermediary of the family considered as society's psychological agency. He in fact interpreted psycho-sociological phenomena as processes of the adaptation of the instinctual apparatus to the economic and social situation. He introduced notions of "libidinal structure", then of "social character", products of the action of socio-economic conditions upon instinctual tendencies, productive forces of society participating in the creation of "ideological superstructures". We find elements of Marxist language there. He also took an interest in and undertook a psycho-sociological analysis of the capitalistic bourgeois mind.

Thus Fromm was principally intent upon studying his contemporary society, the influence of economic factors upon the "instinctual apparatus" of the individual as psycho-social productive force. Moreover, he adopted a fairly critical attitude toward certain Freudian concepts. That is why his analytical psycho-sociology seems quite reductive to me.

Devereux's complementarist ethnopsychoanalysis

By considering that psychoanalysis and ethnology provide complementary, not supplementary, understandings, then by deeming that psychoanalytical investigation must be interrupted at a certain point and at a certain moment in time in order to make room for ethnological investigation, Devereux expressed a certain realism and quite lucid methodological circumspection. Unlike Róheim, he held that, in the ethnographic field, one cannot play the role of ethnologist and psychoanalyst at the same time. Ethnologists will be able to analyse and interpret certain ethnographic data from a psychoanalytical perspective at a later time.

I shall not go back over his rich conceptualisation, over the dialectic relations between culture and psyche, the creation of ethnopsychiatry. Let me say, however, that the psychoanalytical approach of Devereux – who considered himself to be an orthodox Freudian – was inevitably particularly marked by his American training, which led him to underestimate the instinctual dimension of the psyche.

Group psychoanalysis

Anzieu and Kaës made a considerable contribution to the development of group psychoanalysis, a discipline shedding invaluable light on the unconscious aspects of collective products and formations, which could considerably enrich psychoanalytical anthropology.

Kaës taught us that the group experience is one of assembling or fitting together three spaces: that of the group, that of intersubjective ties, and that of the position of each subject in the group. The common identifications, shared phantasies and representations, the formations of the ideal, the common dream matrix, unconscious alliances and phoric functions would then be the points of passage and of rupture between the intrapsychic space and the intersubjective space.

I should also like to bring up again the explanations and clarifications formulated by Anzieu concerning the universality of the unconscious and the relationships of the "individual" unconscious and "collective" unconscious. Deeming the notion of the universality of the unconscious "too vague", he considered it to be justified by the existence of a limited number of unconscious processes, the same everywhere and always, namely the representations-representatives of drives, anxiety, the defence mechanisms and phantasies. However, the organisation of these processes, their ways of combining, vary depending on the individuals, the groups and societies; whence his hypothesis of the independence of individual organisations and collective organisations in terms of their origin and their functioning, each one functioning for its part, in its sector.

This twofold hypothesis of the universality of the unconscious and the independence of the collective and individual formations of the unconscious would, according to him, allow one to guard against the counter-transferential temptation of a narcissistic symbiosis which would lead to misjudging the differences in the organisation of the unconscious, not only among individuals, but among groups and peoples.[64]

Obeyesekere's psychoanalytical anthropology

Obeyesekere's approach is inspired by Freud and Ricœur. Rejecting the instinctual, energetic and dynamic aspect of psychoanalytical theory, it retains its hermeneutic aspect, taking *The Interpretation of Dreams* and the notion of dream work as its primary reference, then the first topography of the psychic apparatus. With his notion of "work of culture", he endeavours to account for the relationships between unconscious deep motivations and culture through the exploration of processes of symbolic transformations of these deep motivations in personal symbols and collective representations. Ricœur's theory of symbols has been a rich source of inspiration for him, while, combining precise description and interpretation, the study of the great Freudian clinical cases has served as a model for him for both psycho-ethnography and ethnography.

Although very enticing, his psychoanalytical anthropology attempts to solve the Freudian puzzle of the intertwining of the energetic and meaning by splitting its two components so as to favour hermeneutics, something which leads to epistemological irrelevancy and impoverishes the procedure, and therefore the data's interpretative and explanatory value.

Notes

1 *Op cit.*, Green, *La Causalité psychique*, p. 119.
2 *Op. cit.*, Kilani, *L'Invention de l'autre*, p. 14.
3 Francis Affergan, "Introduction", in Francis Affergan, Sylvana Borutti, Claude Calame, Ugo Fabietti, Monder Kilani & Francesco Remotti (eds.), *Figures de l'humain. Les représentations de l'anthropologie*, Paris, Editions de l'Ecole des Hautes Etudes en Sciences Sociales, 2003, p. 11.
4 *Op. cit.*, Kilani, *L'Invention de l'autre*, pp. 16–17.
5 *Ibid.*, p. 11.
6 *Ibid.*
7 *Ibid.*, pp. 11–12.
8 André Green, *La Pensée clinique,* Paris, Odile Jacob, 2002, p. 13.
9 *Ibid.*, p. 11.
10 *Ibid.*
11 *Ibid.*, p. 12.
12 *Ibid.*, p. 13.
13 *Ibid.*, p. 27.
14 *Ibid.*, p. 29.
15 Sigmund Freud (1923), "Psycho-Analysis", S.E., 18. London, Hogarth, p. 247.
16 *Op cit.*, Green, *La Causalité psychique*, pp. 274–275.
17 *Ibid.*, p. 283.
18 Paul-Laurent Assoun, *Introduction à l'épistémologie freudienne*, Paris, Payot, 1981, p. 25.
19 Sigmund Freud (1915e), "The Unconscious", S.E. 14. London: Hogarth, p. 181.
20 *Op. cit.*, Devereux, *From Anxiety to Method in the Behavioral Sciences*, p. xix.
21 *Op. cit.*, Francis Affergan, et al., p. 13.
22 Clifford Geertz, *The Interpretation of Cultures. Selected Essays*, New York, Basic Books, 1973.
23 *Op. cit.*, Francis Affergan et al. Ugo Fabietti, "Identités collectives comme constructions de l'humain", pp. 175–214.
24 *Ibid.*, Mondher Kilani, "Cannibalisme and anthropopoiésis", p. 218.
25 Françoise Héritier, "Les fabrications possibles and pensables d'un produit humain", in C. Calame & M. Kilani (eds.), *La Fabrication de l'humain dans les cultures et dans l'anthropologie*, Lausanne, Payot, 1999, pp. 139–152.
26 *Op. cit.*, Green, "Oedipe, Freud et nous", p. 146.
27 *Ibid.*
28 *Op. cit.*, Anzieu, "Freud et la mythologie", p. 136–137.
29 *Op. cit.*, Devereux, *From Anxiety to Method in the Behavioral Sciences*, p. 159.
30 André Green, "Méconnaissance de l'inconscient", in R. Dorey, *L'inconscient et la science*, Paris, Dunod, 1991.
31 Mondher Kilani, "Cannibalisme and anthropopoiésis", in *op. cit.*, Affergan et al., p. 245.
32 *Op. cit.*, Freud, *The Interpretation of Dreams*, p. 245.
33 Sigmund Freud, "'Civilized' Sexual Morality and Modern Nervous Illness" (1908), S.E., 9, London, Hogarth, p. 181.
34 Sigmund Freud, "Thoughts for the Times on War and Death" (1915), S.E., 14, London, Hogarth.
35 Sigmund Freud, *The Future of an Illusion* (1927), S.E., 21, London, Hogarth, pp. 7, 8.
36 *Ibid.*, p. 16.
37 *Op. cit.*, Freud, *Civilization and Its Discontents*, p. 103.
38 Sigmund Freud, "The Dissection of the Psychical Personality" (1933), Lecture XXXI of *New Introductory Lectures on Psycho-analysis*, S.E., 22, London: Hogarth, p. 80.
39 Sigmund Freud, "Three Essays on the Theory of Sexuality" (1905), S.E., 7, London: Hogarth, p. 242.
40 *Op. cit.*, Freud, "Thoughts for the Times on War and Death", pp. 282–284.
41 *Ibid.*, p. 281.

42 Sigmund Freud, "A Short Account of Psycho-analysis" (1924), S.E., 19, London, Hogarth, p. 208.
43 Sigmund, Freud, "The Resistances to Psycho-analysis" (1925), S.E., 19. London, Hogarth, p. 219.
44 *Op. cit.*, Freud, *Civilization and Its Discontents*, p. 142.
45 Norbert Elias, *Über den Prozess der Zivilization*. Basel: Haus zum Falken, 1939. In English: *The Civilizing Process: Sociogenetic and Psychogenetic Investigations*. Oxford: Blackwell Publishers, 2000 (revised edition).
46 *Op. cit.*, Freud, *Civilization and Its Discontents*, p. 103.
47 Arnold van Gennep, *Les Rites de passage*, Paris, Picard, 1981 (1909).
48 Sigmund Freud, "Moses and Monotheism" (1939), S.E., 23. London, Hogarth.
49 Marcel Mauss, "Real and Practical Relationships between Psychology and Sociology", *Sociology and Psychology: Essays by Marcel Mauss*, London, Routledge and Kegan Paul, 1979 (1924).
50 *Op. cit.*, Freud, *The Future of an Illusion*, p. 11.
51 *Op. cit.*, Freud, "The Dissection of the Psychical Personality", p. 67.
52 *Op. cit.*, Freud, "Three Essays on the Theory of Sexuality", p. 234.
53 Sigmund Freud, "An Outline of Psycho-analysis" (1940), S.E., 23, London, Hogarth, p. 185.
54 Sigmund Freud, "Five Lectures on Psycho-analysis" (1910), S.E., 11, London, Hogarth, p. 36.
55 *Op. cit.*, Freud, "Three Essays on the Theory of Sexuality", p. 177.
56 *Op. cit.*, Freud, *Civilization and its Discontents*, p. 121.
57 Sigmund Freud, "Some Psychical Consequences of the Anatomical Distinction between the Sexes" (1925), S.E., 19, London, Hogarth, p. 257.
58 *Op. cit.*, Freud, "Three Essays on the Theory of Sexuality", p. 227.
59 *Op. cit.*, Freud, *Civilization and Its Discontents*, p. 103.
60 *Op. cit.*, Devereux, *From Anxiety to Method in the Behavioral Sciences*, pp. 41–42.
61 *Ibid.*, p. 42.
62 *Ibid.*, p. 161.
63 *Ibid.*, p. xx.
64 *Op. cit.*, Anzieu, "Freud et la mythologie", p. 244.

BY WAY OF CONCLUSION

Towards conditions conducive to fruitful scientific collaboration

This conflictual history and the modest contributions I have been able to make toward understanding it, invite one to think that the determinants and issues are more matters of identity and ideology than of science. In addition, they lead us to consider that psychoanalysis and anthropology, human sciences, ultimately share two common objects, interdependent attributes and components of humanity: the unconscious and culture. Just as the unconscious is individual, intrapsychic and bodily, but is also present within socio-cultural reality, culture as shared, collective reality, is also present in the unconscious psyche of individuals through the agencies of the ego, superego and the ego ideal. These objects therefore act to unify the human sciences. Psychoanalysis and anthropology, henceforth interdependent by virtue of their shared common objects could consequently offer us a complementary understanding of the unity, diversity, and complexity of this human reality. Nonetheless, this situation risks generating identity difficulties with the dangers of encroaching on the other discipline's territory arousing hostile reactions, something which has already been amply observed and related.

I have also found that the conflict crystallised by the problem of the universality of the Œdipus complex, the object of multiple interpretations and manipulations, was the product of a displacement. Indeed, it indirectly expressed that engendered by the discovery of the universality of the unconscious and its two poles, individual and collective, intrapsychic, bodily, and socio-cultural. As long as it remained intrapsychic, its discovery was bearable, under certain conditions, but unpalatable nonetheless. However, by venturing beyond its bounds, *Totem and Taboo* triggered the reactional hostility of anthropologists intrinsic to this very intrusion into their own field but, by afterwardness, this hostility above all also expressed and signified the violence of the rejection of this discovery of the unconscious, which incidentally remains so little understood and quite mysterious even nowadays. Moreover, I find that the Œdipus complex acts to link the unconscious and culture, founder of the "human identity and community", as well as of subjectivity.

In an exemplary fashion, the notion of *Kulturarbeit* accounts for this complex dialectic reality represented by the interrelations between the unconscious psyche and culture. Róheim, then Devereux, also gave voice to this. It could then acquire the status of interdisciplinary concept accounting for this new epistemological reality.

In addition, I have noted that among the "acculturative" disciplines produced in the course of this conflictual history, there was not one, but several, psychoanalytical anthropologies and ethnopsychoanalyses going by different names, not to mention attempts at analytical psycho-sociology. They all show an interest in searching for connections between two fields of knowledge, inevitably involving methodological and conceptual problems and ones of theoretical reference and delimitation of a specific field. They all are based on the recognition of the unconscious and the richness of its socio-cultural manifestations which it would be a matter of exploring in terms of the hypothesis of its presence, as much intrapsychic, individual, as socio-cultural, collective. Nevertheless, the psychoanalytical references differ. Moreover, how is one to detect and identify the unconscious processes and products at work in the vast historical, cultural, and social field? How is one to analyse the processes of transformation and the different stages, going from psychic representations to symbolic cultural representations? As Anzieu emphasised, it is indispensable to differentiate the two types of organisation of the processes and formations of the individual and collective unconscious. How is one to differentiate what would be a matter of unconscious determinism in a socio-cultural fact from other determinisms of, for example, a social, political, economic, ideological, and historical nature – something which obliges one to exercise particular prudence? We could also inquire into the impact of socio-cultural and historical reality on the psyche and on the course of the lives of individuals, members of a given society. Psychoanalytical anthropology should also explore this other direction.

Despite the interest of these multiple approaches inevitably having their own limitations and shortcomings, I am not convinced of the need to create a psychoanalytical anthropology, no matter what the psychoanalytical references and limitations of its field may be in particular. I consider that a proper consideration of the epistemological foundations of psychoanalysis, legitimating its possible exploration of the socio-cultural field, must connect with an anthropology fully acknowledging the existence of the unconscious, its universality, its processes and its collective and individual products, just as a recognition by psychoanalysis and anthropology of the intrapsychic and bodily incorporation of the culture proves to be fundamental. I consider that a psychoanalytical anthropology justifying its existence through a specific, therefore necessarily more profound, approach to an aspect of human reality partakes in this generalised dismembering of knowledge which has conflictual implications for identity and science.

All that has succeeded in convincing me of the need to elaborate principles for collaboration, rather than for the creation of a new discipline or sub-discipline, an "acculturative product of a defensive nature" within this turbulent historical context.

A first principle for collaboration between psychoanalysts and anthropologists would be the recognition, on the one hand, of the existence of two different orders of reality – psychic and socio-cultural; and on the other hand of the extent and complexity of the reality upon which each party works.

A second principle would consist of an indispensable presentation of their respective psychoanalytical and anthropological language and thought, though this is always something difficult and time-consuming. This slow process of acculturation would in fact enable them to be more receptive to the discourse of their colleagues, to understand better, therefore, to assimilate their mode of thought and approach to socio-cultural and psychic facts. In thus dialoguing, they would identify their similarities and their differences, something which would later help them to elaborate a discourse, not common but complementary, regarding certain common objects of investigation.

Some questions need answering. For example, is collaboration always necessary? Are there research objects ruling out the participation of one of the two, in particular when it is a matter of psychic facts unconnected to socio-cultural reality, or of historical, social or cultural, economic, political or technological facts in which no unconscious psychic factor can be made to play a role? Without a doubt, certain objects, both psychoanalytical and anthropological will be favoured in any fruitful pluri- and interdisciplinary collaboration.

The third principle is that, the object having been chosen – psychoanalytical or anthropological – prior work, in accordance with one's own discipline, would be undertaken, then if it is judged necessary or desirable, a complementary approach would be envisaged within a collective framework, within which this work would be presented as good material for further reflexion and the object of collective "free association" between psychoanalysts and anthropologists. In order to be able to understand one another, this would call for vigilance regarding the differences of language. The attempts at collective analysis and interpretation resorting to specific concepts and notions will therefore take place both within this framework and at a distance, in afterwardness.

It is this work of regular encounters and collective reflexion, but also at a distance, in an interplay of proximity and distance-taking that would prove to be a determinant factor in arriving at a richer, deeper understanding of well-circumscribed facts and objects. We are there together in a common interpretative process of translating human realities, therefore, of research having multiple meanings, but in different and complementary languages. It cannot, therefore, be accomplished within the omnipotence of a single discipline or a single researcher, but within the framework of long-term, structured, well-intentioned inter- and pluridisciplinary collaboration. Although potentially conflictual and anxiety-provoking, the welcoming and comparison of differences of thought are also the source of discoveries and innovative conceptual products leading researchers toward interpretations that are original because they are less split apart by their reductive approaches.

A truly scientific dialogue based on reciprocal profound knowledge and genuine interests is thus made possible. It will ultimately, at the very least, free people from entanglement in parasitical identity and ideological issues, as well as from the grip of certain beliefs of a projective nature.

BIBLIOGRAPHY

Affergan, Francis. "Introduction", in Francis Affergan, Sylvana Borutti, Claude Calame, Ugo Fabietti, Mondher Kilani & Francesco Remotti (eds.), *Figures de l'humain. Les représentations de l'anthropologie*, Paris, Editions de l'Ecole des Hautes Etudes en Sciences Sociales, 2003.

Anzieu, Didier. "Freud et la mythologie", *Nouvelle revue de psychanalyse*, Paris, Gallimard, 1970, No.1, pp. 114–145.

Anzieu, Didier. *The Group and the Unconscious*. London, Routledge, 1984. Originally published as *Le groupe et l'inconscient*, Paris, Dunod, 1975.

Anzieu, Didier."Le moi-peau", *Nouvelle Revue de Psychanalyse*, No 9, pp. 195–208, 1974.

Assoun, Paul-Laurent. *Freud et les sciences sociales*, Paris, Armand Colin, 1993.

Assoun, Paul-Laurent. *Introduction à l'épistémologie freudienne*, Paris, Payot, 1981.

Assoun, Paul-Laurent. *Lacan*, Paris, Presses Universitaires de France, 2003.

Bidou, Patrice. "Arguments", introduction to a special issue of *L'Homme,* "Une anthropologie psychanalytique est-elle possible?" January, 1999.

Boas, Franz. "Foreword" to Margaret Mead's *Coming of Age in Samoa,* New York, HarperCollins, 2001 (1928).

Boas, Franz. "Methods of Ethnology", *American Anthropologist,* Vol. 22, No 4, 1920.

Dadoun, Roger. *Géza Róheim et l'essor de l'anthropologie psychanalytique*, Paris, Payot, 1972.

Devereux, Georges. *Basic Problems of Ethnopsychiatry*, Chicago, IL, University of Chicago Press, 1980.

Devereux, Georges. "Culture and the Unconscious", in *A Study of Abortion in Primitive Societies: A Typological, Distributional and Dynamical Analysis of the Prevention of Birth in 400 Preindustrial Societies*, New York, Julian Press, 1955, republished in *Ethnopsychoanalysis: Psychoanalysis and Anthropology as Complementary Frames of Reference,* Berkeley, CA, University of California Press, 1978.

Devereux, Georges. "Ethnopsychoanalytic Reflexions on the Notion of Kinship", 1965, republished in *Ethnopsychoanalysis and Anthropology as Complementary Frames of Reference,* Berkeley, CA, University of California Press, 1978.

Devereux, Georges. *From Anxiety to Method in the Behavioral Sciences*, The Hague, Mouton & Co., 1967.

Devereux, Georges. "Mohave Ethnopsychiatry and Suicide: the psychiatric knowledge and the psychic disturbances of an Indian tribe", Washington, D.C., *Bureau of American Ethnology Bulletin*, No. 175, 1961.

Devereux, Georges. "Normal and Abnormal: The Key Problem of Psychiatric Anthropology", in *Some Uses of Anthropology: Theoretical and Applied*, Washington, D.C., The Anthropological Society of Washington, 1956. Cited here as published in "Normal and Abnormal", Chapter 13 in Roland Littlewood and Simon Dein (eds.), *Cultural Psychiatry & Medical Anthropology: an introduction and reader*, London, Athlone Press, 2000.

Devereux, Georges. "A Sociological Theory of Schizophrenia", *Psychoanalytic Review*, Vol. 26, No. 3, pp. 315–142. Republished in *Basic Problems of Ethnopsychiatry*, Chicago, IL, University of Chicago Press, 1980, pp. 185–213.

Duparc, François. *André Green*, Paris, Presses Universitaires de France, 1996.

Durkheim, Émile. *The Division of Labour in Society*, Basingstoke UK, Palgrave Macmillan, 2013 (1893).

Durkheim, Émile. *The Elementary Forms of Religious Life*, Oxford, Oxford University Press, 2001 (1912).

Durkheim, Émile. *The Rules of Sociological Method: And Selected Texts on Sociology and Its Method*, New York, Free Press, 2013 (1895).

Durkheim, Émile, *Suicide*, London, Routledge, 2002 (1897).

Elias, Norbert. *Über den Prozess der Zivilization*. Basel: Haus zum Falken, 1939. In English: *The Civilizing Process: Sociogenetic and Psychogenetic Investigations*. Oxford: Blackwell Publishers, 2000 (revised edition).

Fabietti, Ugo. "Identités collectives comme constructions de l'humain", in Francis Affergan, Sylvana Borutti, Claude Calame, Ugo Fabietti, Monder Kilani & Francesco Remotti (eds.), *Figures de l'humain. Les représentations de l'anthropologie*, Paris, Editions de l'Ecole des Hautes Etudes en Sciences Sociales, 2003, pp. 175–214.

Foucault, Michel. *The Order of Things: an Archaeology of the Human Sciences*, New York, Vintage Books, 1994 (1966).

Freud, Sigmund. *Civilization and Its Discontents* (1929), S.E., 21, London, Hogarth.

Freud, Sigmund. "'Civilized' Sexual Morality and Modern Nervous Illness" (1908), S.E., 9, London, Hogarth.

Freud, Sigmund. "The Claims of Psycho-Analysis to Scientific Interest" (1913), S.E., 13, London, Hogarth, 1913.

Freud, Sigmund. "The Dissection of the Psychical Personality" (1933), Lecture XXXI of *New Introductory Lectures on Psycho-analysis*. S.E., 22, London, Hogarth.

Freud, Sigmund. "The Ego and the Id" (1923), S.E., 19, London, Hogarth.

Freud, Sigmund. "Female Sexuality" (1931), S.E., 21, London, Hogarth.

Freud, Sigmund. "Femininity, Lecture XXXIII" of *New Introductory Lectures* (1933), S.E., 22, London, Hogarth.

Freud, Sigmund. "Five Lectures on Psycho-analysis" (1910), S.E., 11, London, Hogarth.

Freud, Sigmund. "From the History of an Infantile Neurosis" (1918), S.E., 17, London, Hogarth.

Freud, Sigmund. *The Future of an Illusion* (1927), S.E., 21, London, Hogarth.

Freud, Sigmund. *The Interpretation of Dreams* (1900), S.E., 4, 5, London, Hogarth.

Freud, Sigmund. "Moses and monotheism" (1939), S.E., 23. London, Hogarth.

Freud, Sigmund. *On the History of the Psychoanalytical Movement* (1914), S.E., 14, London, Hogarth.

Freud, Sigmund. "An Outline of Psycho-analysis" (1940), S.E., 23, London, Hogarth.

Freud, Sigmund. *Pre-Psycho-Analytic Publications and Unpublished Drafts (1886–1889)* (1897), S. E. 1, London, Hogarth.

Freud, Sigmund. "Psychoanalysis" and "The Libido Theory" (1923), S.E., 18, London, Hogarth.
Freud, Sigmund. "Psycho-Analysis" (1926), S.E., 20, London, Hogarth.
Freud, Sigmund. "The Resistances to Psycho-analysis" (1925), S.E., 19, London, Hogarth.
Freud, Sigmund. "A Short Account of Psycho-analysis" (1924), S.E., 19, London, Hogarth.
Freud, Sigmund. "Some Psychical Consequences of the Anatomical Distinction between the Sexes" (1925), S.E., 19, London, Hogarth,
Freud, Sigmund. "Thoughts for the Times on War and Death" (1915), S.E., 14, London, Hogarth.
Freud, Sigmund. "Three Essays on the Theory of Sexuality" (1905), S.E., 7, London, Hogarth.
Freud, Sigmund. "The Unconscious" (1915), S.E. 14, London, Hogarth.
Freud, Sigmund & Wilhelm Fliess. *The Complete Letters of Sigmund Freud to Wilhelm Fliess*, Jeffrey Masson (ed.), Cambridge, MA, Harvard University Press, 1985.
Fromm, Erich. *The Crisis of Psychoanalysis, Essays on Freud, Marx, and Social Psychology*, New York, Holt, Rinehart, Winston, 1970.
Fromm, Erich. "Psychoanalysis and Sociology", in S.E. Bronner and D. M. Kellner (eds.), *Critical Theory and Society. A Reader*, London, Routledge, 1988 (1929).
Fromm, Erich. *The Revision of Psychoanalysis*, Rainer Funk (ed.), Boulder, CO, Westview Press, 1992.
Geertz, Clifford. *The Interpretation of Cultures. Selected Essays*, New York, Basic Books, 1973.
van Gennep, Arnold. *Les Rites de passage*, Paris, Picard, 1981 (1909).
Godelier, Maurice. *The Metamorphoses of Kinship*, London, Verso, 2011 (2004).
Gough, Kathleen. *The Traditional Kinship System of the Nayars of Malabar*, Cambridge, MA, Harvard University, 1954.
Green, André. *La Causalité psychique*, Paris, Odile Jacob, 1995.
Green, André. "Inceste et parricide en anthropologie and en psychanalyse", in P. Descola, J. Hamel & P. Lemonnier (eds.), *La Production du social. Autour de Maurice Godelier, Colloque de Cérisy*, Paris, Fayard, 1999.
Green, André. "Méconnaissance de l'inconscient", in R. Dorey et al., *L'inconscient et la science*, Paris, Dunod, 1991.
Green, André. "Le mythe: un objet transitionnel collectif", *La Déliaison*, Paris, Belles lettres, 1992.
Green, André. "Oedipe, Freud et nous", *La Déliaison*, Paris, Belles Lettres, 1992.
Green, André. *La Pensée clinique*, Paris, Odile Jacob, 2002.
Héritier, Françoise. "Les fabrications possibles and pensables d'un produit humain", in C. Calame & M. Kilani (eds.), *La Fabrication de l'humain dans les cultures et dans l'anthropologie*, Lausanne, Payot, 1999, pp. 139–152.
Horney, Karen. *The Neurotic Personality of our Time*, Abingdon, UK, Routledge, 1999 (1937).
Jones, Ernest. *Essays in Applied Pyscho-Analysis*, London, The Hogarth Press, 1951, Vol. II.
Jones, Ernest. "Mother Right and the Sexual Ignorance of Savages", *Essays in Applied Pyscho-Analysis* Vol. II, pp. 145–173.
Jones, Ernest. *On the Nightmare*, London, The Hogarth Press, 1931.
Jones, Ernest. *Papers on Psycho-Analysis*, London, Baillière, Tindall, and Cox, 1938.
Jones, Ernest. "The Theory of Symbolism", a paper read before the British Psychological Society on January 29, 1916 and published in *British Journal of Psychology*, Vol. 9, No. 2, pp. 181–229, October, 1918.
Juillerat, Bernard. *Children of the Blood. Society, Reproduction and Cosmology in New Guinea*, London, Bloomsbury Publishing, 1997 (1986).
Juillerat, Bernard. "Des fantasmes originaires aux symboles culturels: médiations et seuils", *Revue française de psychanalyse*, Vol. 57, No. 3, pp. 139–163, 1993.

Juillerat, Bernard. *Oedipe chasseur. Une mythologie du sujet en Nouvelle-Guinée*, Paris, Presses Universitaires de France, 1991.

Juillerat, Bernard. *Penser l'imaginaire*, Paris, Payot, 2001.

Jung, Carl Gustav. *Psychology of the Unconscious, A Study of the Transformations and Symbolisms of the Libido, A Contribution to the History of the Evolution of Thought*, New York, Moffat, Yard and Company, 1916.

Kaës, René. *Un singulier pluriel*, Paris, Dunod, 2007.

Kardiner, Abram. *The Individual and His Society; the Psychodynamics of Primitive Social Organization*, New York, Columbia University Press, 1939.

Karsenti, Bruno. *L'Homme total*, Paris, Presses Universitaires de France, 1997.

Kaufmann, Pierre. *Psychanalyse et théorie de la culture*, Paris, Denoël « Médiations », 1974–1975.

Kilani, Mondher "Cannibalisme and anthropopoiésis", in Francis Affergan, Sylvana Borutti, Claude Calame, Ugo Fabietti, Monder Kilani & Francesco Remotti (eds.), *Figures de l'humain. Les représentations de l'anthropologie*, Paris, Editions de l'Ecole des Hautes Etudes en Sciences Sociales, 2003, pp. 215–254.

Kilani, Mondher. *L'invention de l'autre*, Lausanne, Payot, 1994.

Kroeber, Alfred. "Totem and Taboo, an Ethnologic Psychoanalysis" (1920), *American Anthropologist,* New Series, Vol. 22, No. 1 (Jan. –Mar.1920).

Kroeber, Alfred. "Totem and Taboo in Retrospect", *American Journal of Sociology*, Vol. 45, No. 3, Nov. 1939, 446–154.

Lacan, Jacques. *Les complexes familiaux dans la formation de l'individu*, Paris, Navarin, 1984 (1938).

Lacan, Jacques. *Ecrits: The First Complete Edition in English*, New York, Norton, 2006 (1966).

Lacan, Jacques. "La Famille", *Encyclopédie française,* Vol. 8, *La vie mentale,* Paris, March, 1938.

Lacan, Jacques. *Family Complexes in the Formation of the Individual.* Cited as translated by Corman Gallagher, School of Psychotherapy, St. Vincent's Hospital, Dublin 4, p. 49. Accessible online.

Lacan, Jacques. *The Four Fundamental Concepts of Psycho-analysis, 1964–1965*, New York, Norton, 1988.

Lacan, Jacques. *Freud's Papers on Technique, 1953–1954,* New York, Norton, 1988.

Lacan, Jacques. "Function and Field of Speech and Language in Psychoanalysis", *Ecrits: a selection,* London, Tavistock/Routledge, 1977 (1949), pp. 9–32.

Lacan, Jacques. "The Mirror Stage as Formative of the *I* Function as Revealed in Psychoanalytic Experience", *Ecrits: a selection,* London, Tavistock/Routledge, 1977 (1949), pp. 1–9.

Lacan, Jacques. "The Neurotic's Individual Myth", *Psychoanalytic Quarterly*, Vol. 48, No. 3, July 1979, pp. 405–425.

Lacan, Jacques. *The Seminar of Jacques Lacan, Book I, Freud's Papers on Technique 1953–1954*, London, Norton, 1988.

Lévi-Strauss, Claude. "The Effectiveness of Symbols", *Structural Anthropology*, New York, Basic Books, 1963.

Lévi-Strauss, Claude. *Introduction to the Work of Marcel Mauss*, Abingdon, UK, Routledge, 1987 (1950).

Lévi-Strauss, Claude. *The Jealous Potter*, Chicago, Chicago University Press, 1988.

Lévi-Strauss, Claude. *The Savage Mind*, London, Weidenfeld and Nicolson, 1966 (1962).

Lévi-Strauss, Claude. *Structural Anthropology*, New York, Basic Books, 1963 (1958).

Lévi-Strauss, Claude. "The Structural Study of Myth", *Structural Anthropology*, New York, Basic Books, 1963.

Lévi-Strauss, Claude. *Totemism*, London, Merlin Press, 1991 (1962).

Malinowski, Bronislaw. *The Family among the Australian Aborigines: A Sociological Study*, London, University of London Press, 1913.

Malinowski, Bronislaw. "On the Principle of the Economy of Thought", in Robert J. Thornton and Peter Skalnik eds., *The Early Writings of Bronislaw Malinowski*, Cambridge, Cambridge University Press, 1993 (1906), pp. 89–116.

Malinowski, Bronislaw. *Sex and Repression in Savage Society*, Abingdon, UK, Routledge, 2001 (1927).

Masson, Jeffrey (ed.). *The Complete Letters of Sigmund Freud to Wilhelm Fliess*, Cambridge, MA, Harvard University Press, 1985.

Mauss, Marcel. *A General Theory of Magic*, London, Routledge, 1972 (1902).

Mauss, Marcel. *The Gift: The Form and Reason for Exchange in Archaic Societies*, London, Routledge, 1990 (1925).

Mauss, Marcel. "Real and Practical Relationships between Psychology and Sociology", *Sociology and Psychology: Essays by Marcel Mauss*, London, Routledge and Kegan Paul, 1979 (1924), pp. 1–33.

Mead, Margaret. *Coming of Age in Samoa*, New York, HarperCollins, 2001 (1928).

Missenard, André. "Identification et processus groupal", in D. Anzieu, A. Béjarano, A. Missenard, and J.-B. Pontalis, *Le travail psychanalytique dans les groupes*, Tome 1, Paris, Dunod, 1972.

Obeyesekere, Gananath. *The Work of Culture, Symbolic Transformation in Psychoanalysis and Anthropology*, Chicago, IL, University of Chicago Press, 1990.

Pulman, Bertrand. *Anthropologie et psychanalyse. Malinowski contre Freud*, Paris, Presses Universitaires de France, 2002.

Pulman, Bertrand. "Aux origines du débat ethnologie/psychanalyse: W. H. R. Rivers", *L'Homme* 1986, No. 100.

Pulman, Bertrand, "Aux origines du débat anthropologie/psychanalyse: C. G. Seligman", *Gradhiva*, 1989, No. 6.

Pulman, Bertrand. "Ernest Jones et l'anthropologie", *Revue internationale d'histoire de la psychanalyse*, 1991, No. 4.

Rivers, William Halse Rivers. "Sociology and Psychology", in *Psychology and Ethnology*, London, Routledge, 1999 (1926). Originally published in *The Sociological Review*, Autumn 1916, pp. 1–13.

Róheim, Géza. *Australian Totemism; A Pyscho-analytic Study in Anthropology*, London, Allen & Unwin, 1925.

Róheim, Géza. "Dream Analysis and Field Work in Anthropology", *Psychoanalysis and the Social Sciences, An Annual*, Vol.1, New York, International Press, 1947.

Róheim, Géza. "Dragons and Dragon Killers", published in Hungarian in *Ethnographia* 22:128–43, 1911, pp. 193–209.

Róheim, Géza. *The Gates of the Dream*, New York, International Universities Press, 1952.

Róheim, Géza. *The Origin and Function of Culture*, New York, Nervous and Mental Disease Monographs, 1943.

Róheim, Géza. *Psychoanalysis and Anthropology: Culture, Personality and the Unconscious*, New York, International Universities Press, 1950.

Róheim, Géza. *The Riddle of the Sphinx, or Human Origins*, London, Hogarth, 1934.

Shand, Alexander F. *The Foundations of Character, Being a Study of the Tendencies of the Emotions and Sentiments*, London, 1914.

Spiro, Melford. *Culture and Human Nature*, New Brunswick NJ, Transaction Publishers, 1994.

Tarot, Camille. *De Durkheim à Mauss, l'invention du symbolique*, Paris, Editions La Découverte, 1999.

Tarot, Camille. *Le Sacré et le symbolique*, Paris, Editions La Découverte, 2007.

Tylor, Edward Burnett. *Primitive Culture: Researches into the Development of Mythology, Philosophy, Religion, Art, and Custom*, Vol. 1. London, John Murray, 1871.

Winnicott, Donald Woods. *Playing and Reality*, London, Routledge, 1971.

Wundt, Wilhelm. *The Elements of Folk Psychology, Outline of a Psychological History of the Development of Mankind*, London, Allen & Unwin Ltd., 1915 (1912).

Zafiropoulos, Markos, *Lacan et les sciences sociales*, Paris, Presses Universitaires de France, 2001.

Zafiropoulos, Markos. *Lacan and Lévi-Strauss, or the Return to Freud, 1951–1957*, London, Karnac, 2010 (2003).

INDEX